BIRTHRIGHT
CHRISTIAN, DO YOU KNOW
WHO YOU ARE?

David Needham

Multnomah®Publishers *Sisters, Oregon*

The 1995 edition of this work was published under the title
ALIVE FOR THE FIRST TIME

BIRTHRIGHT
© 1979, 1995, 1999 by David C. Needham

published by Multnomah Publishers, Inc.

International Standard Book Number: 1-57673-274-6

Cover design by Chris Gilbert
Cover image by FPG Internationl

Printed in the United States of America

Most Scripture quotations are from:
The New Revised Standard Version Bible (NRSV)
© 1989 by the Division of Christian Education of the National Council
of the Churches of Christ in the United States of America

Scripture quotations marked NIV are from *The Holy Bible,*
New International Version, (NIV) © 1973, 1984 by International Bible Society,
used by permission of Zondervan Publishing House.

Scripture quotations marked NASB are from the
New American Standard Bible, © 1960, 1977 by the Lockman Foundation

Multnomah is a trademark of Multnomah Publisher, Inc., and is registered
in the U.S. Patent and Trademark Office.
The colophon is a trademark of Multnomah Publishers, Inc.

For information:
MULTNOMAH PUBLISHERS, INC.
POST OFFICE BOX 1720
SISTERS, OREGON 97759

99 00 01 02 — 10 9 8 7 6 5 4 3 2 1

To Mary Jo, my wife,

who, next to my Lord,
is the sunshine of my life.

CONTENTS

PREFACE

If you are familiar with the first edition of *Birthright, Christian Do You Know Who You Are?* and *Alive for the First Time,* you will discover that this present book contains what, hopefully you will agree, is the best of those two books. Here and there additions and clarifications have been made in both text and end notes.

Because some portions of this book may appear to be nontraditional, I have attempted to do two things. First, the text itself is written in a form I hope you will find quite readable, with ample illustrations to clarify the truth. Second, in addition to the text I have included numerous end notes (some quite lengthy) plus two appendices to aid those of you who wish to interact more in-depth both with the issues and with the perspectives of other writers.

You should not assume that my inclusion of statements by other writers implies that these writers agree with all I have written. Nevertheless, it is my hope that I have been faithful to the writer's intent in my use of any quotation. Though most of my references to the works of others are in some measure parallel with the various emphases of this book, in a few cases they represent an opposing view. I urge you to assume that though disagreeing on one issue, I may very well not only be in agreement with much of what such individuals teach, but may also value them highly for their contributions to God's people.

To write concerning God's truth is a dangerous, almost frightening proposition. That danger is multiplied if the ideas shared appear to be different from traditional statements of the faith.

The danger lies in two areas. First, new expressions of spiritual truth can play right into the hands of the Christian radical whose chief delight lies in upsetting orthodox ideas. Milking every opportunity to fracture harmony in the body of Christ, this misdirected zealot willingly rearranges what is being said to suit his own purpose.

But there is another, more subtle danger.

Many sincere believers have found a comfortable security in neatly systematized statements of theology. Over the years, these systems have grown in prominence and familiarity until they seem as inspired as the Bible itself.

To those who subscribe unquestioningly to these traditional statements, this book will raise red flags. Rather than challenging them to think objectively, it will alarm them into hasty emotional reactions. Recognizing these dangers, I write to you, the individual in that middle group of God's people. You are fully committed to the authority of Scripture. You are also committed to remaining open to the truth. You are a biblicist. If indeed the Holy Spirit is pleased with the following study, then you too will happily respond and praise God for his truth—biblical truth.

INTRODUCTION

While in college, there came a day when I felt I simply could not go on assuming all those victorious Christian beliefs while at the same time knowing that my "good guy" behavior was largely a mask to cover my own self-centeredness. With a passion, I longed for genuineness—a warm heart for God and for people.

Cutting all my classes, I went for a day-long hike up into the hills behind our campus. With almost every step I took, I pleaded with God that he would make himself real to me; that he would set me free from myself.

Never have I prayed harder, nor have I ever ended a day more discouraged. I am sure if I had spent a week in earnest prayer it would have made no difference. Nothing happened. Was it not enough that I had poured out to him the anguish of my heart? What more did he want from me? Was I asking the impossible? Perhaps I simply was never cut out to be spiritual, I thought. Maybe some people have it and some don't. At least now I knew. Yes, I would continue to move toward Christian service. I couldn't go back on that.

And so I did—for years after that day—with little joy and even less hope. I poured myself into the demands of seminary, then youth work, the pastorate, and finally, Bible college teaching. How different those years would have been if only someone had come alongside me back at that crisis point and introduced me to the freedom and freshness of the marvelous discovery that being born again involved a far greater miracle—a living miracle—than I had ever dreamed! The crucial issue for me was not some new type of spiritual discipline or experiential encounter, but truth.

This book is about the marvelous adventure involved in our being the supernatural products of God's new creation—people who are alive for the first time. As we follow this adventure, we will move from tragedy to triumph, from bondage to freedom, from futility to fulfillment, from darkness to light. At times the light will appear too bright and we will be tempted to turn back to the counterfeit comfort of our low expectations. The word *natural* is a comfortable word. We can manage it. But *supernatural*? How do we manage that? Do we actually "not belong to the world" in the same way as Jesus did not belong? That's what he said. Then how are we to understand those obsessive "earthy" feelings we all have?

God tells us we are alive in a way we have never been alive before, possessing a birthright we never possessed before. In that moment when we received Christ, God's miraculous "birthing" act gave us a value, a beauty, a preciousness that lifts us above all earthy measurements. He encourages us to look deep within at his workmanship and make that unexpected discovery of passion for him and a holiness that will set us free to be ourselves—free to live and to love. He invites us to believe the unbelievable about the miracles he has performed in us that enable us to say enthusiastically "Yes!" to him and "Yes" to life, while at the same time saying "Yes" to who we most deeply are.

Could it be that a major reason for the indifference, the epidemic occurrences of moral shipwreck in our evangelical churches, and the shattering of Christian homes is because we have seen ourselves as nothing more than "Christian" forgiven sinners—failing to be what we should be, because we cannot stop being what we think we are?

May we trust that God in his patience will yet awaken his church to the implications of the bigness of the miracles by which we have become the children of God, the sharers of his life—his joy, his purity, his love, his passion, his peace—in a most mysterious fellowship of the saints which reveals, as nothing else has or ever will, the wonder of the glory of God.

CHAPTER 1

What's So Great about Being Human?

This book is about you. It is also about a miracle so gigantic, so spectacular, it belongs in the same class as the miracle of the creation of the universe. In response to that event,

> *"the morning stars sang together and all the heavenly beings shouted for joy"* (Job 38:7[1]).

As the infinite imagination of God splashed his creativity upon the nothingness, the climactic moment came when he shaped human beings from the dust of the earth—uniquely made in his image.

Yet as remarkable as that creative moment was, the miracle that will be the focus of this book transcends it. The product of this miracle is a state higher than Adam and Eve knew, even in their innocence.[2] Though the original creation displayed the wonder of the glory of God, this miracle exhibits even greater divine glory because it displays the full spectrum of his attributes.

Since God described his creative acts as "good," one might expect we would begin this chapter with a great, reverberating trumpet fanfare as the audience is hushed and the curtain is drawn. With a gasp of joy and amazement, there on stage we would see his marvelous masterpiece, the pinnacle of divine creative capacity—human beings.

Indeed, Romans 8:17–21 depicts such a scene—not of that event, but of the greater one—when all creation is described as breathless in eager anticipation of a yet-future moment when at last God will draw back the curtain and unveil the collective exhibit of his majesty: the children of God, the glorious co-heirs with Christ of his eternal kingdom.

This book is about a miracle God either has performed or would like to perform upon you. Despite this major focus upon you, we will discover that the end product of this miracle will be not man-centered, but God-centered. It's the miracle God calls his "new creation."

WHAT DOES IT MEAN TO BE HUMAN?

What does it mean to be a human being? It makes little difference what answers we may find to the other big questions if this one remains a mystery.

Before we turn to God's answer, there is one thing we will need to do that is almost impossible, but we must try. All of us come to the Bible with beliefs about one thing or another that are already well-entrenched, like hardened furrows dug deep in the soil. Furrows are fine if they direct the water in the right direction. But on the subject "What is man?" the furrows we and others have dug go in all sorts of opposing directions.

What we will need to do is try to find an unfurrowed space somewhere in our minds and then allow the Scriptures to make a fresh ditch. Maybe it will go in exactly the direction we anticipated; maybe not. But at least it will be a fresh furrow. It's worth a try, anyway.

Well then, what does the Bible tell us about what it means to be a human being?

The best place to start is in the book of beginnings, the book of Genesis, with one of the first references to man—Genesis 2:7.

Out of the Dust

What do we find? We were made from dust! That's a nice, humble beginning, isn't it? What does this do to your sense of self-worth? But there's more. This verse also says God breathed into man "the breath of life."

That sounds special, but it really isn't. Genesis 7:22 says the same of animals. They too have the "breath of life." In fact, this passage describing animals is even more expressive than the one describing man. Animals have "the breath of the spirit of life." What does this mean? Simply that God is the source of life for animals as well as for man. No difference.

Since we don't want to play into the evolutionist's hand, I fear our temptation as Christians is to latch on to anything that will secure for us our human uniqueness. We try to squeeze out of every passage the last ounce of human dignity we might find. But we can squeeze too hard. Too many have tried to do so with this verse.

A Living Soul

There is one more description in this verse. Maybe it will save our dignity. "And man became a living soul." A living soul—that must elevate us above animals. Yes, we are living souls…but Genesis again is clear in telling us that animals, too, are souls!

If you happen to be looking at your Bible right now, I can hear you say, "But my Bible doesn't say that man became a 'living soul'; it says 'a living being.'"

Is the Hebrew word for *soul (nepes)* really there? Yes, it is, but only one of the English Bibles I have on my desk reveals this fact in a marginal note. For good reasons, translators have chosen to render the word *nepes* by the English words *life* or *living being* or *living creature;* that is what that Hebrew word usually means. As such, animals are as much living beings as humans are.

The word itself says little more than to express the truth that creatures (human beings and animals) have life. The following passages all refer to animals by using the Hebrew word *nepes* (soul): Genesis 1:30; 2:19; 9:15–16; cf. Leviticus 17:11; Deuteronomy 12:23.[3]

Where does this leave us? Are we nothing more than a special class of animals?

In the Image of God

Happily, Genesis 1 provides us with one expression never used of animals: the "image of God." That does sound loaded with dignity. It must mean something special.

Indeed it does. We are more than animals.[4]

There is something about human beings that images God.[5] What is it? One of the first things we discover from Genesis 1:27—especially encouraging to one-half of the human race—is that the text assures us it is not only men who bear God's image, but also women: "in the image of God he created them; male and female he created them."[6] Far too many pages of history (including the present pages) have dark blotches marking the shameful disrespect for one class or another of human beings, even though each person—every one—bears God's image, both Christian and non-Christian.[7] Still, we have yet to uncover what "image" is referring to.

Could it be that we, as does God, possess those qualities of intellect, emotions, and will that give us personality?[8]

Or, since the persons of the Trinity exist in close relationship, is image tied to some sort of relational idea? Building on this possibility, does "image of God" point to a uniqueness in mankind that allows for a conscious interaction between God and people that animals do not have?

Perhaps it is due to some moral parallel between man and God.

As another possibility, might this expression mean *if* God chose to reveal himself physically, the form he would take would be "human" in appearance—that sort of image?[9]

Or is it found in the fact that as God is creative, so we bear God's creative image? How creative are we? Well, creative enough to think up all of these possibilities!

Toward a Working Definition

Surprisingly, the Bible never defines "image of God." Rather than tell us what human beings *are* because they are in God's image, it tells us what they *are to do*. Within the same verse that introduces the image idea (1:26), God declared the role human beings were to play in his creation:

"let them have dominion over the fish of the sea, and over the birds of the air, and over the cattle, and over all the wild animals of the earth, and over every creeping thing that creeps upon the earth."[10]

Interestingly, the first thing we find Adam doing is exactly that.

The LORD God took the man and put him in the garden of Eden to till it and keep it.... So out of the ground the Lord God formed every animal of the field and every bird of the air, and brought them to the man to see what he would call them; and whatever the man called every living creature, that was its name (Genesis 2:15, 19).

From this we conclude that whatever qualities God has that are needed to fulfill this job description comprise the ingredients of the image of God. The powers of thought, imagination, and choice, plus being capable of relating to others, must be key aspects of God's image in people. Clearly, the relating part involved more than grunts; it involved that most remarkable gift—complex language, which allowed for the prospect of a profound relationship with God.[11]

Is the Image of God Mystical?

Through the centuries, both Christians and religious people in general have assumed that being in the image of God pointed to some sort of mystical or nonmaterial, spirit-level, God-conscious quality.[12] Yet to our surprise, we find nothing in Genesis that even hints at this. In fact, the emphasis falls on the fleshiness of humanity (Genesis 6:3, 12, 13, 17, 19; 7:21; 9:9–17).

It is important to understand that in centuries past, a mystical explanation for the superiority of human personality was all anyone had available.[13] But times have changed. Medical and other scientific technology now enable us to identify most human distinctions from animals physiologically rather than mystically.

There is growing evidence that the uniqueness of the human brain provides ample explanations for various human characteristics that used to be viewed as coming from some sort of nonmaterial level of humanness. Scientists are becoming increasingly aware of animals who possess most of the same abilities, though to a far lesser degree. (To humble us a bit more, think of various animals who have capacities you only dream about—the directional abilities of a honey bee, for example. It's so hard to pull into the service station after saying emphatically, "I am not lost!" Or think of the patience of a spider when a customer simply will not make up its mind.)

It is easy to forget that much of what we assume the Scriptures mean has been built on information foundations laid long before anyone undertook the scientific evaluation of animal abilities and before technology was available to investigate the mysteries of brain/mind connections.[14]

Though God's Word remains solid, our theological deductions at times may need to be upgraded. The wonder of Scripture is that its claims concerning human beings are not outdated by more recently discovered truth. (I encourage you to turn to the following extended footnote for excerpts from a fascinating book, *The Amazing Body Human,* by evangelical author Mark Cosgrove. His insights underline this rapidly developing area of discovery.[15])

What Then Is Man?

Man's uniqueness is not found in the fact that God breathed into him the "breath of life" or in his being described as a "living being (soul)." Rather, it is in his being made in God's image and possessing those remarkable capacities of personality that, perhaps most of all, emanate from the gift of complex language. This gift is inseparable from such evaluative qualities as imagination, self-conscious reflection, and choice, which in turn enable deep relationships far beyond the animal level.[16] Why? Unless we read between the lines, the Genesis purpose was for humans to serve as stewards of life on this planet in a dependent, responsive love relationship with God. In fact, the remainder of the Bible reveals that this God/man love relationship idea was the central purpose.[17]

But is this all? Though we are getting ahead of our story, Hebrews 2:6–10, along with many other Scriptures in both the Old and the New Testaments, informs us that God's ultimate intention in creating people was far greater than he first revealed in Genesis! In fact, in light of the New Testament's unfolding of God's awesome, eternal plans he has always had in mind for people, Jesus described the value of a single human soul as being of more worth than all the world! (See Matthew 16:26.)[18]

Since the goal of this book is to capture something of the exhilaration of God's spiritual masterpieces—his new creation saints—in later chapters we will look at another set of passages that use the expression "image of God" in a marvelous, new way. But before we can do that, we must take a painful look at the tragedy that befell those first imagers of God.

THEN CAME THE FALL

One of the best ways to appreciate anything is to see it in contrast. A diamond against black velvet. A lush oasis in the midst of a desert. The Bible does this with people by first telling us what the human race is now—in itself, by itself. Only then, with this as the backdrop, does it tell us about the miracle.

But first, the disaster.

We cannot understand human beings as they now are without first coming to grips with the Fall, the cataclysmic sin of Adam and Eve. At that cosmic crossroad were two trees: the tree of life and the tree of the knowledge of good and evil. One offered the potential for a dimension of life beyond anything Adam and Eve had yet known. The other offered only death. In this supremely tragic moment of history, choosing to believe the serpent rather than God, Adam and Eve chose death (Genesis 2:16–17; 3:1–5, 11–13, 22–24). They were now "alienated from the life of God."

Spiritual Death or Physical Death?

Automatically, Christians have assumed the words "You shall surely die" meant primarily spiritual death.[19] We do know from Ephesians 4:18 that this one act of disobedience placed humans in a state of chosen independence, walking "in the futility of their minds. They are darkened in their understanding, alienated from the life of God because of their ignorance and hardness of heart" (Ephesians 4:17–18).

In that sense, Adam and Eve were dead in their transgressions (Ephesians 2:1). Yet the Old Testament consistently emphasizes that death was the tragic cessation of physical life.

Some argue, since Adam and Eve did not die physically "on the day" they disobeyed, physical death was not in view. The fact remains that on that day the dying process began—they became mortals, embraced by death. In that moment, the dream of immortality shriveled up and died. Satan had lied.

Physical death was certainly on God's mind as he pronounced his judgment on Adam and Eve:

> *By the sweat of your face*
> *you shall eat bread*
> *until you return to the ground,*
> *for out of it you were taken;*
> *you are dust,*
> *and to dust you shall return (Genesis 3:19).*

"Dust you are." How humiliating. How earthy. "And to dust you shall return." From Genesis 4 and throughout the Bible, people are described as mortals,[20] those who are in the inescapable grip of physical death.

Think about human life for a moment, at its best and at its worst. Try picturing a tiny baby in her mother's arms. So soft, so lovable. Picture her again a couple of years later with the sun in her hair. Chubby little hands, sparkling eyes, tiny nose, delicate smile, spontaneous laugh, running across the lawn and calling out, "Daddy's home." Or look at any little boy, four years old, hanging upside down from his swing, wondering why the world looks so strange. Freckles, holes in his jeans, baseball cards—so fully alive! Fifteen years later—so beautiful, so handsome, so expectant. And then…long years, stress, illness, surgeries, wrinkles, pain, sorrow, stooping, decay, dim eyes, the wheelchair, white sheets, jumbled words, a final gasp, death, a box…a grave. That final offense against "the imagers of God."

And as if that were not enough, all through those years there is the ugly side, the evil essence haunting man's highest moments: destructive pride, cruelty, envy, deceit.

The Bible's View of Mortals

To allow this dark truth to sink in, let's look at some of the Bible's many descriptions of human mortality.

> He remembered that they were but flesh,
>> a passing breeze that does not return (Psalm 78:39, NIV).

> For he knows how we were made;
>> he remembers that we are dust.
> As for mortals, their days are like grass;
>> they flourish like a flower of the field;
> for the wind passes over it, and it is gone... (Psalm 103:14–15).

> You turn us back to dust,
>> and say, "Turn back, you mortals...."
> You sweep them away; they are like a dream,
>> like grass that is renewed in the morning;
> in the morning it flourishes and is renewed;
>> in the evening it fades and withers (Psalm 90:3, 5–6).

> All flesh is grass, and all its loveliness is like the flower of the field.
> The grass withers, the flower fades,
> When the breath of the Lord blows upon it;
> Surely the people are grass (Isaiah 40:6, 7, NASB).

More cynical are Solomon's bitter words,

> I said in my heart with regard to human beings that God is testing them to show that they are but animals. For the fate of humans and the fate of animals is the same; as one dies, so dies the other. They all have the same breath, and humans have no advantage over the animals; for all is vanity. All go to one place; all are from the dust, and all turn to dust again.[21] Who knows whether the human spirit goes upward and the spirit[22] of animals goes downward to the earth? (Ecclesiastes 3:18–21)

But What About Human Worth?

"Yes," you may be saying, "but aren't you ignoring all those marvelous qualities of humanness we should rightly treasure with some measure of pride?"

It is most appropriate for us to appreciate quality wherever it is found, including all those wonderful, God-given, unique human endowments. Yes, there is a proper place for a Christian humanism expressed in a respect for the humanities—music, art, literature, the constructive values of the sciences, the many evidences of human kindness, plus all the other special giftednesses that identify us above other life forms on earth. In fact, Christians rightly should be at the forefront of efforts to restore a public sense of the value of human life.

It is true that we are "fearfully and wonderfully made." And we should be most grateful for all those treasured capacities such as sight and hearing and the complexity of all of the systems by which our flesh functions. Yes, we are remarkable. But so is a dolphin; so is a spider.

It is strange how we are so quick to credit whatever an animal does to that vaguest of ideas, instinct,[23] in order to maintain our vast superiority. Are you baffled by the complexity of the DNA molecules that determine so much about us? Then first be baffled by the DNA of a salamander.

Indeed, we have bigger brains, greatly enlarged frontal lobes, plus a highly developed left brain–right brain configuration. We possess the transforming capacity of complex language, which opens the door to reflective thinking, relating past and future, and to imagination, which stirs aesthetics. Still, God has decided that the writers of Scripture should use with considerable frequency the word *flesh* to identify human beings. "Flesh—flesh as grass." *Flesh*. What a gross, humbling word.[24]

In light of this, we should blush when we think of the flip ways we speak of God. The times we toss our prayers upward with the flick of a tongue. In sharp contrast, remember the time when God was ready to kill Moses for his casualness (Exodus 4:24). Then there was Uzzah (2 Samuel 6:6–9) and Ananias and Sapphira (Acts 5:1–11).

Oh! The absolute transcendence of God! The absolute lowliness of man! And then on top of all of this—man's sinfulness! We must never forget God's warning:

> *"Let not the wise man boast of his wisdom*
> *or the strong man boast of his strength*
> *or the rich man boast of his riches,*
> *but let him who boasts boast about this:*
> *that he understands and knows me*
> *that I am the Lord, who exercises kindness,*
> *justice and righteousness on earth,*
> *for in these I delight"* (Jeremiah 9:23–24, NIV).

It is to this one, God says,

> *But this is the one to whom I will look,*
> *to the humble and contrite in spirit,*
> *who trembles at my word (Isaiah 66:2).*

Though the book of Job is packed with the best of man's wisdom, it concludes with God saying, "Who is this that darkens counsel by words without knowledge?" And Job responds, "but now my eye sees you; therefore I despise myself, and repent in dust and ashes" (Job 38:2; 42:5, 6).

Indeed, "the foolishness of God is wiser than man." If God could think a foolish thought, the Einsteins of the world would be forced to bow low beneath such transcendent wisdom. "For as the heavens are higher than the earth, so are my ways higher than your ways, and my thoughts than your thoughts." In fact, God often selects the lesser-gifted individuals to be his channels of wisdom. Why? He tells us—in order to remove any doubt as to the vast distance between God's wisdom and man's—"that no flesh might boast in the presence of God"[25] (1 Corinthians 1:25, 29; Isaiah 55:9).

When speaking of human worth, it would be different if people gave God the glory for the talents they possess. (See Daniel 1:17; 2:30. Contrast Daniel 4:28–32.)[26] Yet there is scarcely a whisper in the world of such an attitude. Take, for example, one of the greatest exhibits of human accomplishment and boasting—the great cities of the world. Proudly they display the best of human creativity—marvelous artistry, advanced technology, phenomenal organization. Yet when was the last time you heard anyone redirect the glory from man to God? In light of this, Isaiah's words are so fitting:

> He humbles those who dwell on high,
>> he lays the lofty city low;
>> he levels it to the ground
> and casts it down to the dust (Isaiah 26:5, NIV).

> [A]gainst every high tower,
>> and against every fortified wall;
> against all the ships of Tarshish,
>> and against all the beautiful craft.
> The haughtiness of people shall be humbled,
>> and the pride of everyone shall be brought low;
>> and the Lord alone will be exalted on that day
> (Isaiah 2:15–17, cf. Revelation 18:10–18).

The Result of Human Autonomy

After centuries of arrogant, independent human stewardship of this planet, what has happened? Everywhere we have left our polluted trademark on all we have touched—the oceans and rivers, the air, the dirt, genetic codes and, most horribly, the moral character of the human race itself. In keeping with this dark reality, listen to Isaiah's description of our planet:

> The earth lies polluted
>> under its inhabitants;
> for they have transgressed laws,
>> violated the statutes,
>> broken the everlasting covenant (Isaiah 24:5).

What is the ultimate end of the great human adventure that began at the wrong tree?

> The earth dries up and withers,
>> the world languishes and withers,

> *the exalted of the earth languish....*
> *The city is left in ruins,*
> * its gate is battered to pieces.*
> *So it will be on the earth*
> * and among the nations....*
> *The earth is broken up,*
> * the earth is split asunder,*
> * the earth is thoroughly shaken.*
> *The earth reels like a drunkard,*
> * it sways like a hut in the wind;*
> *so heavy upon it is the guilt of its rebellion*
> * that it falls—never to rise again (Isaiah 24:4, 12–13, 19–20 NIV).*

The Apostle John, seeing that great apocalyptic moment when God as judge takes his next dramatic step into human history, wrote:

> *The great city was split into three parts, and the cities of the nations fell.*
> *God remembered great Babylon and gave her the wine-cup of the fury of*
> *his wrath (Revelation 16:19).*

Carnival!

I spent my earliest years in the small, sleepy town of Glendora in southern California. But once a year, at least in my childhood recollections, it came alive. During the night, overloaded trucks rumbled into town, depositing all sorts of marvelous contraptions onto a large, ugly vacant lot near our school. The carnival had arrived!

The next day our teachers must have had a terrible time gaining our attention. Never did the clock hands move so slowly. From time to time I would reach into my pocket to be sure those few nickels were still there. All ears, including our teacher's, listened for only one sound—the closing bell.

Moments after, we found ourselves pressing through the brightly colored, beckoning passageway, past canvas walls and into a fantasy world of motion, sounds, and smells. Hours raced by as we slipped past the hawkers, shouting above the sounds of the wheezing steam calliope. Voices tantalized us to win plaster of paris prizes by tossing a ring or knocking down bottles or popping balloons. There were the sword swallower, the fat woman, the maze of mirrors, the fortune teller, the upside-down rides.

This, I thought, was life as it should be—pulsating with excitement and adventure. As darkness arrived, the bright-colored lights mingled with the smells of pink cotton candy and caramel apples. Shadows danced everywhere. Swept along by the noisy crowd, we squeezed our way through the looming bodies of the throng that pressed in around us. From high overhead came the screams from the swirling, neon Ferris wheel. Our sleepy town no longer existed. This alone was real!

All too soon, Mom and Dad would beckon us home. The sounds faded away into the distance while older ones danced long into the night as we were tucked into bed. Then while we slept, the calliope breathed its last, the lights dimmed. Everything came down, was folded away, and long before dawn those huge trucks lurched over the curb and slipped out of town.

Next morning, on our way to school, there it was—that same vacant lot, ugly, dirty, flattened down. Trash caught on crushed thistles; bottle caps and broken glass littered the place. Sticky cotton candy twisted into the sawdust. Had it ever really happened? Could it have been only a dream?

Often when I think of that time long ago, I imagine the world Adam and Eve saw beyond the flaming sword. They were on their own! They were "free" from God. A world to make of their own choosing. Through the centuries, though always "subjected to futility," the children of Adam have attempted to turn this vacant lot into their own "Vanity Fair." Drowning out the screams and groans of human tragedy, the carnival has continued its show. Newer sideshows, brighter lights, voracious video games—until at last we find ourselves on the edge of "virtual reality," the ultimate fantasy.

But darkness will come. There is a day when God will say, "The show is over. Close it down!"

The new wine mourns,
The vine decays,

All the merry-hearted sigh.
The gaiety of tambourines ceases,
The noise of the revelers stops,
The gaiety of the harp ceases…
The city of chaos is broken down…
All joy turns to gloom.
The gaiety of the earth is banished (Isaiah 24:7–8, 10, 11, NASB).

Looking at Infinity

Though the details are fuzzy, I remember a story told about Theodore Roosevelt. After a day spent with the great men of the earth, grappling with weighty issues, evening came. Taking one of his associates, he walked out into the gardens of the White House under the stars. There, they maintained a long, almost painful silence as they stared heavenward. Finally the stillness was broken by Roosevelt's comment,

"Well…now that we see ourselves as small and insignificant as we really are, let's go to bed."

We too must make that kind of effort to get off alone under the stars as David did in Psalm 8, looking long enough to be humbled to the point of utter, almost unbearable smallness. I should warn you if you try to do this, you will not find it easy. You will be tempted to look away. It is so difficult to look at infinity. But don't turn away. Keep on staring into that speckled blackness.

Outdoors on some clear dark night, alone, force yourself to grapple with the vastness of the sky above; vastness that came into existence by a simple word from God. I hope you will see some portion of the Milky Way—those wispy clouds of innumerable stars. Selecting one tiny strand, attempt to narrow your vision to just one of those lesser flickering pinpoints. Have you done that?

Next, exercising that marvelous gift, try to imagine that star is our sun. Then picture yourself standing as you are—way out there—on the dirt of your lonely planet—earth—(a planet far too small to see…one millionth the size of that remote star it circles). This kind of imagination demands the toughest concentration.

Now, broaden your vision again until you see that star as it is, lost among the myriad stars filling the sky. Keep remembering where you are. Where? Way, way off there—standing on a tiny spot of sod on an unseen speck of a speck within a speck within a speck of a single galactic system with billions more beyond. An almost infinite universe.

To do this—to truly do this—is to watch your own sense of importance shrivel to embarrassing nothingness, to the point of almost forgetting to breathe.

Could it be that the brilliance and extravagance of our great cities—the glitter of the Las Vegases of the world—has kept us from doing as David did when he lay beneath the stars, contemplating his own smallness, asking "What is man?" Remember, when he lived he knew so little about the indescribable vastness of the universe, knowledge we take with glib familiarity today. He knew nothing of the billions of galactic spiral universes, each with their hundreds of billions of stars, not to mention the probability of their innumerable circling planets. How much more humbled we should be today!

Then do something else. After looking up, look down and inside and allow yourself to suffer the embarrassing process of contemplating your own fragile flesh—the "bodies of our humble state." Think of the weakness of your will, the fickleness of your emotions. Think about your own pitiably small brain behind your eyes—can you see it? A brain that still is unable to explain the existence of something as familiar as the law of gravity. Think of your own profound mortality. That fleshy pumping heart, the air from your spongy lungs as you feel it whisking through your nostrils. Always, just one breath away from death.

> Those of low estate are but a breath,
>   those of high estate are a delusion;
> in the balances they go up;
>   they are together lighter than a breath (Psalm 62:9).

Out under the stars, force yourself to ask those agonizing questions:

"Where did I ever get the preposterous idea that I could be of any importance to the Being who spoke this universe into existence—that I am significant to him?"

No!

Impossible!

That he would love me?

That he would send his Son to die for me—for me![27]

No! Beyond belief!

Indeed, Paul was right when he wrote of "the body of our humble state." Or Jesus, "that which is born of the flesh is flesh"; or the psalmist's words, "he is mindful that we are but dust" (Philippians 3:21; John 3:6; Psalm 103:14, NASB). To even suggest that we are significant to God would be the worst of human arrogance were it not for one fact:

We are confronted with the voice of this same God who in his Word says that it is true!

We are significant to him. He loves us.

Bow Low before Him

It is time to look back down the furrow we have been digging. Yes, it is true to Scripture. Yes, it is terribly humbling. Even apart from sin, people at their best are still humble creatures in comparison to the God of both the vastness of galactic clusters and the smallness of atoms and quarks.

To this we added the Fall—the monstrosity of human sin, the tragedy of human mortality, and our chosen alienation from God. Dare we yet talk about the dignity of man? Bow low, down on the floor—face and body pressed flat into the carpet. Low and trembling before the God who once said:

> *Turn away from mortals,*
> > *who have only breath in their nostrils,*
> > *for of what account are they? (Isaiah 2:22).*

It is here, in this position, we must begin.

CHAPTER 2

A Cry for Meaning

It would be marvelously refreshing if we could make one simple leap from the lowliness and lostness of human beings as seen in the previous chapter to the loftiness of the new-covenant people of God. But there are two important stepping stones we must consider first. The first one is quite treacherous; it has to do with the issue of sin. Unless we have some clear sense of what is involved, we will lose our way as we try the next step.

These pages will not make for an easy journey. We'll need to walk circumspectly between our preconceived notions and our commitment to get at the essence of biblical truth.

Let's begin by asking some questions about sin. And let's not be satisfied until the answers we find make solid sense. The Bible makes it clear that the lostness, the "dust to dust" despair of humanness, is due to one problem—sin. And we all know what that is. Or do we?

Something Gained...Something Lost

Theologians tell us sin is "any lack of conformity to the moral law of God, either in act, disposition, or state." God says what is morally right; sin is what's wrong.

But why do people find themselves in such a state? Why does sin seem to come so naturally? The answer takes us back to where we were in chapter 1, in the Garden of Eden. Though some writers focus on what Adam and Eve gained—a sin nature—when they fell, the biblical emphasis is on what they lost. There, under the tree of the knowledge of good and evil, Adam and Eve not only lost the hope of immortality (the tree of life), but by choice they lost a dependency-linkage to God's life. They became "alienated from the life of God" (Ephesians 4:18).

They lost dependent life from God. Their relational closeness to him had vanished. Since it was their choice, the loss was actually an act of rebellion.[1] They were now "dead in trespasses and sins." If they were to find meaning in their existence, if they were to make any sense out of the few years allotted to them before their bodies withered and died, they had to do it themselves with what they had—mortal flesh.

God's life flows from no higher source than himself; he draws on no moral law outside of himself. So now Adam and Eve were on their own, severed from any higher source—any moral law other than their own—even as God is "on his own." It was in that tragic sense that they became "like God." At least part of what Satan told them was true. They were now independent creatures, cut off by choice from God's will, from his perfections, from his purity.[2]

From Adam on, all human beings outside of Christ have found themselves unavoidably confronted with their own existence, cut off from both the Subject and the Object of ultimate meaning. Yes, they maintained God's image and the tasks belonging to stewards of life on the planet. But with the love-dependency relationship gone, personal significance vanished with it.

Life for them (if it could be called life) had to be found *within* themselves. In this chosen state of aloneness they were forced to determine how they would handle this thing of *being*. It was unavoidable.

To live is to think.[3]

And to think is to do—to choose, to communicate, to feel.

Yet cut off from the life of God, *to do is to sin.*

"For whatever does not proceed from faith is sin" (Romans 14:23, cf. Romans 8:8).

"Flesh,"[4] that is, everything which made them what they were, became vitally important. Of course it was important, *it was all they had*. Brains, emotions, senses, creativity, imagination, bodies—their own, and those around them who shared the same existence. Life was *right there*, in the flesh. It was nowhere else. My, what potential for those first humans! They were on their own! The grand adventure had begun!

Perhaps the clearest passage describing this drivenness to sin in people still unsaved is Ephesians 2:3. Paul tells us "we were *by nature* children of wrath." This nature, Paul says, was our very life. "Among them we too all formerly lived in the lusts of our flesh, indulging the desires of the flesh and of the mind…" (NASB).

What a tragic paradox. Though Paul used the word *life* in describing such people, it is clear in the context that this life was but walking death. "You were *dead* in your trespasses and sins."

So total is this state of being that God says elsewhere,

> "There is no one righteous, not even one;
>   there is no one who understands,
>   no one who seeks God.
> All have turned away,
>   they have together become worthless;
>   there is no one who does good,
>   not even one" (Romans 3:10–12, NIV).

The why of sin, therefore, is not some mysterious, sinister spiritual gland secreting wickedness within. Rather it is that internal, mental compulsion to fill the emptiness within created by one's rebellious rejection of dependency upon God.

What Makes Life, Life?

What is it that determines how fully alive any person is? What needs to happen during the span of our lives so that at the end of it all we can look back and say, "I have truly lived!" I believe there are two things people require (and not only people, but all creatures God has made): *We must fulfill the destiny for which we were made* while at the same time *being true to who we are.*

One winter, years ago, a stray tomcat showed up at our home. It wasn't long before he had stolen our young daughter's heart. Each day she would find that cat by our back door and shower on him more love than I am sure he had ever known. Because it was so cold outside, our daughter called him "Shivvers." Though he soon had the run of the house, the name stuck. After a few years, Shivvers died and we buried him on the hillside. It was sad, but not too sad, because we knew one thing about Shivvers, and that was that he had truly *lived*. He had done everything a cat was supposed to do—eat at his leisure his own gourmet meals, sleep in his own special spots 80 percent of the time, chase birds, scare off dogs and, best of all, receive the love and pampering of a little girl. There were also those times when Shivvers would disappear only to return after a few days, showing off a few new battle scars, plus what I was sure was a special gleam in his eyes. Yes, Shivvers had truly lived—*fulfilling his destiny* and at the same time *being what he was.*

It is always sad to know of people who in one way or another have died before they have truly lived. An eagle confined in a tiny cage. An Alaskan Husky trapped in a high rise apartment. An artist who never finishes her ultimate masterpiece. A composer whose stroke forever locks his greatest symphony within the prison of his mind. Athletes who are injured just before they compete for an Olympic gold medal, never to have another chance. Even a master thief who is shot just before he completes his perfect crime! (Have you ever rooted for the bad guy?)

Yet Solomon tells us that even if the artist had completed the painting or the composer his symphony or the athlete had gained the gold, all of them would still have missed life. How did this king of old discover this truth? By trying every option he could dream up as to what might make life, *life.*

> I said to myself, "Come now, I will make a test with pleasure; enjoy your-
> self." But again, this also was vanity. I said of laughter, "It is mad," and of
> pleasure, "What use is it?" I searched with my mind how to cheer my

body with wine—my mind still guiding me with wisdom—and how to lay hold of folly, until I might see what was good for mortals to do under heaven during the few days of their life. I made great works; I built houses and planted vineyards for myself; I made myself gardens and parks, and planted in them all kinds of fruit trees. I made myself pools from which to water the forest of growing trees. I bought male and female slaves, and had slaves who were born in my house; I also had great possessions of herds and flocks, more than any who had been before me in Jerusalem. I also gathered for myself silver and gold and the treasure of kings and of the provinces; I got singers, both men and women, and delights of the flesh, and many concubines....

Whatever my eyes desired I did not keep from them; I kept my heart from no pleasure, for my heart found pleasure in all my toil, and this was my reward for all my toil. Then I considered all that my hands had done and the toil I had spent in doing it, and again, all was vanity and a chasing after wind, and there was nothing to be gained under the sun....

So I hated life, because what is done under the sun was grievous to me; for all is vanity and a chasing after wind (Ecclesiastes 2:1–8, 10–11, 17).

One by one he tried each option. Quite a list!

> The luxury of endless possessions.
> Slaves enough to set him free from drudgery.
> Beauty enclosing him.
> Every sensual delight known to man—every taste,
> sound, fragrance, sexual fantasy.
> Every rush.

He tried them all.

Imagine grasping as your own *everything your eyes desired*. Wandering through the world's greatest shopping malls after winning the lottery would scarcely begin to tell Solomon's story.

But even if you won the lottery, Solomon still had two things you and I do not have. Because he was the king, he could get away with just about anything he chose to do. And because he was the wisest man who ever lived, not only could he dream bigger dreams, he could mentally sort them all out when he was through.

It wasn't that he didn't get his rush. He did (see 2:10). But when it was over, he declared he "hated life." Everything was futility, "chasing after wind." Try as he might, he could not escape the bitter reality that he had missed life.

Where Then, Is Life?

In the Bible, the concept of sin is inseparable from the issue of meaning. Although we lack Solomon's gold, we do have our own ambitions and fragile fantasies. For these we struggle and sacrifice, envy and steal (quite subtly, of course). Unfortunately, we do not possess Solomon's wisdom. Thinking we've made it, we cling tenaciously to our idols and respectable pride, unwilling to admit to ourselves or anyone else, "Is not this thing in my right hand a fraud?" (Isaiah 44:20)

By nature (because of Adam), human beings are committed to this sometimes colorful, ofttimes suspenseful, unavoidably self-centered, but always "dead-end street" existence. Sin, then, is not simply a capacity or a sinister spiritual force. It is rather *the unbendable bent of every person who does not possess life from God.* People have no alternative but to struggle with the "futility" of their minds (Ephesians 4:17–18), forced by birth into a state of rebellion, to live in a world "subjected to futility" (Romans 8:20).

No choice but to deal with the issue of meaning, significance, purpose—
>   to search for it,
>   fight for it,
>   envy it in others,
>   react against those who might take it from us,
>   grieve because it has been lost,
>   or perhaps (most deceptively and pitifully) be deluded into
>   thinking we have found it.

To give up is suicide. But to continue existing in meaninglessness—is that so much better?

This is sin. It is not merely something a non-Christian has, it is his most basic nature.

It would appear that through much of history only the rare person ever stopped and asked why we exist. Probably for most, the job of survival was so demanding there simply wasn't time to ask questions. For others, unquestioned commitment to family or king or religious system appeared to fill the vacuum. Yet the question Why? has ever lurked in the shadows, refusing to leave. The conscious or unconscious issue of meaning has driven every person who ever lived.

Few of us have stopped to realize the dramatic effect the last two hundred years of the industrial (and more recently, electronic and genetic) revolution continue to have upon man and his struggle with meaning. It has given multitudes the time and means to discover entirely new counterfeit reasons for living. The multiplied billions spent each year on advertising has not been a poor investment. Spot TV commercials and lavish full-color magazine ads confidently point us to where we can find life. Whether it's a new car or toothpaste, the line is the same. There must be millions who are so captivated by materialism as to make it profitable for some TV channels to provide nothing but endless commercials!

With more leisure time, we grab at entertainment with its many faces, each one beckoning us away from our own world into someone else's. Whether their world is real or simply another fantasy doesn't make much difference, at least it isn't mine. And to think that just around the corner I will have the ability to create my own virtual reality!

For some—the dedicated executive, the political activist, the environmental crusader, the innovative public relations man, the loyal employee who attaches a father image to either his company or his union—the continuing revolution itself represents meaning in life.

For others, this revolution has stolen the only meaning left to them—the challenge simply to survive. Promising cradle-to-grave security, it has resulted in psychotic boredom. This is all too evident in the epidemic of drugs, growing fascination with gambling, sex perversion and exploitation, thrill killings, zealous crusades for empty causes. Then there are those far more socially acceptable symptoms that surface: an addiction to television or an obsession with more and more spectator sports.

Most recently, the increase of ethnic wars, power struggles, and economic skullduggery have changed the whispered *whys* into bold cries no thinking individual can fail to hear. Unless people are able to practice some form of self-deception, they admit to a strange emptiness invading even their more productive moments. It is an emptiness marked by both a sense of futility and loneliness—the foreboding doubt that perhaps what they had assumed was *life* is not really life at all.

THE TWO-FOLD TRAGEDY OF EDEN

If only we could grasp the absolute, unutterable horror of that tragic day in Eden! It was a two-fold tragedy, both man's and God's.

Imagine for a moment you are a judge who is also a master woodcraftsman. With supreme skill you carved a gavel, uniquely shaped to be held in your hand as an extension and expression of yourself. Imagine further that somehow that choice gavel is removed from your hand—the one for whom it was made. Imagine it being picked up and used for hammering nails or pounding in bean poles or scraping the moldy insides of garbage cans. No matter how productive that gavel might be, or how destructive if used as a club, every use, every act, would be a most ugly offense to you, the gavel maker.

So also must the human race have become an offense to God. The very creatures who were to express God's glory—his mind, his will, his love—were aborting and perverting that display.

But the tragedy was not God's alone.

The tragedy was also man's.

This crime against God resulted in a curse settling over the world. It settled on all creation so that it, too, "was subjected to futility" (Romans 8:20). But it settled most pointedly upon people. They "became futile in their thinking" (Romans 1:21); "a mere phantom, going to and fro, bustling about, but only in vain" (paraphrase of Psalm 39:6, cf. NIV); caught in a web of "futile ways" (1 Peter 1:18; cf. 2 Kings 17:15; Jeremiah 2:5). It was heard in the shouts from the crowds as they erected the tower of Babel. "Let us make a name for ourselves" (Genesis 11:4). It was repeatedly echoed in the words, "And all the people did what was right in their own eyes" (Judges 17:6, 21:25). Perhaps Solomon gave it its most eloquent expression when he cried:

> "Meaningless! Meaningless!"
>   says the Teacher.
> "Utterly meaningless!
>   Everything is meaningless" (Ecclesiastes 1:2, NIV).[5]

The Master of My Fate, the Captain of My Soul

And so it has remained through all the centuries. As a representative child of Adam, I have rejected all of God's efforts to communicate with me. I stoned his prophets. I mocked his Scriptures. And then—two thousand years ago—I killed his Son, the One who came to bring me the only hope, his very life. Since that day, my journey through the darkness has only accelerated. I have become adept at inventing counterfeit lights—bright-colored, flashing lights, pseudo rainbows, artificial sunsets, celluloid stars. My carnival.

More recently I discovered that God is dead, anyway. I am a product of organic evolution, a cosmic accident. A unique moment in a mysterious thirty-billion year process. It is an adventure filled with suspense *and* cruelty *and* meaninglessness. And though I do not know what is ahead, never fear—I am on my way!

> It matters not how strait the gate,
> How charged with punishments the scroll,
> I am the master of my fate,
> I am the captain of my soul (William Ernest Henley).

Even today, after reading the morning news and the latest issue of *Time* magazine, and even though I acknowledge countless gallons of human tears produced by an endless cycle of agonizing tragedy, I, along with the world's majority, maintain that Adam made *the right decision*. Even as I swallow my tranquilizers, rush to my psychiatrist, take that extra drink, endure my third divorce, and watch my children reject all the ideals I have tried to pass on—I still say there is hope!

> You grew weary from your many wanderings,
>> but you did not say, "It is useless."
> You found your desire rekindled,
>> and so you did not weaken (Isaiah 57:10).

A Fresh Definition of Sin

This, then, is the essence of sin. Though the traditional theological definition of sin is accurate, what we need is a definition that looks more at the mechanics of sin. I suggest that sin is more pointedly

the expression of man's struggle with the meaning of his existence while missing life from God. It is all the varieties of ways man deals with and expresses his rebellion against his Creator as he encounters the inescapable issue of meaning.[6]

Adam and Eve voluntarily placed themselves in this rebel position of independence from God. They chose to be the determiners of significance in life.

Our first parents would decide what was to be good and what was to be bad; where values were to be found; where life was to be found. So "sin came into the world through one man, and death came through sin" (Romans 5:12). Sin is a transgression of the law of God. And to reject life, to determine a will different from the will of God (which is the law of God), is the most heinous crime a person can commit.

In that instant of the Fall, self-sovereignty became the driving force of human life. This, by the way, is the reason for secular humanism's hostility toward biblical Christianity: It would usurp the primacy of human beings. *The essence of sin, then, cannot be separated from the issue of meaning.*

Perhaps someone is voicing an inner objection at this point.

"I think you are playing lightly with the horrible nature of sin," they say. "How can you describe it so casually as a struggle with meaning in contrast with those scathing descriptions in Romans 1 and 3? You are not doing justice to those forceful biblical descriptions."

Just the opposite is true! Isaiah 53:5 most literally says, "He was pierced for our *rebellion*; He was crushed for our *perversions*."[7] In rebelling against God's perfect intention and perverting the qualities of humanness toward self-centered ends, man has committed the ultimate offense. For the wrath of God to be aroused—for the lake of fire to be man's ultimate end—*is* justice.

"The Deeds of the Flesh"

For the non-Christian, this combined *will to live* and the *will to discover meaning* find expression in what Paul calls "the deeds of the flesh."

> Now the works of the flesh are obvious: fornication, impurity, licentiousness, idolatry, sorcery, enmities, strife, jealousy, anger, quarrels, dissensions, factions, envy, drunkenness, carousing, and things like these (Galatians 5:19–21).

The first three deeds, *fornication, impurity,* and *licentiousness,* obviously relate to man's attempts to get at meaning through his body—his glands and senses, his fantasies. *Idolatry* is very broad. An idolater is one who has made up his mind on where and how he will find life. And whatever it is, he will work feverishly to get it, guard it, sacrifice to it, and worship it. To lose it is to lose life.

Sorcery focuses on the search for meaning in the occult. *Enmities, strife, jealousy,* and *anger* reflect the standard reactions of one who is frustrated with a given set of circumstances. Either some supposed meaning in life has been taken from him, threatened, or kept just beyond his reach.

Quarrels, dissensions, and *factions* point to conflicting ideologies as to where life really is, where values are. *Envy* is clear enough. You and another person are nominated for senior class president or cheerleader…and you lose. Your best friend steals the girl you had your eye on. Your associate at work gets a promotion and raise and you don't. You got the smaller scoop of ice cream. Someone else has made it, and you want it.

I believe at moments like these, consciously or unconsciously, we feel threatened by whatever we thought made living significant. Meaning—even as lowly a meaning as "right this moment, life for me is a stomach full of ice cream, stimulated taste buds, a satisfied nose"—has been hurt. Someone else got the bigger scoop.

The final two deeds, *drunkenness* and *carousing*, reveal that we have given up.

We no longer have any desire to seek meaning.

We've tried and tried to make some sense out of life.

We're through trying.

We want out.

Please Don't Tamper with My Idol

Of the various expressions of the deeds of the flesh, *idolatry* seems uniquely captivating, especially the socially acceptable types of idolatry. We grasp so tightly to our fulfillments. And from the point of view of human welfare, it is good that we do. We find meaning in our work, our community service, our artistic creations. Our idealistic humanism, instead of attacking others or escaping responsibility, is actually contributing to the well-being of others. But let someone threaten our idol and watch out! You'd be surprised how quickly we can react.[8]

Perhaps my particular idol is that of being a popular, much-admired teacher. And then some better teacher comes along. I begin to hear that students are flocking to sign up for his section (to the detriment of mine). Stand back! My protective reflexes are as quick as a panther. I say to myself, "That new teacher seems smooth enough…probably covering his own insecurity! Just give him a few weeks and the veneer will wear thin. Anyway, students are poor judges of what makes a good teacher."

Such "wholesome" idols are so terribly subtle because I can say to myself, "But isn't 'being a teacher every student would love to have' a worthy goal?" And of course the answer is "Yes!" But a goal can easily become *the* goal and as such it becomes *the* measurement of where life or meaning is to be found. It then becomes an idol—a very fragile idol at that. As an idol, it cannot help but cast a shadow on the priority of God—his joy, his sufficiency, his glory—and my relation to that priority. It is so difficult to separate one's *identity* from the particular *channel* through which God might desire that identity to flow.

There are so many potential idols. Maybe yours has been to be attractive to the opposite sex. And at last your efforts appear to be rewarded. Someone has found you attractive. Oh, what a feeling! And then comes that faint coolness and reserve followed by tactful rejections and finally that blunt, cold breakup. That would be shattering enough to your idol, but then you discover that she (or he) has not only rejected you, but has found someone else. Someone more fun, more attractive than you. Devastating, humiliating. Out of this terrible hurt you either fall into depression as you feel life slipping through your fingers or you pick yourself up and once again fight to protect your idol.

"She wasn't good enough for me, anyway. Didn't appreciate my fine, inner qualities. Knew all along she couldn't be trusted. They deserve each other. She'll get burned by him for sure."

With that, your idol, your sense of meaning and fulfillment in life, is once again safe and secure.

Some idols are especially wholesome, but they are still idols.

An individual's life may be entirely submerged in his family. He has carefully constructed his priorities, and his family is number one. Then one day some drunk careens across the center line and his entire family is wiped out in an instant. Yes, he grieves, almost more than he can bear. But it is more than grief. In losing his family, he has lost the only reality that gave him life and meaning. There is nothing left! Unless he soon discovers some other goal, some worthy idol, he will turn to embrace any one or more of the other works of the flesh we've discussed from Galatians 5. He might even choose the ultimate escape, suicide, which is no escape at all.

It is both surprising and discouraging to discover how many sins we Christians commit that are really nothing more than flesh-level efforts to protect some idol.

Remember how you felt when someone said, "Say, you're putting on weight!" or "I didn't know you were losing your hair." Maybe you controlled it, but it was there nevertheless—you were angry, offended, just a little bit hateful. This was especially true if you were criticized in some area in which you had taken pride in yourself, such as in speaking or in sports or in being a good cook or a loving, generous person. Inwardly, at least, the sparks flew and you flushed with emotion. You might even have told just a little lie to keep your idol intact.

That Dangerous Meaning Vacuum

Putting it in such terms makes it sound so simple; but it isn't. The lust of sin often strikes with poignant, consuming force. It may be food. It may be sex. It may be one of a thousand obsessions which so captivate us that for a time we find ourselves unable to think of anything else. Why is that?

Usually we become gripped with an obsession to sin when some other more respectable or righteous fulfillment in life is being frustrated. Perhaps some relationship which should have been realized, some dream dissolved, some disappointment in our own ability to fulfill a task or to use our heads. Nothing opens the door to sin faster than failure. (Unless, perhaps, it is success.)

Since it is simply unthinkable to be alive without some degree of satisfaction that can bring sense into life, I automatically reach out for whatever object or experience is readily obtainable. That is why physical or sensory lusts are so especially quick to arise. My vacuum of meaninglessness can be filled in an instant! There are times when simply stuffing my mouth satisfies. And for those moments, life seems to be making sense. Shallow sense, but then, any sense is better than an aching vacuum.

Sometimes it takes a little more time. If the lust is sex, it may take a little while to find that person, that video or magazine, that "something" which will awaken this fantasy of meaning. I must consider my reputation of course and my financial resources, it may require some careful planning and delay, but that's okay. For you see, from the very moment I set my mind on lust, *I am moving!* My mind is alive—planning, anticipating.

And something else that's remarkable. Even if I cannot lay my hands on whatever object or experience lust demands, I can easily slide into fantasy. For those few seductive moments, I can forget the real world. I can push aside the haunting frustration, the emptiness, the broken plans and dreams. I can even forget my lackluster life.

(What I have just described is equally valid if the lust is in the area of possessions, power, or recognition.)

Then, of course, if my fantasies can be followed by actual experience, I have doubly lusted, doubly lived. Little wonder lusts are so consuming! Temporary? Oh yes. And invariably followed once again by the gnawing emptiness of that powerful meaning vacuum.[9]

Portrait of a Gallery

Try to imagine for a moment the entire human race as though it were an art gallery full of picture frames. Long, long halls. Billions of picture frames—*without any pictures!* Empty. Can you visualize it?

Some of the frames are very carefully carved. Some boast delicate gold leaf, others are rather gaudily painted. A few are dirty, chipped. But every frame is wrapped around—*nothing*—emptiness.

Is it possible that the human race is seen in such a way by God? An art gallery with no paintings!

Each human being was intended to frame an inimitable, individual masterpiece of God's own reflected glory. But where God should be, there is only emptiness, a bare patch of wall. Since the frames are conscious, however, the fact of emptiness is simply too devastating—too self-destructive—to acknowledge. And so humankind becomes obsessed with the only thing left to it: its own flesh. The frame. Life, if it is to be found at all, must be found in one's own frame and the frames around him.

So, ingeniously and carefully, man lights his gallery, carpets and air-conditions the halls, creates all sorts of special displays, and leads community crusades to clean up the dirty and broken frames. In solemn conferences he formulates long-range plans to deal with the rapidly increasing quantity of frames brought about by mass production and new preservation techniques. The antique section of the gallery presents a special challenge.

Compromises must be found to lessen the tension between frames demanding individualistic displays and frames committed to a group identity. Calm must be restored to those remoter wings of the gallery that have been so neglected and now demand equality with the more privileged wings.

Since one must naturally protect the welfare of one's own frame, and since growth now appears beyond control, it seems that the gallery rules must be changed. Forget that dark hall, those jumbled rooms. Dismantle those old frames. Abort the delivery of new frames, euthanize the old ones. No, wait. It wasn't supposed to work out this way! We thought all our new inventions and progress would solve the difficulties and…if only we had more time! But the air's getting foul. Lights are beginning to flicker. Sounds of confusion are coming from every corner.

And anyway—*there are no pictures.*

We all know that.

Emptiness. Everywhere emptiness. What difference does it all make, anyway?

Oh, the tragedy of Eden! Rejecting dependence upon the will and character of God, Adam and Eve rejected *life!* Looking for fullness, they found instead a fathomless despair. Even if in some twisted sense they fulfilled by sinning what they were—sinners—they still were missing the destiny for which God had created them. Their one bridge to meaning, their fundamental reason for existing, lay collapsed in hopeless ruin before them. Man's essential nature was now "in the flesh." And the Bible says that "those who are in the flesh cannot please God."

So, by his very nature, man is a sinner.

Cut off from his Creator.

Cut off from any hope of meaning.

A rebel trapped in futility.

That is what sin is all about.[10]

IN SEARCH OF HOPE

To appreciate the wholesomeness of authentic Christian personhood, it must first be seen over against the biblical picture of the lostness of people and the fundamental nature of sin. When we rebelled against a dependent love relationship with God, we were left without the prospect of fulfilling the primary reason for which we were made. For all other creatures, to be who they are and to fulfill the destiny for which they were made mean essentially the same thing. The one great exception is people. For us, these two goals are hopelessly in opposition.

So it was, long ago in the Garden, human beings forced upon themselves the task of self-fulfillment without any hope of success. Authentic meaning, significance, and purpose lay always beyond their grasp. It is this fact that underlies the darkness of evil. This then, is sin—a tragedy for human beings and an offense to God. Apart from God's intervening miracle of changing us, there is no hope.

CHAPTER 3

More
than
Justified

We've looked at the tragedy of sin long enough. It's time we focus on what it means to be a Christian. By the time you finish this chapter, I hope it will be clear that the answer to the problem of sin and the despair of meaninglessness is found in discovering the vast scope of the miracle God performed when he saved you—a miracle that actually changed you.

SELF-CONSCIOUSNESS, GOD'S SPECIAL GIFT TO PEOPLE

I doubt if you'll ever bump into a turtle or a frog who is seriously contemplating his own existence. I may be wrong, but I have trouble picturing such a creature involved in self-interrogation as it basks in the afternoon sun.

"I wonder who I really am, or why I am at all?"

I can't see it.

But God has made men and women to be self-conscious beings, beings who reflect on their own identity. In a passage we considered earlier, listen to David's voice:

When I look at your heavens, the work of your fingers, the moon and the stars that you have established; What are human beings that you are mindful of them, mortals that you care for them? (Psalm 8:3–4)

I believe God has given to us this unique ability of self-consciousness, of thinking about who we are and why we are alive, for a very important reason. Without it, no one would ever respond to Jesus.

By the Way, Who Are You?

With many non-Christians, it was this very questioning that broke down the barrier of resistance to the conviction of the Holy Spirit. Perhaps this was the way it happened in your life. You came to the place where you began asking yourself, "I wonder what life is all about, anyway? This squirrel-cage existence doesn't make sense at all. There *has* to be something else."

This ability of self-awareness can also serve as a special means of grace to lead a believer deeper and deeper into the real meaning of life.

We all do a fair amount of thinking about ourselves. Yet I've been surprised to discover that many people don't like to be pressed too far in answering the question of their own identity.

"Pardon me, but who are you? Have you thought about that?"

"Well, sure. I'm Sam Jones."

"No, I mean *who are you?* Not just your name."

"Oh…well, I live in Portland, and—"

"Excuse me, but let's try again. Who *are* you?"

"Aw, you know, I'm the guy who drives that yellow Corvette. I work at the service station on the corner. My sister married the mayor's son."

"No, you misunderstand me. I'm asking you who you are—way down deep inside. Who are you?"

"Come on. I'm a member of the human race. What planet did you come from?"

No, people don't like questions like that. Even Christians become ill at ease.

"Who am I? I'm a Baptist. No, wait, I get you now. I'm a Christian— you know."

"Tell me."

"Well, a Christian is a person who has accepted Christ."

"But I didn't ask you what you've done. I asked you who you are."

After fumbling around a bit he might respond, "I'm going to heaven when I die" or "I'm a person who has been forgiven of all my sins. I'm a believer." Then again, he might think he knows what you're driving at and say, "Sure, I know who I am. I'm just a plain old sinner saved by grace."

In this chapter, my hope is that you will come to grips with who you are in a way you perhaps never have before. *Just who are you?*

Fragile Identities

Generally, when we think of our own identity, we focus on some particular position we have (or hope to have). We are fathers or mothers, students or teachers, baseball players or farmers. Yet when we stop to think about such identities, we have to admit they are all so fragile, so tenuous. *"I'm a mother!"* you say. And that is beautiful. Just great...as long as your children are alive. But who would you be if a tragedy takes them from you? What is your identity then? *"I'm a businessman."* That sounds solid, until the bottom drops out. You're bankrupt, business gone. Who are you then? *"I'm a vocalist."* Yes, you are...until that dreaded surgery makes a mockery of the title.

"Who are you?"

"Oh, someday I hope to be—"

"Who are you?"

"Aw, I don't have to worry about that. I'm retired!"

An Identity Pilgrimage

I wonder—would you be willing to follow me on an identity pilgrimage? It is a rather private one. My own. Parts of it are stupid, even silly. Some of it sad. But it all leads to the most glorious event I have ever consciously experienced. A new beginning!

I'll have to go back to when I was a little boy, walking down an aisle at the conclusion of a church service to let everyone know I was trusting Jesus as my Savior. From then on, I knew that I was forgiven; that I would go to heaven when I died; that God heard my prayers. I was a Christian.

As time went along, I did most of the things a Christian boy was expected to do—Sunday school and church, evening youth group, rallies, summer camps. One camp was decisive. I remember saying to God (with considerable fear of the consequences), "Oh God, my life is yours to do anything you want with it." I was fourteen, six feet tall, gold-rimmed glasses, embarrassingly skinny. The biggest reason for my decision? I saw it as the lesser of two fears. Sitting next to me in his wheelchair was a boy terribly crippled by polio—my own secret fear. It wasn't as though the speaker used the crippled boy as an illustration, but he did send shivers down my spine as he warned of the danger of backing away from total commitment to Christ. Thus, 90 percent out of dread and maybe 10 percent out of love for God, I responded. "Lord, if I don't give my life to you now, you're going to take it one way or another! So here it is."

I was now a dedicated Christian.

A Sack of Weed Seeds

I soon discovered that my decision seemed to create more problems than it solved. First, my concept of dedication kept colliding with all sorts of self-centered desires and fantasies. Second, these repeated collisions underlined more than ever how sinful I was. What little positive self-image I had was now shattered. I knew that "nothing good dwells within me." I knew that for sure. I was a sinner—a dedicated Christian sinner. So much for self-image!

Soon after that, a youth rally speaker declared (with considerable enthusiasm) that we were God the Father's love gift to his Son. He had us turn to John 17 where repeatedly the expression occurs: "those whom you gave me." As I listened, I thought to myself, *if someone gave me a gift like that, I would call it a dirty trick! For God to give me to Jesus would be like giving a doctor a bottle of germs or a farmer a sack of weed seeds.* Yet as I read John 17, it sounded as though Jesus actually was pleased with his gift. How could that possibly be?

Oh, to Be Somebody!

So desperately I wanted to really be somebody. Just to hit a home run at summer camp with all those girls cheering along the side! But every time at bat was the same old thing. My middle name could well have been Clumsy. Compounding my awkwardness, I refused to wear those ugly, wire-rimmed glasses. Naturally, the balls just swished past my bat and home-run glory became just one more fantasy.

In this struggle for some sense of personal worth, friends are terribly important. A friend is someone who thinks you are somebody even when you don't see how you could possibly be of value to anyone. There was the one cute girl with long, blond hair who actually wanted to walk with me to the last campfire. Grasping her hand, I glanced up through those tall, dark pine trees and thought, *Say, God, maybe I'm not such a nobody after all!*

One day, walking down the hall in high school, the basketball coach spotted me—now 6-feet-3-inches of bone tightly wrapped with skin. He told me I would make a fantastic basketball player.

Say, maybe he could be right!

And I really tried. Being a Christian would be so much easier if Coach's prediction proved true. But somehow my elongated appendages wouldn't cooperate with my fervent desires. I might as well have dressed the part of a clown out on the court—I had everything but the costume.

But there was one day of glory. In the middle of an exciting game I found myself loping down court, rather than occupying my usual niche on the bench. Someone threw the ball at me. Hard. Right at my stomach. Doubling up and falling to the floor, I desperately threw the ball up…and made a basket! The hometown crowd erupted. I read my name in the school paper, even the town paper. I didn't have the courage to tell anyone I hadn't aimed for the basket; the goal was sheer chance. I simply hurt too much to do anything else. But oh, it felt so good to be somebody!

"Nothing Good Dwells in Me"

The time finally came when I couldn't put it off any longer. I had to decide what I was going to do with my life. Wouldn't it be great to have such evident talent that a decision was unnecessary? An artistic flair, a mechanical knack, a beautiful voice. I had a friend in college with such a voice. All he had to do was learn a few more things about music, get up, open his mouth, and everybody would marvel. (They still do.) Self-worth, identity, meaning? He had it made!

As a Christian, I often struggled to live up to "the expected" level, whatever that was. But always close to the surface lurked a surging supply of feelings and desires vividly supporting my "biblical"[1] conclusion "that *nothing good* dwells in me." Speakers told me that God would take away all my old desires. He didn't! No, I didn't drink or smoke. Dancing was out; only Disney movies were okay. But what I couldn't do in public, my imagination dreamed in private. I was sure that deep down inside, something about me was very bad. And I didn't think there was a thing I could do about it.

I remember a warm, summer evening when two girls from the East visited our youth group. As the group's president, I was more than willing to extend a very friendly welcome. Especially to one of them—simply beautiful. My thoughts flickered rapidly as we smiled through small talk. With the local girls, I had to maintain my committed Christian image. No fooling around—word spread fast in our group. But a visitor…I drove her home. She was as delightful to sit next to as I had imagined. But to my disappointment, all she wanted to do was talk about spiritual things, all the way to the door. I didn't even get to hold her hand.

With all my burning fantasies (quite innocent by today's standards) still intact, I drove home. A long, long drive home. Piercing me deeper than any disappointment was the knowledge that my heart was "deceitful above all things and desperately wicked." How could it be that my desire to please God could fit inside the same person who was so captivated by desires that were just the *opposite* of what pleased him? What was I anyway? A spiritual failure, that was for sure.

Trying Harder

In order to muffle those inner cries of failure, I tried hard to do the things I figured God wanted me to do. I took every college Bible course available.

Every weekend, all the way through college, I worked in struggling rural Sunday schools. Not that I wanted to, but it seemed the way to please God. Then there were four years of seminary, four years of youth ministry, four years in the pastorate. I was committed to become someone for God—a youth leader, a pastor, a husband, a father, a teacher, a *something*.

And God was gracious. Again and again he showed me mercy and honored his Word. He did love me! I knew "the answers" and I taught them well, with all the sincere, emotional energy I could muster. Yet I remember one night driving home after speaking on the subject of spiritual victory. "David," I said to myself, "what you told them tonight is true. At least according to the way you were taught. But David, it isn't working for you, is it? It isn't working at all."

I had reckoned myself "dead unto sin" dozens of times. I "claimed by faith" that sin's power had been broken. I pled with God with all my heart for victory and joy. I confessed and received forgiveness countless times. I wore out my little packet of memory verses. I sincerely tried to lay hold of the fullness of the Holy Spirit in earnest faith. It was real faith.

And it did not work.

Why? Wasn't I right in what I believed, in what I was taught? The answer is both yes and no. The yes side of the answer is truly wonderful. It is an answer in which we can take great joy. It is only as we truly understand it—and value it—that we can then turn to look at the no side of the answer.

The yes has to do with one of the greatest words in the Bible, a big word that in itself might tempt you to stop reading because it sounds so theological. Please don't! It's too important. It's the word *justification*.

What Is Justification?

Yes, I knew that I had been "justified by faith." Eventually I even found out what it meant. Because its biblical meaning has little to do with the way the word is commonly used today, let's take some time to be sure we're clear about it. To do this we will need to exercise that gift we spoke of earlier—our imaginations.

Let's imagine GOD in his absolute moral perfection at the very top of the picture below. He is a God of absolute justice. That's just the way he is. All earthly comparisons fall short.

Down at the bottom, let's place me (or you), the SINNER.

GOD

(ABSOLUTE JUSTICE)

W R A T H

GUILTY
REBEL
SINNER

Could God in any way receive me?

Of course not!

In my sin I was the opposite of everything he is. In God's judicial record book, everything listed under my name was laced with one word: sin. The only thing I deserved from him was his wrath.

But wasn't I just a wee bit lovable? No, not a bit. On my own I was at heart a rebel, "a child of wrath," trapped in the power of my own sin (Isaiah 64:7).

We are so used to compromises and plea bargaining that it's difficult for us to accept the truth that God cannot fudge even within himself. For him there is no chapter 13 bankruptcy escape clause—ever. His moral laws are so much a part of him that to change them would be to change himself. They are unbendable.

The greatest proof of this fact is the cross. Because of the evil of our essential natures, no matter how much God might have wished to forgive us, the eternal punishment we deserved still *had to be administered.* Could there be a substitute? Yes. But that substitute had to be a perfect substitute. Of course, the substitute would have to be a human being (to take our place), but also a *perfect* human being who needed no punishment himself. Not only that, if the punishment was to be completed—since it was an eternal punishment—*and* if it was to be enough for every human being, it required someone no less than God himself to be that substitute, he who is the infinite Lord of eternity.

But he did love me, didn't he? Yes he did, with *agape* love.

God was deeply moved to give himself to me in my complete unlovableness. Yes, he loved me, but *not because of what I was or even because of what I could become.* Instead, it was because God is a remarkably self-giving person: "God is love." He simply *chose* to give himself to me—and to you, whether or not we would respond.

So what did he do? God's divine Son willingly became a human being, fulfilling a perfectly righteous human life. At the cross, having now taken into himself the sins of the entire world, the Father crushed him with the weight of his wrath. It was an act of *perfect justice.* (Read Isaiah 53:4–10; 2 Corinthians 5:21.)

In the midst of my lostness, God brought me under his convicting grace and I received Christ as my Savior. In that moment God installed a marvelous "screen" between himself and me, the sinner. That screen is Jesus and everything about him—his perfect life, his substitutionary death.

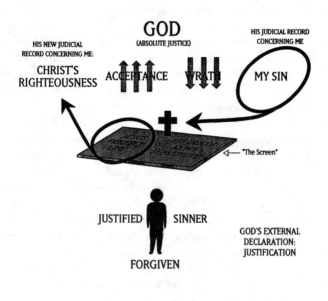

At the cross the Father took the entire condemning record against me—the sum total of all of my lawlessness—and placed it on Jesus, "nailing it to the cross" (Colossians 2:13–14). Because the punishment Jesus received perfectly satisfied the Father's justice, I heard God say to me, "David, you are hereby totally forgiven!"

But God did more than that. He next replaced my old record in his judicial record book with the perfect record of Jesus' own righteous life. Because of what he saw, *he declared me to be as righteous as his Son.* What a fabulous screen! Simply amazing! In other words, because of that screen, when God looks my way, what he sees is not my sin, but Jesus' righteousness.

But if for a moment—horrible thought!—that screen were not there and he saw me as I really am, he would call me what I am, a SINNER. But

God would not do that; he is committed to always seeing me "in Christ." He no longer remembers our sins (Hebrews 10:17).[2]

This is a most wonderful truth. I can rest in the fact that God accomplished this without any dubious "book juggling." Before the infinite Judge of the universe, according to his own flawless reckoning, I now possess total forgiveness and acceptance.

I am justified!

I am judicially righteous, positionally righteous. This is the way God sees me. On that screen he sees his Son.

This is no minor matter. For Paul especially, the wonder of forgiveness and acceptance before God was a marvelous truth. It is the centerpiece of Romans 3–5.

> *Therefore, since we are justified by faith, we have peace with God through our Lord Jesus Christ (Romans 5:1).*

During the long, dark centuries of the Middle Ages, the church almost drowned in despair because it had lost this awareness.

Never able to satisfy God's righteousness.

Endless confessionals.

Agonizing penance.

And always awaiting the dread of purgatory.

In Martin Luther and John Calvin the light that broke through that darkness shined most of all on the great truth that produced the Reformation—*justification by faith.* It was as though that great doctrine said it all.[3] That truth alone became the heart and soul of what "Christian" meant.

This then, is the yes answer regarding what I believed. But it is critically important to understand that "justification takes place outside the believer." This act of God *changed nothing whatsoever inside of a believer.*[4]

How Do We Become Godly?

True, God sees me (remember the screen) as he sees his Son in union with him. That is so good to know. But justification doesn't change *me.* Millard Erickson's illustration is helpful:

This union is like that of a couple who, when they marry, merge their assets and liabilities. With their property held in joint tenancy, the assets of the one can wipe out the liabilities of the other, leaving a positive net balance.[5]

This helps us to understand Paul when he stated that God "justifies the ungodly" (Romans 4:5). In other words, this act of God—justification—does not *make* anyone godly. Well then, if I haven't changed, sinning will be as natural for me after being saved as before. If that is so, then my agonizing struggles described earlier were what I should have expected. Of course that was very discouraging, but at least I knew I was as normal as anyone else.

It is certainly good to know what God sees when he looks my way (the screen idea again). But what a terrible dilemma I now face! Mine is the impossible task to try fulfilling the destiny for which I was originally intended: I am to be holy. Yet at the same time, I must somehow stop *being myself!*

Of course I know what I actually am. But I am somehow to ignore this fact and instead try to see myself the way God sees me. That's tough to do! And to think I heard someone once say, "God has a wonderful plan for your life." What *wonderful* plan? Trying to be what I am not?

But there is more. This wonderful plan involves my going to heaven someday. I like that. But wait, does it ring true? I, an ungodly-yet-justified sinner, walking around in a holy heaven? That couldn't be! I would dirty up the place as soon as I got there.

"Yes," someone will say to me, "but God sees you in Christ." Great! Is heaven a place where God will never see me for who I really am? Will he always keep me hidden behind that screen, somehow enclosed in a sterile "bag" so that I won't be able to infect heaven with my inborn virus?

I should be most thankful that God's act of justification delivers me from his eternal wrath. But since it does not change me, *it does not qualify me to fit in a holy heaven.*[6] That's not only true, but it is very important to realize how true it is.

Do We Become Holy When We Die?

"Oh," someone will say, "don't worry, you will become a different kind of person when you die. You will be holy then." True, our behavior will be perfect then. *But nowhere does the Bible tell us that after we die God changes our essential nature.* There is no heavenly "car wash" at the pearly gates. The Bible says only one thing about what happens to Christians when they die: They leave their bodies behind (Romans 8:18–23; 2 Corinthians 5:8; Philippians 3:21; 2 Peter 1:13–15).

It is common for people to use the words of 1 John 3:2 ("we will be like him") to prove that when we die (or when Jesus comes back) God will at last clean us up and we will be holy as Jesus is. But a careful look at the passage reveals such an idea was not in John's mind at all. In fact, John later stated "as he is, so are we in the world" (1 John 4:17). His joyous hope was in anticipating the day "we will see him as he is." Why will we see him "as he is"? Because we too will have glorified resurrection *bodies.* Bodies—eyes, emotions, minds—capable of not only enduring, but enjoying the God "who dwells in unapproachable light, whom no one has ever seen or can see" (1 Timothy 6:16). We will see him then "as he is!" (The result of this awareness is that we commit ourselves afresh to walk in purity "just as he is pure," while still in our sin-prone, unredeemed bodies.)[7]

Well then, if God doesn't make me a different kind of person when I die, then I must be what I thought I was all along—nothing more than a forgiven, justified sinner. If that is so, even forgetting the problem of heaven for a moment, what choices do I have as to how I make it now?

What Are the Options?

One option is to conclude that Christianity is telling everybody about an impossible ideal. But at least it gives us something to dream about.

Or maybe I should assume that holiness really is possible if I work at it very hard. Since I do love God, no matter how discouraging life is, I should try my best to be holy. Perhaps I could carry around some sort of tiny electric shock device, programmed so that every time I started to entertain a lustful or proud or generically sinful thought, I would get zapped. Maybe if I suffered enough zaps for all the wrong things I did, I might eventually get cured.

Is this what the Christian life is? Gritting your teeth, toughing it out with harsh discipline so that who I truly am never has a chance to express itself?

Here's another option. The Bible tells us that God gives us the Holy Spirit. Maybe his task is to help me wear a "Jesus mask" so no one will see me for who I actually am. Could this be what Galatians 2:20 is talking about? (But God forbid if the mask slips and people see the real me!)

Or perhaps holiness is something that finally takes place in some special moment in my life at some great conference or prayer retreat when the Spirit moves and "it" happens—some marvelous, second saving act of God—and I am never the same again. Though stories abound of such experiences, the Epistles never present holiness as coming by this route.[8]

Well then, instead of that, could holiness be a sort of "split second" thing that exists in between the point when I confess my sin and experience forgiveness, but before I pick up where I left off and start sinning again?

Or maybe... No, we have speculated long enough.

There is an answer, God's answer. He *does* have a wonderful plan, a plan that involves *more than justification.*

Earlier, when I was describing my own sad pilgrimage, I stated that though there was a wonderful yes regarding what I believed, there was also a no. No matter how wonderful one side of God's truth—justification— was, my failure to see the other side became a major hindrance in discovering the fullness of joy that God intends for each of his children. It is to that side we now turn.

More Than Justified

This side involves two changes God has made *inside of us.* Though the second change will be our major emphasis, we will need to catch something of the wonder of the first change, because it forms a most important bridge to the second one. Listen to Paul:

> *But God proves his love for us in that while we still were sinners Christ died for us. Much more surely then, now that we have been justified by his blood, will we be saved through him from the wrath of God. For if while we were enemies, we were reconciled to God through the death of his Son, much more surely, having been reconciled, will we be saved by his life (Romans 5:8–10, emphasis mine).*

In that moment when you received Christ as your Savior, not only were you justified and delivered from God's wrath (the screen idea), but God made a very special change inside of you—he changed your attitude about him. Before that, with your back toward God, you were "alienated and hostile in mind" (Colossians 1:21, NASB). But now, realizing that the offense of your sin has been removed by the blood of Christ, you turn around. What do you see? You see the compassionate face of a loving God with open arms reaching out toward you. What do you do? You run into those open arms. You are no longer hostile! You have been reconciled to God.[9] William Robinson said it so well:

> By the shedding abroad in our hearts God's love for us, the Holy Spirit makes the reconciliation wrought in Christ effective in us. Thus he brings the prodigal back from self-seeking rebellion into grateful, loving obedience in the Father's family.[10]

To your surprise, you discover that you love him. Not only do you love him because "he first loved you," but you love everything about him. Deep within, you "delight in the law of God" (Romans 7:22). You truly want to please God. How often David in the Psalms expressed this same attitude, for he too knew what it meant to be reconciled to God.[11]

This would seem to take care of everything—justified and reconciled. But it doesn't. It is to that second change *inside of us* we now turn. It involves a biblical truth that is so marvelous we might easily hesitate to believe it. To best understand it requires that we try to slip into the sandals of one earnest, seeking Jewish Pharisee.

A New Kind of Species

Nicodemus wanted to make sure he would be in God's kingdom. We may assume he truly wanted to please God. Yet he must have sensed that even with his commitment to God, something was missing.

Jesus could have said, "Nicodemus, don't worry. If you have placed your faith in God as Abraham did, all is well." But he didn't. In fact, he spoke words no one had ever heard before, even though they were implied in several Old Testament promises.

Jesus answered, "No one can see the kingdom of God unless he is born again.... You must be born again" (John 3:3, 7, NIV[12]). Since Jesus added, "Flesh gives birth to flesh, but the Spirit gives birth to spirit," it is clear he did not mean "birth" as some vague, symbolic, initiatory term. No, he was talking about a radical new kind of life.[13] He was talking about regeneration (new birth). That alone would qualify someone to live in a holy heaven!

By physical conception my parents gave me "flesh" birth. It involved much more than my "getting something." I *became* someone. I became a real, full-fledged, "flesh" person. (Remember what we discovered in chapter 1 about being human.) Similarly, by the new birth *I became a brand-new kind of person.* In fact, Leon Morris states: "Jesus is referring to the miracle which takes place when the divine activity *re-makes a man*. He is born all over again by the very Spirit of God"[14] (italics mine).

It was far more than a passing statement when Paul said, "Thus it is written, 'The first man, Adam, became a living being [soul]'; the last Adam [Christ] became a life-giving spirit" (1 Corinthians 15:45).[15]

Jesus did not say being born again equals getting the Holy Spirit. He said it equaled *becoming* spirit. No, my DNA genetic code didn't change. I am still a human being (I always will be!).[16] But "Spirit gives birth to *spirit.*" At the heart of my humanness—spirit—there is life where there was never life before. Even saying "by the new birth we receive a new nature" clouds the picture. It is not *getting* something; it is actually *becoming* a different kind of person.[17] (This will be the focus of chapter 4.)

God is spirit and angels are spirit, yet they are as much "persons" as we are. "Spirit personhood" is not so strange after all. Still, you may find it more comfortable to say "spiritual" than "spirit." That's fine, as long as you don't water down that word.

One writer goes so far as to describe a Christian as "a new kind of species." He then says:

> These two segments of the human race are at opposite poles, they are basically in antithesis. They dwell together because they are both members of the *Family* of man. They are one *Genus,* to use the zoological term. But something has happened to cause them to separate into two *Species* within that *Genus,* and this separation is at a far deeper and more fundamental level than mere genetics. The division is the result of a spiritual transformation that really constitutes a new creation—nothing less, in fact, than rebirth. It is not a symbolic rebirth, like that achieved by ritual in some pagan religions of antiquity and even of today. It is a fundamental change in human nature, so great a change that it amounts to a genuine form of speciation.... We indeed remain *in* the world, but we are no longer *of* the world.[18]

You Are Not the Same

This concept of identity, so fundamental and yet so mysterious, was well known within the leadership of the early church. Their words were clear, their analogies simple and striking. They spoke without hesitation, unencumbered by the creative complexities theologians have dreamed up over the centuries.[19]

They knew they were "not of the world" *anymore than Jesus was*—even as he had said in his great prayer in John 17, anticipating the transformation of his own disciples, which soon would take place.[20]

They knew they were "aliens and exiles" (1 Peter 2:11).[21] Now their citizenship was in heaven (Philippians 3:20). As such they saw themselves as ambassadors in a foreign land (2 Corinthians 5:20).

Perhaps this "new personhood" idea seems far away from the daily reality of your life. That still doesn't change the basic fact. If you have received the Savior, you simply are *not* the same person you were before. When you were *"in the flesh"* (Romans 8:9), life and meaning for you had to be found right there—and there alone. Your brain, your emotions, your senses, your creativity, your glands, your world environment, your relationships—this was life. It could be found nowhere else.

But if you have been born again, this is not so anymore, *whether you know it or not!*

You may weigh the same,

look the same,

feel the same,

but you are not the same.[22]

That is why Jesus could look a man or woman straight in the eyes and say, "I have come that you might have life." They thought they were alive; Jesus said they were wrong. But weren't they doing everything "live" people were doing—eating, walking, loving, dreaming, planning, working? Yes. Yet the Bible says "in him was life."

Don't Water It Down

That's radical. We dare not water it down! And how could we do that? By saying: "Yes, I know I have a new nature."[23] Or "God has 'clothed me with righteousness!'"

But what you *have* isn't the point. It's *who you are* that's the issue. By saying, "Oh, I'm just a sinner saved by grace, indwelt by the Holy Spirit," you're watering it down. You're casting an undeserved shadow on the greatest miracle God has ever performed concerning you. Don't do it! God has not only justified you and reconciled you, he has also birthed you.

Listen to John's voice for a moment: "How great is the love the Father has lavished on us, that we should be called children of God! And that is what we are!... Dear friends, now we are children of God" (1 John 3:1–2, NIV). It is almost as though the apostle were writing along and as he came to the words "children of God," he paused in amazement.

Could this really be?

"Children," not by adoption, *but by birth.*[24]

Did the miracle-working love of God go that far? That we should be called *the children of God?*

Yes, emphatically, it is true.

Because John was so deeply moved by what he had just written, he adds, "And that is what we are!"[25] We dare not take the edge off John's excitement.

The Apostle Peter shared this same sense of wonder when he wrote that we are "partakers [sharers] of the divine nature." Paul adds, "We are [God's] workmanship, created in Christ Jesus" (2 Peter 1:4; Ephesians 2:10, NASB). Did God create something unclean? Is God's workmanship—his master-piece—simply adding a little spiritual lump onto sinful clay? Listen to God's answer: "So if anyone is in Christ, there is a new creation: everything old has passed away; see, everything has become new!" (2 Corinthians 5:17).

Perhaps you are saying, "But how can that be? I know what's inside of me and it's hardly 'God's masterpiece!'" Happily, this book has just begun. In chapters 8 and 9 we will focus on some very practical steps you can take to transform an *actual* truth into an *experienced* truth. But right now it is crucial for each of us to take Scripture for what it says.

Twin Bins

One of the most powerful forces any of us must deal with is the power of our own mental programming. Ways of thinking have cut very deep ruts across the fields of our minds. Even when we know a different way of thinking is right, it is difficult to break out of those smooth, well-worn paths.

I am convinced that the major reason this revolutionary truth was so hard for me to grasp was because I had been programmed to assume that all biblical truth falls into either of two big bins.

The first bin is called *positional truth.* Into it falls that most wonderful, foundational doctrine called "justification by faith." The other bin, *experiential truth,* includes all that becomes part of our conscious experience either at salvation or progressively as we grow spiritually.

Therefore, as I read my Bible, it is my task to decide whether the truth

I am reading about is to be understood as either positional or experiential. Most discussions place sanctification in this second bin. What about regeneration? Since that miracle may not be consciously experienced, it doesn't fit well in either of these bins.

When something doesn't fit, it is easily ignored. Of course, we make a big point of it in presenting the gospel—"You must be born again!" But then we turn right around and explain it by saying, "Well, that means to be forgiven of all your sins." (Of course, that is justification, not regeneration.)

A Third Category

I am convinced there is a third classification that deserves the title *actual truth*. It involves facts that certainly are not positional and may or may not be experiential. As we already have seen, those crucial miracles of reconciliation and (especially) regeneration fit in here.

Maybe an illustration would help. Let's suppose a young girl possesses a very beautiful singing voice. Because her parents are fearful she will become proud, they keep telling her that she has a terrible voice—nobody would want to listen to it. Assuming that her parents must be correct, she determines never to sing. But since people around her might consider that too strange, she muffles her voice so that it rises a little above a whisper. True to what her parents said, there *was* nothing beautiful about the sounds she made. Years go by, silent years. Then one Sunday in a worship service she becomes so caught up in a melody that she forgets herself. With an overflowing heart she sings out—strong and clear—in full voice. Immediately the people around her cease their singing in order to hear this lovely, haunting voice.

"My!" they exclaim after the song. "You have a wonderful voice!"

"Oh no," she stammers, embarrassed. "I—I know I have a terrible voice. Please forgive me. I'm sorry I bothered you with it. I'll try to be more quiet."

"No! Really your voice is beautiful, even captivating. Please sing more!"

This is what I mean by actual truth. All through those songless, whispered years, this girl had a beautiful voice—that was the real truth. But it wasn't experiential. And it certainly wasn't positional (that is, a recording of someone else's voice but with her name put on the label).

Many Christians assume that unless something is being experienced, it must be positional truth rather than actual truth. If I don't *feel* a given truth from Scripture, I throw it into the positional bin. All too often we don't feel like new creations, so it is easy for us to say, "Well then, that must be a positional truth."[26]

What does Scripture say? If you have received Jesus Christ as Savior, God says that in the deepest sense of personhood, you are not a sinner—no matter what you have been told, no matter how much you feel the pull of sin.

You are righteous!

But what "you" are we talking about? Not the "justified" you, the image seen because of the screen, but that most fundamental you.

The you that most deeply and eternally gives you authentic personhood.[27]

The you that goes to heaven when you die.

The you that is *already qualified* "to share in the inheritance of the saints in the light" (Colossians 1:12).

Remember, we're talking about reconciliation and especially regeneration, not justification.[28]

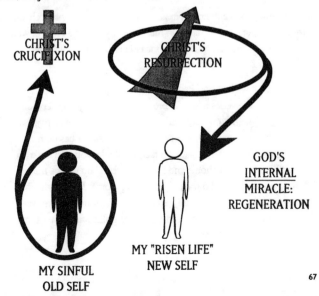

CHRIST'S CRUCIFIXION

CHRIST'S RESURRECTION

GOD'S INTERNAL MIRACLE: REGENERATION

MY SINFUL OLD SELF

MY "RISEN LIFE" NEW SELF

A Few Illustrations, Bad and Good

Many contemporary sayings and illustrations roll in like a fog to obscure our true identity. You've heard a few.

Like the bumper sticker: "Christians aren't perfect, they're just forgiven."

Like the pious little saying: "A Christian is just one beggar telling another beggar where to find bread."

Really? Peter says we are a royal priesthood!

Perhaps you've encountered this illustration that has been used to explain Paul's statement that our "citizenship is in heaven":

> I was a native of a very wicked country, Satan's country. I stood for everything my country stood for. And then came the day I received Christ. Jesus took over that part of Satan's territory where I lived. The boundary lines were changed. Then Jesus came to me and said, "By the way, you're in my territory now. So you'd better start changing the way you act to conform to your new citizenship."

Maybe the little story has a point, but it misses the biggest point. Being born again involves a radical change of *being*. It is not simply a change in citizenship papers; it is a change in me! I was "by nature a child of wrath." No more. By *nature* I am now someone else: a "by birth" child of God.

Here's another illustration:

> I've been a wicked boy. Recently I was caught in the act of one of my many thieveries and was brought before the judge. Looking down on me, he pronounced a huge fine I could never pay. But then the judge paused, stepped down, and stood beside me. "I will pay your debt," he said. "In fact, I will take you into my own family to live in my home and eat at my table. You will be trained by a private tutor." So the judge took me home. My new life has begun as my tutor (the Holy Spirit) is teaching me how to wash my hands and hold a fork and how to be polite and clean up my language.

But I'm still me! You see, the illustration simply doesn't go far enough.

Let's try one more. There you are at home, sitting in an easy chair in front of the TV. Nothing to do and nobody there but you.

You didn't exactly plan it this way, but there on the set a program begins that you know good and well a Christian should not be watching—no question about it. The program's prime purpose is to stir you to lust (whatever kind of lust happens to tantalize you). In a few moments you're hooked. You want to watch it even though you know you shouldn't. You slide the chair a bit closer.

Then the thought comes flashing into your mind, *What if somebody walked by the house and looked in the window and saw what I was doing? It would sure ruin my testimony!*

You check the curtains. But still, someone could come in any moment. "I just can't take that chance," you say to yourself. So reluctantly you click the remote and sit back—frustrated, but at least secure that your witness hasn't been messed up.

Is that victory? Hardly. Let's take it a step further.

Same program, same circumstance, except the door is locked (or you are in some distant motel). Once again, you are captivated. Then you make a horrible discovery—"*God can see me!* I can't escape that. No curtain will solve that! I have enough problems already without getting into deeper trouble with him. I know, he can be pretty tough. Drat it—I guess I'll have to turn it off. But I sure don't want to."

Yet you do turn it off, after you pause to take that one last, delicious look. There you sit, mumbling to yourself, "Why did I have to do that? God, I hope you realize the sacrifice I made!"

Well, is that victory over sin? Oh, it's better than watching, but it isn't victory. In fact, it's bondage, even when the TV is off. Let's try again.

Same thing, same place, when suddenly you are hit with a fresh thought. *I know if Jesus were here it would disappoint him to see me watching this. He went to the cross and died for me. He paid for my sins—this sin. How can I keep on grieving him? I know he loves me and I really do love him. I truly do want to please him.*

Anyway, I am supposed to see myself the way he sees me [that screen again] *even though that's not what I am. If I were dead to this sin, I wouldn't be feeling it the way I do! Yet I'm to reckon myself dead, even though I know I'm not. And of course, God knows that too. He knows what* actually is. *He knows what's going on. Sure, I don't have to watch it. I can turn it off. In fact, right now, I am going to trust God to give me the strength to turn it off.* And you do—after taking that one last look. "That was hard!" you say. "It hurts to say no to myself."

Why does it hurt? Because you, the person, really wanted to keep on watching. Your curious mind, your churning hormones, your stirred emotions all urged you on. "At least it shows how much I love him," you say. Then you settle back into your chair, trying your best to stop imagining that next scene you're missing.[29]

Victory? I think some people would say "Yes, that's what it's all about. You said no to yourself and yes to Jesus. That's it; denying yourself and taking up your cross."

But that's not victory at all because you still want to watch it. And the Bible calls that the sin of coveting. *But how can you stop wanting what you want?* Coveting is an irresistible force if your essential nature is sinful. You cannot stop being what you are. "Well then, there's no hope. I'm sinning even when I am not watching. Oh well, thank God I am justified."

Finding True Victory

No hope? Let's try this illustration one last time. There's the television set. There you sit. The same thing is on the screen. But this time a very different thought confronts you.

Wait a minute, David. Just who are you anyway?

"Well, I'm aware that I have fleshly desires; I don't deny that."

But is that what you most deeply are? Just a physical being, with a mind, will, and emotions, connected to glands and senses that cause you to respond one way or the other to what's on the television set? Is that what you most deeply are?

"No, it isn't! I'm born again! I am a 'partaker of the divine nature.' As such, my essential nature is 'dead to sin and alive to God.' Even though my fleshly feelings are saying one thing, I, as his divine workmanship, am saying the opposite. Sin is not my friend but my hated enemy."[30]

Well then, David, in view of who you most deeply are—and God cannot lie—do you want to watch that?

At that moment something most wonderful happens as I hear myself say, "No!" For the first time, I'm free. Free to be what I most deeply am. Instead of feeling as though I am making a great sacrifice for Jesus, I am experiencing *life*.

Dear reader, this is what regeneration is all about. This is New Covenant Christianity. When this truth finally dawned on me, it was the most dramatic event I had ever known. (I was too young to remember much about my conversion.)

After so many years of merely existing as a Christian, I felt free to live as I had never felt free before. I had discovered that the life God called me to live was actually the fulfillment of my own deepest desires—desires that I scarcely knew were there.

What is life? Two things: *to fulfill the destiny for which you were made while at the same time being who you are!* No longer were these concepts poles apart.

Up until that time, to follow the will of God so often required my saying no to everything I was in the flesh, which meant, *to everything I thought I was.*

Indeed, it is true there are no's to be said to fleshly desires. I believe this is what Jesus meant when he talked about denying yourself. But God has called us to lives of yeses far more than to no's. Yes to *Life*. Yes to the freedom of being who we are. Regeneration is that big of a miracle!

Christian, are you listening? Are you thinking? What does the Bible say? *Who do you think you are?* Is the Spirit right now bearing witness with your spirit that you are both reconciled (a new relationship) and born again (new focus of being—a new sphere of life)? Do you hear his convincing voice?

So Much More

Contrary to much popular teaching, becoming a Christian is more than having something taken away (sins forgiven), or having something added to you (a new nature plus the assistance of the Holy Spirit); it is becoming someone you had never been before. It is justification + *reconciliation* and *regeneration*.[31]

This new identity is not on a flesh level, but on the deepest level of one's inmost self. This miracle is more than a judicial or positional act of God. It is an act so actual that it is right to say a Christian's essential nature is righteous rather than sinful.

In a sense, one could say that justification is salvation as viewed from above, where God sits as a righteous judge issuing his judicial declaration. Reconciliation touches both "above" and "down here" as it affirms that since the wrath of God has been satisfied through Jesus' blood, we who were once enemies are now friends. We have responded to God's love by loving him and all that he is. Regeneration is salvation viewed from below, where we experience God's internal miracle of being alive with the life of Jesus by the Spirit. These together not only remove us from God's wrath, but qualify us to fit—to actually fit!—in his righteous kingdom through the possession of Jesus' risen, eternal life in a restored relationship.[32]

It is not surprising, then, that such a miracle would usher in a new age for human beings. It is to this new age that our thoughts will now turn.

CHAPTER 4

The People
of the
New Age

With such a chapter title, you might well wonder where this book is going. Sadly, terms best used by Christians have been so usurped and twisted by various cults that we fear to use them. Think of the name Jehovah's Witnesses, for example. What better description of a true believer who bears witness to Jesus as the person he actually is—Jehovah!

The same is true of the term *new age*.

THE COUNTERFEIT NEW AGE

Recently an ancient Eastern view of man has experienced a remarkable renewal through what is commonly called the New Age Movement, described by B. J. Williams in *The Oregonian* as "a sort of intellectual Velcro dragged across history, picking up odd bits of philosophical lint from unlikely and often contradictory sources."

Typical of New Age thinking is Adam Ford, an Anglican priest who wrote,

> We are more than the sum of our chemical parts, and our spirit is a new thing with its own unique reality before which the vocabulary of science falls short. The human spirit, an emancipated product of matter, has power over matter.[1]

73

Later he says,

> For billions of years the reconnoitering has been done through
> evolution by sleepwalkers. The changing forms of plants and ani-
> mals have explored and occupied the various niches in the
> environment, without purpose or plan, as unthinkingly as hollows
> are filled by running water. Evolving life has capitalized on every
> available opportunity for living space, from the oceans to the skies,
> from the driest desert to the wettest rainforest. But in humanity the
> sleepwalkers awake. The human mind is exploring the world of
> thought at an accelerated rate and is pushing its way into all the
> opportunities latent in creation. Everything apparently new under
> the sun, physical or mental, is simply the coming into being of
> what is logically possible.[2]

Man as his own god stands at the threshold of a glorious, limitless
adventure—the new age! That sounds so exciting. The Age of Aquarius,
the age of the spirit. Satan's promise fulfilled.

What a total, tragic lie. Remember the carnival illustration? It would
appear that those in darkness will grasp at anything by which they can
trash the humbling, biblical "flesh" evaluation of humanness. In its place
they will exchange some type of elevated "spirit" level of being. As we noted
earlier, Solomon was right: Man in himself is destined to futility.

God's Glorious New Age

Among the most expressive books in the Old Testament is the book of
Isaiah. With that wonderful gift of an imagination, let's slip our feet into
Isaiah's sandals and see through his eyes—feel with his heart—as we listen
to his despair:

> *We wait for light, and lo! there is darkness;*
> *and for brightness, but we walk in gloom.*
> *We grope like the blind along a wall,*
> *groping like those who have no eyes....*
> *We wait for justice, but there is none;*

> *for salvation, but it is far from us.*
> *For our transgressions before you are many,*
> > *and our sins testify against us (Isaiah 59:9–12).*

Isaiah wrote these words after giving us one of the most vivid descriptions of the wickedness of man in Scripture (used by Paul in Romans 3). Utter hopelessness. The human race was bankrupt and Isaiah knew it. Yet out of that darkness, the Holy Spirit led him to capture the dream of a new age that God, not man, would bring.

> *Arise, shine; for your light has come,*
> > *and the glory of the LORD has risen upon you.*
> *For darkness shall cover the earth,*
> > *and thick darkness the peoples;*
> *but the LORD will arise upon you,*
> > *and his glory will appear over you (Isaiah 60:1–2).*

Some day, a new covenant age would come.

A Redeemer would arise.

God would send His Spirit.

His people would "all be righteous."

Forever God would rejoice over his people "as a bridegroom rejoices over a bride."

Finally he would create a new heaven and earth, and the past would never again be remembered (Isaiah 59:20–21; 60:21; 62:5; 65:17).

Jeremiah dreamed that same dream: a new covenant age.

> *"I will make a new covenant.... I will put my law within them, and I will write it on their hearts; and I will be their God, and they shall be my people. No longer shall they teach one another, or say to each other, 'Know the LORD,' for they shall all know me, from the least of them to the greatest," says the LORD, "for I will forgive their iniquity, and remember their sin no more" (Jeremiah 31:31, 33–34).*

Ezekiel described it in these words:

> *"A new heart I will give you, and a new spirit I will put within you; and*

I will remove from your body the heart of stone and give you a heart of flesh.... And you shall be my people and I will be your God.... And it shall be an everlasting covenant with them" (Ezekiel 36:26, 28; 37:26).[3]

The New Age Is Inaugurated

Isaiah, Jeremiah, Ezekiel—none of them lived to see the promise (Hebrews 11:39). Centuries passed. Then a baby was born. A generation later the land of Israel stirred with messianic hope. Had the time arrived?

One Passover night in an upper room, that messianic man held a cup filled with red wine and spoke words no one had ever heard before: "This is *the new covenant* in my blood." By the next day he was dead.

Even after it was known the Savior had risen, seven weeks passed before anyone grasped the pivotal importance of his death and resurrection. Finally on the Day of Pentecost, the fire fell; the Spirit came. From deep within, "rivers of living water" flowed, just as Scripture—as Jesus—had promised (John 7:38). The risen Christ was dispensing LIFE (John 1:4). By the new birth, realized in its fullness on the Day of Pentecost, life was theirs as they had never before experienced it. "From his fullness we have all received, grace upon grace" (John 1:16; cf. 1:12). How expressively this was underlined by the angelic message to the apostles: "Go, stand in the temple and tell the people the whole message about *this life*" (Acts 5:20, italics mine).

Later the book of Hebrews announced that the new covenant promise had been realized. "The completion of the ages"—"the consummation"—had arrived (Hebrews 8:8–13; 9:26). The new age had dawned.

Paul declared that the law, once written on "tablets of stone," was now written on "tablets of human hearts." Life was now "resurrection life." The persons they used to be, persons who knew only life in the flesh, had been crucified with Christ. They were "risen with Christ," "alive to God" as they had never been alive (2 Corinthians 3:3; Romans 6:2–11; Colossians 3:1–4).

Familiarity Breeds a Yawn

Are these texts familiar to us? Yet I fear we Christians have become so used to these expressions, they scarcely stir us.

What do they mean?

What does it mean to you that you are living on *this side* of that point in history? Only a change in perspective?

Is it simply that before this point, people looked ahead to the cross, and now you look back?

An increase in divine help—more of the Holy Spirit now than before?

Yes, but something far greater than these!

Citizens of God's New Age

What does this all mean? It means that by the new birth, you and I are now participants in the ultimate new age of God's eternal purposes. We are living within the fulfillment of the prophets' aching dreams and God's promised miracle. We are now, actually, the internally transformed citizens in God's kingdom of righteousness—where Jesus reigns, within the kingdom of our hearts.

> *For it is the God who said "Let light shine out of darkness," who has shone in our hearts to give the light of the knowledge of the glory of God in the face of Jesus Christ. But we have this treasure in clay jars, so that it may be made clear that this extraordinary power belongs to God and does not come from us (2 Corinthians 4:6–7).*

One of the earliest writers on this passage, Chrysostom, the Golden Mouth (A.D. 400), contrasted this passage with that moment in creation when God brought light into existence:

> Indeed he said, "let it be and it was:" but now he said nothing, but himself became Light to us. For he said not, "hath also now commanded," but "hath" himself "shined."… For seeing he had spoken many and great things of the unspeakable glory, lest any should say, "And how, enjoying so great a glory, remain we in a mortal body?" he saith, that this very thing is indeed the chiefest marvel and a very great example of the power of God, that an earthen vessel hath been enabled to bear so great a brightness and to keep so high a treasure. And therefore as admiring this, he said,

"that the exceeding greatness of the power may be of God and not of ourselves."[4]

God did not say, "Let some light shine into David." No! "God himself has shined in our hearts"! We are not only "children of the light," but we are the people in whom God dwells as the light. Not a fading light as with Moses, but a glory that transforms us "into the same image from one degree of glory to another" (2 Corinthians 3:13–18).

"The same image." This takes us back to our first chapter when we considered the nature of man as being made in God's image. There we noted that later in this book we would see this expression in a marvelous new way. Here it is!

Christ in Us, the Hope of Glory

Christ, the "life-giving Spirit," is now reproducing himself progressively in the lives of the saints. We are "predestined to be conformed to the image of his Son" (Romans 8:29). Remember, "The first Adam became a living being [soul]." As such, he imaged God within the confines of his flesh. Now "the last Adam [Christ]" having become "a life-giving spirit" [or more accurately, Spirit][5] is reproducing his very life—his image—in us! (1 Corinthians 15:45). The "image" concept is now more glorious than Adam, even in his innocence.[6]

This is the new age. The consummation of all the ages has begun. We are now by birth, by the Spirit, "the children of God," pulsating with the risen life of Jesus. Some day, perhaps soon, it will reach its apex when at last our "physical [soulish] bodies" will be transformed into "spiritual bodies"—at "the redemption of our bodies." At last there will be no more conflict between our spirits (as inseparable from Christ, the life-giving Spirit) and our soulish, fleshly bodies. Finally, the last tear will have been shed; "death…swallowed up in victory." The King returns! (Romans 8:23; 1 Corinthians 15:44, 54; Revelation 19)

Johannas Behm describes this new age this way: "The *new aeon* [age], which has dawned with Christ, brings a new creation, the creation of a new man" (italics mine).[7]

Having stated that "the union with Christ which brings justification also brings the new life," Millard Erickson quotes J. A. Ziesler, "The believer enters not just into a private relationship with Jesus, but a new humanity, in which he becomes a new kind of man."[8]

J. Knox Chamblin comments, "Jesus Christ is no less than the inaugurator of *a new humanity*" (italics mine).[9]

New age, new humanity, new creation. We are—both corporately as the church *and* individually—part of something which is the capstone of everything God ever has or ever will do.

One of the most amazing statements pointing to this fact is found in Matthew 11:11. Jesus, after saying, "among those born of women no one has arisen greater than John the Baptist," then added, "yet the least in the kingdom of heaven is greater than he." How could this possibly be? One writer answers,

> The ancient order of things [old covenant] and the new are separated by such a gulf, that the least in the latter has a higher position than John himself. The weakest disciple has more spiritual intuition of divine things than the former. He enjoys the dignity of a son, while John is only a servant. The least believer is one with this Son whom John announces.[10]

Do you feel you are part of something this momentous? No? Is your mental programming, *I am but a forgiven sinner,* so deeply ingrained it is impossible for you to imagine yourself any other way? Have you been so used to using Old Testament examples of the good and the bad that you never considered the new covenant age to be *that* different?

Perhaps you are saying, "Oh, I know it's different. Expressions such as 'risen with Christ' prove that. It's just that my own spiritual failure proves that whatever those words are supposed to mean haven't touched me. I don't feel risen at all. In fact, I have begun to wonder if they were ever meant to be understood. Not just those words, but others too, such as,

> *'Our old self was crucified with him'*
> *'Consider yourself dead to sin and alive to God'*

'Those who belong to Christ Jesus have crucified the flesh'
'Those who are born of God do not sin'"
(Romans 6:6, 11; Galatians 5:24; 1 John 5:18).

Those words! They sound so powerful, so radical, yet so out of reach. Did God really intend them to be beyond our reach? I wonder if you would consider looking at them one more time?

WHERE DO WE BEGIN?

One tough beginning point would be to suggest we do a detailed study of the standard passages: John 3; Romans 6–8; Galatians 3–6; Colossians 1–3; 1 John 1–3. Are you ready to jump in and do that? Probably not, at least not right now. (Perhaps you might have time to simply read through these passages before we move on. See also the Appendix, "Suggestions toward an Understanding of Romans 6–8.")

Our first step will be to assume that you and I agree that being a Christian is both an external fact—the screen idea (justification)—*and* an internal fact. Your relationship to and attitude toward God has been changed (reconciliation). And you are alive as you have never before been alive (regeneration). God has actually changed *you* (the closing emphasis of chapter 3).

How big was that change?

Big enough so that if you died right now—separated from your body—you would fit in a holy heaven. Apart from any spiritual growth; apart from added inner transformation; you, as you are, would fit.

But still, what actually changed about us?

Illustrations to the Rescue

Often when Jesus wanted to get across some very deep truth, he would use parables, illustrations, to serve as lights to shine on truth. Time and again in my own life I have found if I could only illustrate some difficult truth, at last I could see it.

We need light when confronted with this question, "What actually changed about us?" Perhaps an illustration I have in mind may serve as that light. Once again, with that gift of imagination, picture that you (as an unsaved person) *are a tree*—a little tree. What kind? How about a crab apple tree? A very sour, wild apple. Recently I came across one in the woods. One bitter bite of its fruit was all I needed!

Crab apple is your essential nature (Ephesians 2:3). Then one day a momentous, momentarily terrifying thing happens to you. Someone takes a razor-sharp knife and makes a long diagonal cut and slices part of you off a few inches or so above the soil. The entire top of you is gone. Quickly this same someone takes a fresh green section of stem, cut with a matching diagonal slice from a different tree, and splices it on to what's left of you. Carefully, the splice is wrapped and sealed. Then a tag is attached to you that reads "golden delicious."

In the days that follow, the buds above that splice burst with life. Eventually they blossom and produce. What will they produce? That's right—golden delicious apples. Why? Because this is who you now are. No one who knew what had taken place would ever think of calling you a crab apple. You are not even a crab apple + a golden delicious. You *are* a "golden delicious."

But what about *below* the graft? What if sprouts were allowed to flourish there? What would they produce? That's right—crab apples. Yet if that happened, they would be considered usurpers, aliens, deserving of only one thing: removal.

When I was in high school in southern California, I began a small tree nursery that involved exactly this process, except I raised a rather exotic subtropical fruit tree called cherimoya. (Happily, it paid my way through college!) Once I had grafted one of my young seedling[11] trees, I never thought of its nature as anything other than that of the parent tree from which I had taken a special, short stem (called a *scion*). That small tree was now new. A "Booth" or "Bays" or some other choice, marketable variety.

Though this was true, I had to maintain constant vigilance because the buds below the graft still wanted to grow. If I failed to deal with them, those lower shoots could so dominate my little tree, its true identity could scarcely be seen, surrounded as it was by the lush wild growth from below the graft. "Suckers" we called them, for obvious reasons. Yet even if this happened, *I didn't change the name on the tag.* No, it still retained its new identity. Sometimes it almost hurt to cut the suckers away, because they looked so healthy, so right. But they had to go because they no longer represented what that little tree was.

Do you have this picture in your mind?[12] Hold on to it as we overlay it on Scripture.

Crab Apples into Golden Delicious

The moment you were born again, the unregenerate person you used to be—your old self (crab apple)—was sliced off, crucified. What you had been by nature, "a child of wrath," you are no more. There it lies on the ground, dead. At this same moment (the *scion* grafting moment) you became a genuine new self, a golden delicious. The name tag that is now yours is not there simply because this is the way God sees you on that screen (justification). No! It now truly represents who you are (regeneration).

Yes, the root and stock below the graft remains. Nothing has changed there at all. *But that part is no longer the determiner of your identity.* (This is so important to understand.)

As with most illustrations, this one has its weak points. If only it were true that crab apples thrive in the darkness and golden delicious grow only in the light, then we would have a perfect illustration. (Since we are imagining anyway, why not imagine crab apples *do* grow only in darkness?)

We, as golden delicious, are "children of the light." It is because God himself "has shone in our hearts" that we are alive with the risen life of Jesus. On the other hand, unregenerate life lives in darkness (John 3:19; 2 Corinthians 4:6–7; Ephesians 5:8; 1 Thessalonians 5:5; 1 Peter 2:9).

Does this mean your flesh root stock has no importance? Not at all. God's intention for you was not simply to change your nature in some unseen inner way, but to enable you to produce actual, visible fruit. This requires a physical body plus your own distinctive, flesh-level uniqueness—but only as expressed *above the graft.*

In fact, in tree grafting, though a particular type of apple root stock cannot change the essential golden delicious nature of a tree, it may have significant effects on the expression of its nature—such things as the size of the tree, its suitability for a particular climate, or resistance to certain diseases. The same is true for us. The flesh distinctives each of us have, including types of personality, will allow us to express who we are (golden delicious) in distinctive ways through various circumstances.

It is true that Paul called your body a "body of sin." But I am sure he was not saying that our bodies in themselves are sinful. Yes, our energies, if expressed *below the graft,* would burst out with suckers. That innate mental bent toward sin is *still there.* But those same energies, when rising *above the graft,* infused with risen life by the Spirit, are wonderfully transformed. This is a marvelous thing! When joined to life from God, they enable holiness to become a physical, visible reality.

Suckers Below the Graft

Where does sin operate and where do the suckers grow? Only in that independently functioning flesh level of our total personhood—below the graft. Romans 7:23 expresses this so well: "the law of sin that dwells in my members."

With these thoughts in mind, let's take a look at one of those key Scripture passages.

> *We know that our old self [crab apple] was crucified [severing of the tree from the small stock and root below] with him, so that the body of sin [the part below the graft which could still produce crab apples if given the chance] might be rendered powerless,[13] and we might no longer be enslaved to sin [producing crab apples]. For whoever has died [that severing event] is freed from sin [no longer obliged to produce crab apples].... So you also must consider yourselves dead to sin [the kind of tree you once were, crab apple] and alive to God [the tree you now are, golden delicious] in Christ Jesus.*
>
> *Therefore, do not let sin [crab apple sucker growth] exercise dominion in your mortal bodies [in particular, below the graft where sucker growth arises]...but present yourselves [you, the entire tree] to God as those who have been brought from death [crab apple existence] to life [golden delicious life], and present your members [everything that comes from your root stock] to God as instruments of righteousness (Romans 6:6–7, 11–13).*

Paul's final command, "present your members," is so important because, as we noted above, God's intent in the new birth is more than changing your nature (to qualify you for heaven). He also had in mind changing your behavior *now*—in your mortal body—to golden delicious behavior.

It is so important to note that even though this crucifixion and resurrection (crab apple severing + God's golden delicious grafting) took place so that our bodies of sin might be rendered powerless, *it is still possible* for sin to reign in our mortal bodies (Romans 6:12). Earlier in my sad autobiography, I grieved over that painful discovery. Even though I was told that "sin's power had been broken," I found that it *had not been broken at all*. In other words, sin was still reigning. Yet if new birth was mine, how could this have been?

Two Momentous Events

Back to our illustration. Two things happened in that moment of grafting. Not only has the identity of the tree been changed, but also all those surging energies from the stock below the graft have an entirely new direction to flow. But *they must be encouraged to flow upward through the graft.* If they aren't, they will instead pour their strength into those eager buds below the graft.

As a young Christian, I still assumed I was a crab apple—a forgiven crab apple. Therefore, not realizing that God had performed such a radical grafting act upon me, I had no idea that I was a new person—golden delicious.

Because of that ignorance, I believed that crab apple growth *was what I was*. No matter how many branches I chopped off, they came right back. I tried dying to self dozens of times. But the sap had to flow somewhere. To me they weren't alien suckers. They were who I was and nothing else. What could I do? (Remember, "to live is to do.")

Since I had my well-developed list of the proper do's and don'ts of Christian behavior, I became an expert at attaching imitation golden delicious fruit to my chopped-back crab apple branches. I imagine that, at times, I was so successful other people assumed what they saw was the real thing.

Then came an enlightening thought. Instead of imitation apples, what God was after was the real thing—the "fruit of the Spirit." Because his fruit would be alien to crab apple trees, it would require a major step of faith to trust him to hang his golden delicious fruit on my gnarly, half-pruned crab apple branches. This is the way I saw myself—sort of like a Peanuts cartoon Christmas tree.

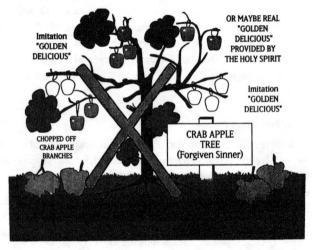

I am sure this is a very common view of the Christian life. It is put forward in statements such as "You are to live *as though* you had been crucified and raised with Christ."[14] Or "This is your position in Christ" (back to the screen idea).[15] No wonder the world is not very impressed. No wonder so many Christians give up the battle somewhere along the way.

There is another teaching on victory over sin that is also very popular. It says,

"Yes, God performed a radical 'grafting' miracle when you were born again. He gave you a brand new nature, a new disposition. Now, rather than having only the old one—your sin nature—you also have a new nature. You now have *two* dispositions. God has given you the Holy Spirit to assist you in hindering the old disposition's activities. Therefore, you simply have to adjust to this dual identity."[16]

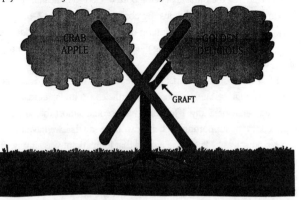

Sometimes those who hold such a view are quite frank to say your sin nature (crab apple nature) is your *essential nature*.[17] If this were true, the next passage we will consider, 1 John 3:9, would make no sense at all.

Those who have been born of God [you are now golden delicious] do not sin [produce crab apples], because God's seed [the essential nature of the scion, hence the tree] abides in them; they cannot sin, because they have been born of God.

But what did John mean by "cannot sin"?[18] When John used the word *cannot*, I believe he was trying to communicate a critical point. Sinning (crab apple producing) is so utterly irrational—so stupid—*no one in their right mind would ever consider sinning a reasonable behavior.* In other words, it is as unthinkable for a Christian to sin as it is for a golden delicious to produce crab apples (even though that is still possible below the graft, a possibility John allowed for, as seen in 2:1, "if anyone does sin"; see also 5:21). Sinning would still be reasonable if one-half of your essential nature were sinful. But nowhere in John's epistle did he suggest that a Christian was a "two-dispositioned" person (see above illustration.)[19]

Radically Righteous

John considered the miracle of being born of God so radical, it produced a person who was truly righteous. By observing 1 John 3:3, 7–8; 5:18, it is obvious that John was not thinking of justification (being *declared* righteous), but of regeneration, (being *made* righteous by the infusion of Jesus' life).

I fear most of us as Christians have allowed ourselves to assume that sinning, though certainly wrong, is nevertheless an understandable, to-be-expected behavior. Sadly, 1 John 1:8 has become almost threadbare by its repeated use in supporting such a view. "If we say that we have no sin, we deceive ourselves." Many have argued that John's point was simply, "There is always some measure of sin in our lives." Yet if this is what he had in mind, why just three verses later did he write "My little children, I am writing these things to you so that you may not sin. But if anyone does sin, we have an advocate"? *"If* anyone sins." "If." Did he really mean "If"?

What Did John Really Mean?

Let's try to slip our feet into John's sandals and see through his eyes. Remember, for three-and-one-half years he had watched a man who always practiced righteousness—a man, as we will see in chapter 7, who used *the same resources available to us.* He had heard his Savior say: "My sheep hear my voice…*and they follow me."* Like Peter, John knew he was to follow in the steps of the One who "committed no sin, and no deceit was found in his mouth." He also caught the obvious implications of Jesus' words, "as the Father has sent me, so I send you" (John 10:27; 1 Peter 2:22; John 20:21).

Long years had gone by since the Day of Pentecost, years when exciting theory might have been wasted away by the cold realities of life. But not for John. The truth of being a "born one of God" (1 John 3:1) was ever more captivating, ever more practical. So practical, he found it impossible to imagine himself or any believer being irrational enough to choose sin. With this brief background, let's read 1 John 3:6–10 again.

John certainly allowed for the possibility that Christians might occasionally sin (1 John 2:1); but his assumption for himself and for his brothers and sisters was that such times would be totally out of character. To draw any other conclusion from 1 John is to be out of step not only with John, but God himself. (Please see chapter 6 for an extended look at this and other passages in 1 John.)

Sin = Temporary Insanity

I wonder what effect it would have upon us if we realized that every time we chose to sin, we were choosing to act as *temporarily insane?* I would be the first to admit such times. But how stupid! That's exactly what any nurseryman would think about me—every time I would choose to let a sucker grow on my little golden delicious tree. Why? Because I would be choosing to frustrate the true nature of that little tree. "Crazy," they would say, and rightly so.

I hope you would not find it too difficult to look back at some point in your life, when for a brief time, even a few seconds, you were totally captivated with God—his love, his forgiveness, his faithfulness. No space for any other thought. I hope you can. Well, how about five minutes when no other thought crossed your mind? Was there any sin during that time? Of course not. Nothing to confess! Can you imagine a period of time when you were so completely wrapped up in the needs of someone else that there were no self-centered motives, simply a heart reaching out in love and compassion? I am sure you can. Was there any sin during that space? No!

What strange mindset has taken hold of Christendom that we can't allow ourselves the joy of times when we are 100 percent pleasing God?[20] Why must we assume the grace of God and the Spirit's power *are inadequate* to fulfill in us the risen life of Jesus, the fruit of the Spirit and the pure motives of 1 Corinthians 13? When the apostle wrote, "walk by the Spirit and you will not carry out the desire of the flesh,"[21] was he presenting a genuine possibility or only a fantasy?

Life beyond Fantasy

Once again, with the grafting illustration in mind, let's consider some radical statements in Galatians:

> *And those who belong to Christ Jesus have crucified the flesh [everything below the graft is now dead to me in regard to who I now am] with its passions and desires [crab apple making].… May I never boast in anything except the cross of our Lord Jesus Christ, by which the world [everything that might encourage crab apple sucker growth] has been crucified to me [golden delicious], and I to the world (5:24; 6:14).*

As a tree, are you aware of the insistent urgings below the graft? Of course you are. Not only are you aware of them, but it is easy to imagine that if those budding suckers were allowed to flourish, you might falsely assume they *were* your true identity. Of course, those crab apple buds are there; they will be there until you die. But they are no longer where *life* is for you. *They are really dead to you as being your life* (Galatians 5:24). Not only that, but anything that might encourage them to grow—the world— is also dead to you (Galatians 6:14). You *are* a golden delicious.

Nevertheless, it is asking quite a bit of that more shallow level of our being (below the graft) to adjust to the idea that it is not the master of our total personhood.[22] This shallow level of mortal consciousness has to back off and admit to a deeper level of being that will eternally outlive its own mortality. Is that easy to do? No![23]

Still, because this is your essential identity, anything that might show up below that graft is alien to your life and deserves to be put to death (Romans 8:13) as quickly as possible. Yet even before the "cutting off the sucker" action is taken, those suckers were *already* dead to you *as being where life is*. They were, even before you knew it! They became the opposite of life the moment you became a golden delicious!

Finally, let's look at Galatians 2:19–20.

> *I [the crab apple tree I was] have been crucified with Christ [severing of the tree]; and it is no longer I [as I was] who live, but it is Christ [the parent tree, the source of the grafted scion] who lives in me. And the life I now live [I, the golden delicious tree producing golden delicious fruit] in the flesh [still joined to the root and stock] I live by faith in the Son of God [total confidence in the authenticity of the life source of the scion], who loved me and gave himself for me.*

"The life that I live *in the flesh*"—is there any value in the root stock? Even though if left to itself it would produce sin? How thankful we may be that God's answer is an emphatic yes! Our present mortal, physical state is very important. Apart from it, the scion would have nothing to be attached to, no way for it to fulfill its physical golden delicious destiny.

So what am I to do now? I present my members (root and stock below the graft, and the resultant energies flowing up through the graft) "as slaves to righteousness." Why "slave"? Because apart from making my body my slave (1 Corinthians 9:27), it will automatically start producing crab apple suckers. But as a slave, it actually supports my true identity—golden delicious.

Happily, someday when my present root and stock gets old and dies, the scion and its resulting growth—my true identity all along—will be kept alive by God in order to someday be attached to a marvelously new "glorified" root and stock. And from that point on I will never have to be concerned about crab apple suckers again!

Are you ready for another illustration—a mini-melodrama? This time imagine that you are a typical high school boy who likes two things most of all: food and girls (in either order). If someone asked you who you were and you were honest you would have to express both your identity and your reason for living in those terms (with a long list of other ones, of course).

One day you're standing by your locker in the hall and the track coach spots you. He takes you by surprise when he strolls purposefully over to your locker to talk to you. (The *track* coach talking to *me?*)

"Say, I've been watching the way you walk—gotta lot of bounce to your step. Whether you know it or not, you're a sprinter. With a little training you could be setting records in the 100-yard dash. I just know it!"

"Aw c'mon, Coach. I'm no sprinter. I might win a gold medal in eating or girl-watching, but a sprinter? You've got to be kidding."

"No, I'm not kidding. And I'll prove it to you. This afternoon—at practice."

Now he's hooked you. You go to practice that afternoon…and every afternoon for weeks to follow. Your first clockings aren't that outstanding but you sense a strange exhilaration as you run that maybe, just maybe, the coach was right. In the days that follow you read biographies of great sprinters; you watch films of great races. You run and run and run. It hurts so much sometimes, yet always deeper is a growing sense of identity. You *are* a sprinter! Before long the whole shape of your life bends to this new sense of personhood. If someone walks up to you on the street and asks, "Who are you?" you spontaneously respond, "I'm a sprinter at Madison High! The big meet with Wilson High is this Saturday—you gonna be there?"

And Saturday comes. The crowd stirs as you walk across the cinders to your starting block. Suddenly the prettiest girl from Madison High walks straight up to you with a large, juicy piece of apple pie fresh from the oven and topped with a big glob of ice cream. "Hi," she coos. "I brought this for you…just for you."

Now comes the decision. You are free to do what you want. But what will you do? It all depends on who you believe you most deeply *are*.

Who are you? Are you a skin-wrapped package of taste buds, salivary glands, and sex drives? If this is your identity, there isn't much question where you will find meaning.

Or are you aware of something else? A new identity. An identity reinforced by a relationship you've built with your coach, by a new focus on personhood, a new set of values. If these things are true, your response to sweet Sue will be automatic—and conclusive. On the other hand, if you have missed out on track practice, if you have allowed your mind to focus on those very tangible, fleshly things where you had always found life before, you will respond in one of two ways: "All right! Who cares about the race anyway. I'd much rather be with you, Susie." Or, if not that it will be, "Sorry Sue, I want that hunk of pie but I can't have it."

What is your response as the sprinter you now know yourself to be? With scarcely a second look at her pretty face, you turn to focus on that tape 100 yards away.

"Sorry, Sue. I'm a sprinter. I don't *want* that apple pie (not simply I can't have it). Life for me is touching that tape before anyone else. What you offer just doesn't fit in. Thanks anyway."

"Oh, you must want it…and me."

"No, Sue, there's something far deeper about me than that. I'm not just a mouth connected to a stomach; I'm not just a guy who gets turned on by good-looking girls. *I'm a sprinter,* Sue. That's who I am. That's living. There's nothing like it in all the world. I'm gonna win, Susie!"

BANG! Off you go…and you win.

Oh Christian, do you get the point? If you don't know most deeply who you are—if you have allowed your sense of personhood to be shaped by your own flesh, by Satan, and by the meaning-mad media that saturates the world—you are either consciously or unconsciously a most miserable, frustrated Christian. Your Bible reading, such as it is, is self-condemning. First John 1:9 is your life verse. God is almost your adversary. Strange that he could be both Savior and adversary. But it's true. It seems as though the things you want most in life he says you should want least or not at all. In your view, a Christian is one who must continually say no to himself, no to his dreams, and no to his desires, all the while saying yes to God and his demands.

To such statements Paul would shout with flaming indignation, "God forbid! What travesty! Whoever had the audacity to paint the Christian life in such a way? What a shambles of God's truth. For me *to live is* Christ!" For you see, even as Sam discovered a deeper identity, so God's intention is that every believer become literally obsessed with LIFE—dare we say it—*new age* life.

LET THE NEW AGE ROLL!

Has the new age arrived? God's answer is an enthusiastic yes! In the New Covenant, the consummation of the ages began (Hebrews 9:26). Resurrection life is the new age. From the moment of regeneration, each child of God possesses "the mind of Christ" (1 Corinthians 2:16). "There is a new creation: everything old has passed away; see, everything has become new!" (2 Corinthians 5:17).

But there is even more to come!

From that initial bursting of golden delicious life, the process continues of actually producing the fruit of that life—"the image of Christ," "from glory to glory." The zenith of that new age awaits the arrival of the King, when what we most deeply are will be joined eternally to a golden delicious body—"like unto His glorious body." Only then will "the eager longing" of creation be rewarded when at last the children of God are revealed (Romans 8:19). Only then will the dignity, the majesty of God's masterpieces find their fullest expression as both the bride and the co-regents with their groom, the Lord Jesus Christ. The divine image is now complete.

CHAPTER 5

Two Kinds of People, Two Kinds of Life

Imagine with me that you were given a beautiful, diamond-studded, golden pendant strung from a golden chain to hang around your neck. One day as you picked it up, you made a startling discovery. What you had assumed was delicate filigree along one edge was actually a tiny hinge. A quick search exposed an equally tiny latch. A moment later, the pendant reveals its treasure within: an exquisite, miniature etching depicting with absolute perfection the face of someone you love most of all.

The gift of receiving Christ as Savior is something like that. The gift in itself is most wonderful: "justified by his blood…saved from the wrath of God…reconciled to God." That would seem to be enough. But it isn't! For the locket opens as we read on in Romans 5:10, "much more surely, having been reconciled, will we be saved *by his life.*"

Not only has God forgiven me, delivering me from his wrath, but he has placed his very life within me! It was this truth that captivated Paul: "Christ in you, the hope of glory…Christ, who is [our] life." Life for Paul was one word: Christ (Colossians 1:27; 3:4).

If the only Scripture we had was 2 Corinthians 4:7, "we have this treasure in clay jars," we might have assumed that we have not changed a bit, except that Christ is now in us—*yet as totally distinct from us.* We were sinful clay jars before; now we are forgiven sinful clay jars, with Jesus inside. If this were so, then when we die, the "Jesus in us" would depart back to heaven, but we wouldn't. Why not? Simply because we are still what we always were—sinful clay jars, hardly qualified to fit in a holy heaven.

Happily, God has protected us from such a false belief by informing us in a variety of ways that "Christ in us" actually changes us. Our true identity is now something deeper than flesh. Call it "spirit" or "inmost self"; the point is that life for us is now to be found in a new dimension where there was never life before.

Since we have been using terms such as *inmost self* and *mortal self,* it is time we stop and get our bearings as to the meanings of some very common biblical words, especially the words *flesh* and *spirit.* As we do this, we will wrestle with the mystery of what it means to be a person, a "self." Only when we arrive at some point of rest with these terms will we be able to see the broader picture of authentic Christian personhood.

COMING TO TERMS WITH TERMS

Human language is both a marvelous thing and a frustrating thing. Imagine how convenient it would be if the definitions of individual words determined their usage, with each word having only one meaning. Since in reality it is just the opposite—with usage determining definitions—words end up with all sorts of shades of meaning because of the way they are used. This quirk of language requires that we must do more than spot individual words and attach a meaning to each one. Instead, we must try to discover how a writer is using each word in the particular context of his thoughts.

For the most part, we do this automatically. But when it comes to crucial words—crucial biblical words—the task requires conscious effort. This is especially true when we come to the group of words the Bible uses to describe human personhood—words such as *heart, soul, mind,* plus those mentioned above. How much we want clear-cut definitions! Since word meanings underlie what we believe about anything, it would be so helpful if each of these words had their own precise meanings.

Why didn't God supply us with his own official list of definitions?[1] Apparently, he assumed that through the valued process of searching the Scriptures, our discovery of how words are used would provide us with just enough understanding to fulfill the life he has called us to live. What is that "just enough" level of understanding? Unfortunately, I am sure it is not as much as we would like. We prefer precision that allows us to say that people are composed of three parts or two parts or even no parts—a single unity.[2] God has his own reasons for frustrating our wishes. Perhaps he wished humanness to retain a touch of mystery.

Regardless, the Bible could not be clearer when Jesus declared there are two kinds of people—people who are flesh and people who are spirit (John 3:6). Though we will not escape the mystery aspects of humanness, I believe our grappling with these words, *flesh* and *spirit,* will bring us much closer to appreciating the marvelous miracle of being the children of God.

The Physicalness of Flesh

Though other words referring to human beings are used more often (man, woman, child, people, souls, etc.), none are as descriptive as this surprisingly common word, *flesh.* It is such a graphic, seeable, physical word. As we shall see, it was chosen for that very reason.

The Bible starts, "In the beginning God created…" and finishes with descriptions of God's marvelous *physical* creativity: "and the one who was seated on the throne said, 'See, I am making all things new'" (Genesis 1:1; Revelation 21:5)[3]. When God made human beings from the dust, he said "it is good!" Physicalness, as God intended it, is always good.[4] (Plato was wrong.)

As we saw in chapter 1, nothing was stated in those early chapters in Genesis to suggest human beings were anything other than physical. But doesn't the Bible inform us that all human beings have some measure of continuing existence apart from their bodies after they die? Yes. But that does not change the fact that biblical teaching in general places humanness prior to death within a primarily physical sphere—that is, until God informs us of those interior miracles we considered earlier in this book.

After the Fall, human physicalness suffered significant loss. With the Tree of Life beyond their reach, that first couple trembled as they heard "you are dust, *and to dust you shall return*" (Genesis 3:19). Who could miss that sense of lowliness wrapped up in God's later words, "My spirit shall not abide in mortals forever, *for they are flesh;*[5] their days shall be one hundred twenty years," or the psalmist's pitiable reflection, "He remembered that *they were but flesh,* a wind that passes and does not come again" (Genesis 6:3; Psalm 78:39, italics mine)?

Throughout the Old Testament, *flesh* is used to describe human beings in their physical, mortal frailty.[6] When we say *physical,* one should not conclude that we are thinking only of something that is weighable. How much does an emotion weigh? A thought? A choice? Yet increasingly science has become aware that these expressions, though minuscule by comparison, also are found in the animal world.

In other words, there is no nonphysical, mystical attachment to this word.[7] It is most important to remember this as we turn to the New Testament because, I believe, *the New Testament writers followed the same pattern.*[8] Sadly, a number of newer English translations reflect a view that the New Testament writers—especially Paul—dreamed up a new, mystical, nonphysical meaning for *flesh* by rendering this word as "sin nature." (Please see extended footnote regarding this.[9])

To the contrary! When Jesus said, "What is born of the flesh is flesh," this is what he meant. Whatever is born of fallen, physical humanness is simply that, and as such is not adequate for existence in God's kingdom.

Of course, we dare not forget that apart from God's intervention, flesh (mortal humanness) as such, functioning independently from God, has an unavoidable bent toward sin (see chapters 1 and 2). This explains why we find the words *sinful flesh* or expressions such as "what the flesh desires is opposed to the Spirit" when the focus is on human beings and sin (Romans 8:3; Galatians 5:17). At other times, an ethical or moral issue is not central, and the word *flesh* simply is another word for "people as mortals." Parallel with this is Walt Russell's statement:

The heart of my thesis is that *sarx* ["flesh"] does not change its basic sense by metonymy [substituting a word for another that is related to it] in any of the passages where Paul uses it in an ethical or moral sense. Rather, the term's basic bodily sense is simply enriched by Paul's use of redemptive-historical reasoning.[10]

The point is that regardless of what possible hidden nonphysical aspects of humanness may exist (such as spirit), all human beings apart from the grace of God find their present existence within the limits of physicalness or flesh. These brains/minds, along with the rest of the body, are "where it is." Of course, after people die, they continue to exist. The issue here is, *before they die,* where is life expressed?[11]

To make such a statement raises all sorts of questions. At the heart of most of them is the common Christian belief that Christians and non-Christians alike are fundamentally spiritual beings. We have thoughts and emotions that are not weighable, not physical in themselves. But that doesn't make them *spiritual* (a term we have yet to consider), unless we allow for animals also being spiritual. One writer, in listing the deeds of the flesh in Galatians 5:16–17, states, "only five out of the fifteen describe what we usually call bodily sins; the rest are 'sins of the spirit' (hatred, discord, jealousy, and the like)."[12] Yet we know animals experience these same things. Are they spiritual?[13]

Christian philosophers may argue long and hard, but our authority must remain with Scripture. Yet even here, we must make those difficult choices between what we may have been told the Bible teaches and what it actually teaches.[14] This brings us back to the word *flesh*. If we allow its evident Old Testament meaning to carry over into the New Testament, it's not too difficult to understand.

What Is Flesh?

Flesh, according to John 3:6 (and enlarged upon in the epistles) is everything that humanness is apart from the new birth. It may be good flesh, the kind described in Philippians 3:4–6 or 1 Corinthians 13:3—

- personal sacrifice, "give all my possessions to the poor,"
- willingness to die for a cause, "surrender my body to the flames,"
- wise statesmanship,
- esthetic works of art in sight and sound,
- creative scientific advancement.

(How often are these used—even in Christian circles—to measure personal worth?)

Or it may be bad flesh, the kind described in Galatians 5:19–21, plus all the other standard observable sins and those secret ones involving motives and desires.

Whether motivated by Satan or simply as the product of human proneness to sin, "whatever does not proceed from faith is sin" (Romans 14:23). Yet flesh is not merely what people do; it is who they are—*apart from the new birth.*[15]

Because of the physicalness of this word, it is often interchangeable with the word *body* (see Philippians 1:20–24). Second Corinthians 4:10–11 provides us with another good example. When Paul said that he was "always carrying about in the *body* the dying of Jesus...that the life of Jesus also may be manifested in our mortal *flesh*" (NASB, italics mine), he was referring to the same thing. To be "absent in the flesh" is equivalent to being "absent in body" (Colossians 2:5; 1 Corinthians 5:3).[16]

This is also true when sinfulness is the issue. The expressions, "deeds of the body" and the "works of the flesh" are getting at the same idea (Romans 8:13; Galatians 5:19). When Paul mentioned "the body of sin," there is every reason to believe he was referring to human physicalness.[17] Since sins do not originate in our mouths or eyes or hands, he obviously was including the thinking activities of a person in the word *body*. For example, the only sin Paul mentioned in Romans 7 was the sin of coveting, which is clearly mental. Yet he recognized "the law of sin" as "dwelling in [his] members," in his "flesh" (7:23, 25). In fact, without the truth of Romans 8, his only hope of deliverance from sinning was to be rescued from "this body of death," including the thinking mechanisms of his body.[18]

Listen to Russell once again:

> Therefore, to be "fleshly" is to be "non-Christianly." It is to be living as if your only standards and resources were what you could muster. It is to live as if, in this bodily existence, you were on your own and unaided by God's Spirit. Such a life stands in stark contrast to the Christian who is spiritual (1 Corinthians 2:15) and whose pattern of behavior should reflect that identity.[19]

Though still "in the flesh"—our bodies are not yet redeemed—we "have no confidence in the flesh." If individuals walk "according to the flesh," their "life" is nothing other than the kind of existence they had before they knew Christ. But we have been born again. In fact, we have "crucified the flesh" in the sense that it is truly dead to us as being our source for life.[20] The old age has passed away; the New Covenant age has arrived (Philippians 3:3; Romans 8:4; Galatians 5:24; 2 Corinthians 5:17).

Though we look forward to the "redemption of our bodies," already we are urged to "present our members to God as instruments of righteousness" as the Holy Spirit enables us to "put to death the [sinful] deeds of the body" (Romans 8:23; 6:13; 8:13). Why must we do this? Because the natural proneness of our flesh—our bodies, most particularly its thinking mechanisms—is toward sin.

Happily, some day we will have a brand new kind of flesh as different as a plant is from the seed from which it came.

> *What is sown is perishable, what is raised is imperishable.*
> *It is sown in dishonor, it is raised in glory.*
> *It is sown in weakness, it is raised in power (1 Corinthians 15:42–43).*

Though we look forward to that day, we enthusiastically lay hold of the fact we have *already* been set free to fullness of life by the Spirit, even while still in unredeemed bodies.

Only by having some grasp on the kind of people we were can we now turn to that second word, *spirit,* which points us to the wonder of the people we now are.

Human Spirit and the Holy Spirit

"Two kinds of people, two kinds of life." Few places in Scripture are more expressive of this fact than 1 Corinthians 2:13–15. Those two kinds of people are the "soulish" people and the "spiritual" people—those whose life center is soul and those whose life center is spirit,[21] as inseparable from the Spirit.

"No fuzziness, you say? Yes, my Bible uses the word *spiritual,*[22] but I don't find the word *soulish,* not even in my old King James! Where is it?"

Looking at those two verses, whether you find the words "those who are unspiritual" (NRSV) or "the natural man" (NASB, KJV) or "the man without the Spirit" (NIV) or "the man who isn't a Christian" (Living Bible), the Greek text clearly states "the soulish person." *Soulish* simply means "that which pertains to the soul or life…the life of the natural world."[23] Gordon Fee describes this word as meaning "humanity in its natural, physical existence."[24] Leon Morris goes so far as to say that it "has reference to animal life."[25] (Why the translators have chosen to hide the word *soulish* from the reader, both here and elsewhere, I am not sure.[26] They have no such hesitancy with the word *spiritual.*)

In light of Paul's later criticism of the Christians in Corinth for their "fleshly" attitudes, where he told them they were acting like "mere men"—like the world (1 Corinthians 3:3, NIV)—we may be confident he would have considered the expression "in the flesh" identical with "soulish." Both of these parallel terms describe unregenerate people.

Opposite this group are "those who are spiritual."[27] But what does that mean? The answer to this question should captivate us to a fresh sense of wonder, optimism, and joy.

But will it?

Unless we're careful, there's a good chance it won't. We've heard it all before—at least we think we have. Since it did not make much of an impact on us then, why get excited now?

Please look again!

The greatest trademark of the kind of persons called spiritual is that *they have received the Spirit as a life-transforming reality.*

In eager anticipation of this, Jesus cried out:

"Let anyone who is thirsty come to me, and let the one who believes in me drink. As the Scripture has said, 'Out of the believer's heart shall flow rivers of living water.'" Now he said this about the Spirit, which believers in him were to receive, for as yet there was no Holy Spirit [given], because Jesus was not yet glorified (John 7:38–39).

Little wonder that Peter on the Day of Pentecost was so enthusiastic. The Spirit was now being given![28] "Rivers of living water" were flowing from deep within! They were alive as never before. It was only after this Paul could have written,

He saved us…through the water of rebirth and renewal by the Holy Spirit. This Spirit he poured out on us richly through Jesus Christ our Savior, so that, having been justified by his grace, we might become heirs according to the hope of eternal life (Titus 3:5–7).

What a marvelous salvation package. Not only justified but born again—so renewed by the pouring upon us of the Holy Spirit that we are now, as spirit, alive to God! Though we rightly speak of "receiving Christ," it is significant that Paul felt fully at ease in describing that moment of new birth as "receiving the Spirit." It was that significant (Galatians 3:2, cf. 3:14). Apart from this miracle, a person remains in that first class—a *soulish* individual.

Yet no matter how important receiving the Spirit is, the crucial issue involves what the Spirit does.

The Old Gives Way to the New

In Old Covenant times the Holy Spirit came upon people for a variety of reasons:

- to give craftsmanship abilities, as with the builders of the tabernacle;
- to give wisdom, as with Solomon;
- to give divine revelation, as with the prophets;
- to give physical power, as with Samson;

- to give enablement in performing miracles, as with Elisha;
- to give courage and the capacity to lead, as with Moses, Joshua and David.

For those who have assumed there is little difference in the ministry of the Holy Spirit between Old and New Covenant times, it should come as a major surprise to discover that never in the Old Covenant is the Spirit described as giving spiritual life to anyone other than in promises looking ahead to the New Covenant. And with the possible exception of Psalms 51:10–13 and 143:10, the Spirit is never described as producing behavioral holiness in a believer, though we should assume he was active in bringing people to faith and giving them hearts that delighted in God and his law.

Yes, the Spirit continues to provide enablements similar to those listed above in our times. He continues to reconcile people to God, to teach, to be our counselor, and to give all sorts of spiritual gifts. But there is one thing above all else that marks his work in the New Covenant age.

The Holy Spirit is now installing in God's people the actual, risen life of Jesus to the degree that his life *is their life*. To receive the Spirit is to receive Christ. Not simply accepting him, but *receiving* him. To look at the heart, the essence, of the new birth, is to see this. By his birthing act, the Holy Spirit *actually changes us by placing in us the life of Jesus*. We were once only flesh; we are now spirit (John 3:6). This alone qualifies us to belong in God's eternal kingdom.

Peter Davids writes,

> First John 3:9 describes new birth so literally that he says God's "sperm" (usually translated "seed" but the same word is used for the sperm or semen of a male) remains in the child of God. According to 1 John, because this or that person is born of God he or she does not sin. This is because the nature of the Father is in them.[29]

Spiritual people are not only those who have received the Spirit of life, but they are products of his birthing power. "Whatever is born of the Spirit is spirit." Jesus Christ's very life—his risen life—is in them as *their life*.[30] They are now "participants of the divine nature" (2 Peter 1:4).

"And by this we know that *he abides in us,* by the Spirit that he has given us." Paul spoke of "Christ *who is our life*" (1 John 3:24; cf. 1 John 4:13; Colossians 3:4).

Levels of Self

All of us are used to functioning with "levels of self."[31] Consider those times you have driven down the highway, negotiating turns and avoiding oncoming cars, only suddenly to realize you had just covered miles of roadway while your mind was somewhere else! For a moment we are baffled how we could have covered that stretch of highway without being conscious of all those twists and turns. We know how! All during that stretch, two levels of mind and will were functioning: one was handling the driving; the other was far away, captivated by other thoughts. It is not therefore so strange to affirm that for the believer there is a *deeper level of self* than either of these—spirit.

For each of us, in that instant of new birth, our lives as "in the flesh" (soulish life) tumbled from their throne, forever replaced by life as spirit "in the Spirit." G. Appleton states,

> There are two levels of existence; the one is the sphere of the flesh
> and the other of spirit. On each level like produces like. A man can
> only pass from the lower order, the realm of flesh, into the higher
> order, the realm of spirit, by being born again.[32]

Yet it is not as though, before our new birth, that level of humanness called "spirit" did not exist. Rather, as Donald Guthrie states, "it is more reasonable to assume that man's natural spirit, which in his unregenerate state is inactive, is revived at conversion by the Spirit of God."[33]

Do you remember the little epitaph,

> Here lies Sam Pease
> Beneath the sod.
> It's not really Pease;

It's just the pod.

Pease shelled out

And went to God.

Though it is an oversimplification, it has a point. Normally, the shape of the shell gives us some idea of the shape of the seed inside—big or small, fat or skinny—but not always. Sometimes, for any number of reasons, the shell may be covered with warts, bumps, or creases. And yet, when we remove the shell, we may find that the irregularities have no connection at all with the nature of the seed inside.

You look at me, you may even live with me. Do you know me? I hope so. I sincerely hope the outward "flesh" man that you see bears a close resemblance to the shape of the deep person I most truly am. It would be so good if my spirit and my behavior were saying the same thing. No, I am not two people, but there are most certainly levels to my personhood. There is the deep level of self (inner man)[34] and my more shallow level.

Shallow self is so quickly affected by circumstances. And if shallow self is not made a "slave to righteousness," there's no telling what strange warts and bumps and creases you may see. My mannerisms, voice pattern, even my temperament may be circumstantial rather than reflective of my true personhood. You may observe me when I'm so busy protecting some supposed self-image, or catching one I think I'm supposed to have, or grieving over one I think I've lost, that you wouldn't have the faintest idea who I really am. And neither would I. But I have a dream...

I hope it is more than a dream.

I dream that you might see when you look at me, live with me, a unique, human, personable expression of Jesus. Like no one else.

People as Light Bulbs

The following illustration should bring us closer to understanding ourselves, that second kind of people who possess a new kind of life.

I am sure there are thousands of kinds of light bulbs in the world. Different shapes and sizes, colors, and designs; little bulbs, big bulbs; skinny ones, stocky ones; some formed with the sensitivity of a master glass blower, others quite plain; some of brittle, fragile glass, others quite tough. Yet each one was made to fulfill some distinctive purpose, to fit in its own special place.

Inside each bulb is a filament. Even here the differences could be endless, all the way from delicate, weblike threads, laced from point to point, to filament that is nothing but a thick, stubby wire.

Can you see them? Each in their assigned places—Christmas lights, refrigerator lights, fog lights, signal lights, night lights, stadium lights, landing lights, flashlights—on and on—by the millions. Each one representing an individual human being. But all are missing the one quality that alone justifies their existence—*light*.

Then, as we watch, here and there, in an instant, single bulbs come alive with light—the new birth!

What actually happened? Did anything about the bulb materially change? No.

Let's go a step further and say that the filament is a person's spirit, or one's inmost self. Did it change? Well, yes and no. The substance itself didn't change, but as you look at it you can scarcely see it for the brilliance of the light flooding from it. In fact, the filament, the glass bulb itself, is now virtually hidden within the light. Also, though the light originates in the filament, it affects the entire bulb.

So is the miracle of regeneration. It isn't simply that a Christian becomes a spirit person (a shining filament person), but rather, the whole person, as one unity, shines.

Yes, God, the Holy Spirit himself shined into our hearts (the filament). And the shining is nothing other than the risen life of Jesus. But this "treasure" (2 Corinthians 4:6–7) is not the exclusive property of the filament; rather, Paul says, "we have this treasure in clay jars" (the glass bulbs). God's intent is that this quickening miracle affect everything about us.

What if someone decided to start giving out awards for the best light bulb? How would they decide what makes a "best" bulb? With each light in its proper place, fulfilling its purpose, how could one be better than another?

By brightness? No. Who would want a 1000-watt night light?

By artistry of craftsmanship? Hardly. When the light is shining, it is the light which is the point of interest, not the glass.

In fact, the only way one could ever give out awards would be to turn off every light. With the light gone, all that's left is filament and glass. And yes, that could be judged and awarded. But how foolish! Bulbs were made for light.

So also the wonder of God's miracle. "Therefore from now on we recognize no man according to the flesh" (2 Corinthians 5:16, NASB).

When one is born again, God not only infuses light into what would otherwise be our darkened (though very distinctive) mortality; but now, not only is every part of our being in some way touched by light, *but the light becomes what we most truly are!*

We don't say, "Turn on the bulb," but "Turn on the light!" So the one who is joined to the Lord is "one spirit." We cannot claim that we *in* ourselves, or *of* ourselves, are light. The only way we are light is because of our *dependent* union with God, who is Light. This, by the way, protects us from ever thinking that we become little gods.

One thing, however, remains unmistakable: Life for us no longer is found in the distinctive shape of our bulb, the quality of its design (our bodies), or any other unique refinements we may possess. Remember, when we are functioning as lights, the glass and the filament are scarcely seen. Not only that, but even the light as it exists within the bulb is usually not the center of attention. It is rather what the light *does*.

So also is God's expectation for his children. We are not to be self-conscious, nor should we expect others to center their attention on us. Rather, both we and they rejoice in the effect of those lights—love, sensitivity, warmth, purity—all the beautiful fruit of the Spirit.

THE MYSTERY OF THE NEW BIRTH

Is this mysterious? Yes![35] Why should we not expect mystery when we have been touched by the creative finger of the incomprehensible God? How tragic if we attempt to remove the mystery by suggesting that no interior change took place when we were born again—that we are simply forgiven sinners (justified) who have been given the Holy Spirit to override our badness with his goodness.

Of course, God could have done that. He could have said, "At this point I save you. From now until you die you will be exactly the same as before you were saved, except you are forgiven. So don't expect too much. The change comes only when you die."

The point is, he did not say that!

We have resurrection life *now.*

Spiritual life *now.*

Eternal life *now.*

Who we most deeply are *now* is who we will be eternally.

And it is *now* that God's loving purpose of visibly expressing his life as our life—in our flesh—is being fulfilled. How better could he demonstrate the greatness of his power than to perform this marvelous, continuing miracle in the midst of our sin-prone circumstances?

Hidden Identities

"When I see Grampa in heaven will he look like he did just before he died?"

"Will babies who die always be babies in heaven?"

"Am I stuck with this inadequate brain of mine forever?"

Known only to God is an understanding of the authentic personhood of each of his born ones. In some cases, that deepest level of selfhood is scarcely observable due to whatever tragic limitations their frail or diseased or in some way handicapped mortality has placed upon them. Yes, such individuals are very much spiritually alive, but the temporary inadequacies of their light bulbs may so limit the display of light that perhaps God alone is aware of their inward glow.

Think of the multitudes of dear Christians who in years gone by were locked away in madhouses because they were epileptic or suffered from some endocrine or blood sugar problem. Who were they? Perhaps the cruelty of their very circumstances turned them to madness. Not only was their normal flesh-level personality altered, but so were the facilities necessary to express their deepest level of selfhood. (Please see the following extended footnote.[36])

Many of us know someone who has suffered extreme brain damage due to some accident. We say, "They are not the same person they used to be." No, in the flesh, they are not the same. But even if they were, are you certain the person *you knew them to be* was a true representation of who God knows that person actually is? What circumstances, what performance demands, what internal or external pressures caused them to appear as something other than the distinctive, God-shaped spiritual being you will know them to be when you meet them in heaven? Sadly, some of God's new creation lights have allowed themselves to become so captivated with their own glass, they have dressed it up with so many layers of eye-catching colors, it is next to impossible to see any light at all!

Imagine the thousands of truly born again people whose true identities have been hidden behind some very earth-oriented image they have created for themselves. Perhaps it was an obsession with athletics, or building a business empire, or their physical appearance, or material possessions. Did you ever truly see *them* as they actually are—God's spiritual masterpieces?

What if someone someday pulled off the impossible and gathered in one place all of Michelangelo's marble statues? Some of them are still crated, and by all appearances have no value other than the box itself. Others are in various stages of unpacking with strands of protective wrappings hanging here and there, quite unattractive. A few are already polished and on display—there in all their beauty.

Yet the hidden ones, the dusty ones, the cluttered ones, are as precious as those on finished display. What a tragedy, what mockery if the boxes and the wrappings themselves *became* the display. How often does this happen among God's spiritual masterpieces?

It is one thing if, by unavoidable human tragedy, the masterpieces will be seen in their beauty only when Christ returns—those who die in infancy, those who endure a lifetime of minimal expressiveness. But it is another thing when the masterpieces could have been seen in all the perfections of the life of Jesus, but missed by a lifetime of quenching the Spirit's work.

The Crucial Issue

There really are two kinds of people, the soulish and the spiritual, who are as different as darkness is from light. Before we expend our energies trying to draw fine lines of distinction in each biblical reference to the human soul and spirit, we must recognize that the crucial issue relates to two kinds of life: life in the flesh and life in the Spirit. Remember, the kind of life we possess determines the kind of persons we are.

We who possess an entirely new kind of life, totally by God's grace, dare not allow ourselves (or anyone else) to degrade God's miracle by measuring our selfhood with superficial flesh-level yardsticks. Yes, we still have flesh life, but what is a bulb without the light?

Is this as radical as it sounds? Jesus said, *"they are not of the world any more than I am of the world."* His expectation was that your life would be as revolutionary as his was—a kind of life the world had never before seen. A kind of life the world *must see* in our times if the church is to fulfill its calling.

Our next step will be to take a careful look—for some, a revolutionary look—at how big Jesus' expectations actually are.

CHAPTER 6

God's Expectations for His Miracle Children

With great enthusiasm we believe the new creation age has arrived. With equal enthusiasm we who are born again know that we are a different kind of people with a new kind of life to live. What kind of life? A life that expresses the invisible God being made visible in human lives—in us. Our lives are the expression of his perfection, his purity, his love.

"But wait a minute," someone says, "let's not get carried away. We have to be realistic. We all know that Christians are messing up all the time. In fact, who's to say Christians sin any less than non-Christians? Certainly you are not suggesting that God expects our Christian lives to be marked by consistent holiness, are you?

"Yes, I know Jesus said, 'Be perfect, therefore, as your heavenly Father is perfect.' And, yes, Peter echoed the same thought when he urged his readers 'as he who called you is holy, be holy yourselves in all your conduct.' But let's face the real world. Not only do Christians blow it, but the Bible says right there in 1 John, 'if we say that we have no sin, we deceive ourselves.' That's the way it is. You know what I mean. It's one thing to be challenged to live a holy life, but come on now. God knows we won't. He never really expected us to, did he?" (See Matthew 5:48; 1 Peter 1:15; 1 John 1:8)[1]

If we are committed to taking God seriously, it would be difficult to imagine any issue we should be more sure about than this. We dare not be fuzzy in our thinking.

Is Sinning Normal for the Child of God?

To be sure we are clear, there is an ample supply of Christian speakers and writers who appear eager to soothe our consciences by asserting that sinning is quite normal for all of us. Of course they will use 1 John 1:8 ("If we say that we have no sin, we deceive ourselves") to prove their point. If that were not enough, they will throw in a few choice Old Covenant Bible biographies of sinning believers to eliminate any doubts we might have.[2] Just like the bumper sticker says, "Christians aren't perfect, just forgiven."

How many times have you heard someone say,

"Didn't Paul say that he was the foremost of all sinners? Well then, why should we expect to be any better? Not only that, but he claimed to be the very least of all the saints. He urged Christians to regard others as better than themselves. He knew he had not yet arrived—that he wasn't perfect. In fact, he confessed his own painful moral failure by writing, 'for I do not do the good I want, but the evil I do not want is what I do…wretched man that I am!'" (See 1 Timothy 1:15; Ephesians 3:8; Philippians 2:3; 3:17; Romans 7:19, 24)

As if this were not enough, we are reminded that the epistles are loaded with evidence that sinning was common enough in the early church. Why should we, two thousand years removed from the time of Christ, expect anything better?

Well then, is the case closed?

No, not until we take a second look at these passages to see if they mean what we've been told. Since the focus of this book is on the radical nature of the new birth miracle, let's begin by checking out the message of the man who used new birth terminology more than any other writer, the Apostle John.

The Beloved Apostle Looks at Sin

Perhaps you noted back in chapter 4 that I took a less-than-popular approach to the meaning of 1 John 3:9. I am convinced—and I hope you will be, too—that what was stated there is what God wants us to believe. In fact, I doubt if there is any other section of Scripture in which normal meanings of passages have been so skewed to make them fit typical Christian behavior. How you understand 1 John will have a major impact on how you view sin and the Christian.

Let's begin by looking at a few of John's most radical statements:

> No one who abides in him sins; no one who sins has either seen him or known him.... Those who have been born of God do not sin, because God's seed abides in them; they cannot sin, because they have been born of God.
>
> We know that those who are born of God do not sin, but the one [Jesus] who was born of God protects them, and the evil one does not touch them (1 John 3:6, 9; 5:18).

That's right. And that's radical. In fact, these statements are so radical, so opposite to common Christian experience, we find ourselves searching the rest of his little book for whatever support John might give us that will allow us with a clear conscience to reject the apparent intent of these verses, while still preserving our high regard for God's Word.

Could it be that John had in mind our *status* rather than our actual *behavior*? (Once again, the screen illustration—the way God sees us in Christ.) But no, that won't work here because throughout this little epistle his focus is on very practical matters related to how we are to live.

Well then, there must be other things John said that will protect us from this unrealistic—and some would say, dangerous—belief that Christians should not expect to sin. Does our search *appear to be successful?* Some Bible teachers would answer yes by pointing first to 1 John 1: 8–10, and then by pressing a grammatical point on the passages quoted above.

With haste they remind us that John already has stated, "if we say that we have no sin,[3] we deceive ourselves, and the truth is not in us," and "if we say that we have not sinned, we make him a liar, and his word is not in us" (1 John 1:8, 10). With a sigh of relief, we reaffirm our expectations not only that Christians sin, but that sin is so tenacious we must never imagine a time in our lives when it is not in some way expressing itself—a time, no matter how brief, when we have no sin.

Now, if this is what John was teaching, we will have to solve the problem of that little word *if* used just two verses later when John wrote, "*if* anyone does sin."

"Of course," some respond, "sometimes when we say *if,* we actually mean *when.* That must have been John's meaning here.[4] Not only that, but since we always 'have sin' (and isn't this what John said in 1 John 1:8, 10?) then *when* must mean *always.*"[5]

There. Problem solved! Sin is normal for a Christian.

Still, with this type of logic, we haven't cleared up the meaning of those verses quoted earlier; at least we may rest assured they do not mean what they appear to mean. That's good! Or is it?

Right now, would you be willing to set aside your need of justifying sin in your life long enough to be open to a different way of looking at 1 John 1:8–10?

Let's begin with something I trust we all believe—that people cannot be saved apart from admitting both that they have sinned and that they are sinners. Yet there is evidence that John began his epistle quite aware that somewhere in his audience were false teachers who did not believe that at all.[6] They had no need of a Savior because they had never sinned. These people were unsaved. I. H. Marshall writes,

> It seems likely that the claims John denies at the beginning of the Epistle represent those who were false teachers. They were people who claimed to have fellowship with God and to be sinless (1:6, 8, 10). They said they knew God (2:4).... They did not believe that Jesus was the Christ or the Son of God (2:22; 5:1, 5).... If they

denied that Jesus was the Christ, they probably also denied that his death had any significance; if they claimed that they had no sin, *it would follow that they felt no need of atonement and the cleansing by the blood of Jesus* (italics mine).[7]

For any of us who have grown up in a Christian context where we were told numerous times that 1 John 1:8–10 is a passage written to remind us that sinning will be a normal characteristic of believers until they die, it takes a concerted effort even to consider the possibility that John had another purpose in mind. This purpose is well stated in Daniel J. Harrington's summary of an article by Sakae Kubo:

> In 1 John 1:8 the author is answering the Gnostics who claim they have no sin, while all the time they live a life of sin. They could make this claim because their own definition of sin allowed them to do so. Because their understanding of sin is different from that of orthodox Christians, the Gnostics have claimed to be sinless (1:8) and to be born of God (3:9) but *their actions have belied their claims* (italics mine).[8]

Think about it. What is one of the first things non-Christians must do if they are to be saved? That's right, they must confess that they are sinners. In other words, they must express a "1 John 1:9" kind of response. Apart from this, it is meaningless for them to believe Christ died for their sins! Those who would say they have not sinned certainly would not admit to any need of a Savior—and of course, to any need for forgiveness. It is also obvious the "we" of verse 9 has the same individuals in view as the "we" of verses 6, 8 and 10.[9]

How constructive it would be if Christians, once and for all, stopped using these verses to defend the idea that sinning is normal Christian behavior! Not only is that not the intent of 1 John 1:8, 10, but it also contradicts 1 John 2:1. Yes, we Christians *do possess* in our flesh a propensity toward sin (Galatians 5:17). But to admit that as true is a far cry from assuming John's intent was to support the idea that succumbing to the desires of the flesh should be thought of as characteristic of Christians.[10] I wish I knew some way to underline the importance of recognizing this fact.

Of course, it is also true that once one obeys 1 John 1:9 and has therefore become both forgiven and a child of God, the practice of confession should continue as the need arises—whenever the person becomes aware of specific sin in his life. But within its context, this does not appear to be the main purpose of John's inclusion of 1 John 1:9.

(Even if one holds the view that this passage represents false claims made by true Christians, it still does not support the belief that Christians are always in need of confessing sins because sinning is unavoidable. It is true that Christians have in their flesh a disposition to sin (1:8). It is also a dishonest expression of arrogance for anyone to say "I have not sinned." But neither of these facts opposes the joyous expectation of a life in which sinful behavior is an unnecessary aberration as is emphasized throughout 1 John.)

By readjusting our understanding of this passage, perhaps we are ready to take an honest look at those remarkable verses, 1 John 3:6, 9; 5:18.

A Halfway Solution

Earlier I mentioned that many Bible teachers believe the claims of these verses are not as bold as they might first appear. They conclude that when John said "Christians do not sin," he had in mind *habitual* sinning. They support this on the basis of John's use of present tense verbs.[11] One writer goes so far as to say that John has in mind "continuous" sinning.[12] Most English versions have willingly cooperated with this idea. In one way or another they modify the NRSV rendering of John's words quoted earlier. Most typically, the "cannot sin" idea is changed to "cannot go on sinning" or "does not continue to sin" (NIV); or "practice sin" (NASB). In other words, these versions express the idea that even though people who are born again will sin occasionally, they will not *always* be sinning, *habitually* sinning.[13]

Of course, this is only a halfway solution, because all of us know someone—probably ourselves—who went through times where a habitual pattern of sinning—pride, envy, self-centeredness—seemed almost unshakable. Yet most of us are hesitant to assume perhaps we were not saved at all.

Also, the "habitual sinning" idea is no solution at all to those who believe Christians are continuously sinning to some degree (see endnote 5).

Well then, a halfway solution is no solution at all. Not only that, but a variety of recognized scholars warn that this "habitual" idea requires stretching the limits of Greek grammar too far.[14] What, then, was John expressing? Could it possibly be he actually meant to say born again people do not sin?

After describing and rejecting several approaches to this passage,[15] Marshall suggests John is depicting "the ideal character of a Christian," yet an ideal *that was not sheer fantasy.* He then draws some rather startling conclusions.

> We may now conclude that our texts express the possibility which is placed before every believer, the possibility of a life free from sin.… It is a reality which is continually threatened by the tensions of living in a sinful world, and yet one which is capable of being realized by faith.
>
> Despite its apparent subtlety this view is probably the most satisfactory of the various alternatives we have discussed.… John summons believers to become what they are, in the same way as Paul urges the "saints" to live as saints. Sinlessness is not a negative virtue: it includes full observance of God's positive commands. John speaks of Christians as those who do observe God's commands, and yet he has to counsel them to keep those very commands.…
>
> We can regard this verse [3:6] as a practical conclusion to what John has been saying in the previous verses. Sin is incompatible with being a child of God. God's intention is that the believer should be free from sin.[16]

I wonder if we might find a parallel if someone we knew started doing things anyone in their right mind would never do. Imagine a person who raises prize-winning roses deciding to head up a "Protect the Aphids Society" or inventing a faster mildew maker. What would we say? "You can't do that! You're out of your mind. No one would do such a thing!" Dunn puts it this way:

To claim to be a child of God, and yet to be indifferent to moral obligation, is to confuse the whole issue. Of the personal problem raised for one who acknowledges all this, and yet is conscious of sin, *he is not at this moment thinking* (italics mine).[17]

As stated earlier, John did not deny the possibility of sin in the Christian's life. Yet we may be sure John assumed his commands regarding righteous behavior would be obeyed (2:3–6, 9–11, 15; 3:11–15; 4:7–8). From his perspective, why would anyone who possessed eternal life, who is a child of the Light, a citizen in the New Covenant age, be insane enough to live as though they were, to use John's words, "in darkness"?

Is it possible for a Christian to practice temporary insanity? Yes.

Is sin *ever* a rational behavior for a Christian? Never.[18]

Might a Christian remain in an extended state of temporary insanity? I imagine so. (I know of no other explanation for such times in my own life.) Some examples of sinful behavior described in 1 and 2 Corinthians appear to support the possibility of an ongoing state of sinful behavior. Note especially 2 Corinthians 12:21. Nevertheless, Paul viewed this with such alarm he felt it necessary to warn those in the church to examine themselves to make sure they were truly "in the faith" (2 Corinthians 13:5). Another example is found in 1 Thessalonians 3:14–15, involving those who were unwilling to obey Paul's commands. They were still to be regarded as believers. In this case it is probable their reason for disobedience was not so much an act of rebellion against God as it was an expression of their lack of respect for the apostle. Nevertheless, Paul still regarded it as sin.

It should be noted that most sins Christians commit are the products of spiritual weakness overwhelmed by the power of temptation rather than expressions of rebellion. Such weakness may express itself in boredom due to the absence of the flow of true meaning in life, forgetfulness, or mental confusion. Even if willfulness is present, often the Christian hears him(her)self saying, "I know this is wrong, but I simply can't help it." I believe one of the evidences of the regenerating work of the Spirit is the degree to which we Christians will try to avoid a mindset that might suggest we are in open defiance against our Savior.[19]

I wonder—how would you respond to some particular temptation to sin if you paused long enough to acknowledge (1) that your thoughts (sin always begins with thoughts) were not motivated by the Spirit, but by your own self-centered flesh, and therefore were the enemies of authentic life; (2) that to continue to entertain those thoughts in light of who you most deeply are would be to choose to function as temporarily insane?

If your essential selfhood were "in the flesh" ("crab apple" life), sinning would at least be true to who you were. John's enthusiastic little book shouts to every "born one of God"—"Be what you are—golden delicious!" The Spirit makes it possible.

C. H. Dodd expresses this most encouraging truth so well:

> In other words, the renewal of our nature consequent upon accepting the Gospel is such that our whole bent is away from sin, and our normal condition one of sinlessness. It may happen that, under stress of temptation, we commit a sinful act; in that case we make our peace with God by virtue of the sacrifice and intercession of Christ, and revert to our normal condition of sinlessness. For, whatever happens, we are children of God, and sin is abnormal and unnatural for us. It cannot be that, while God's word remains in us, we should so belie our heavenly parentage as to be set in sinful courses.[20]

Are these statements radical? Very much so!

Are they in keeping with New Covenant truth? Yes!

From the pen of the Apostle John is ample evidence that the new birth is a miracle far greater than many of us have been willing to accept. It was because of this actual "God's seed abides in us" miracle, that truly consistent, righteous behavior is a reasonable expectation (1 John 3:9).

The Apostle to the Gentiles Looks at Sin

So much for the Apostle John. But what about Paul? What about his claim to be "the foremost" of all sinners (1 Timothy 1:15)?

It's true he used those words. So then, what hope is there for any one of us? But wait. We dare not miss the fact that he clearly had in mind his life *before he was born again.*

Paul was *"formerly* a blasphemer, a persecutor, and a man of violence" (1:13, italics mine). Paul could think of no sin worse than persecuting Jesus and his people, even though he had done it in ignorance. Paul's whole point was, if God's grace had reached low enough to save him, "the foremost of sinners"—after what he had done—God could save anyone!

The apostle touched on the same idea in 1 Corinthians 15:9 when he said he was "the least of the apostles." Why? Because he currently was such a sinner? No! Rather it was because he had "persecuted the church." Probably this same thought was in Paul's mind in Ephesians 3:8, "I am the very least of all the saints."[21]

Some have pressed their point using Philippians 2:3. "There," they say, "Paul urged believers to see themselves as worse sinners than anyone else because the passage says 'regard others better' than themselves." But in view of the immediate reference to Jesus and the overall emphasis on humility, the idea of "better" in the sense of "more important" (NASB), not only fits the context, but also agrees with the meaning of the Greek word used.[22] Proper humility does not in itself require a person to believe they are the worst sinner in the world. Paul also reminded each of us "not to think of yourself more highly than you ought to think, but to think with sober judgment." May we never forget that whatever worth we find in ourselves is there only by the grace of God (Romans 12:3; cf. 1 Corinthians 4:7).

Still others would argue from Romans 7:14–25 that Paul's life continued to be marked by personal moral failure—"for I do not do the good I want, but the evil I do not want is what I do.… Wretched man that I am!" To add support to the view that Paul believed this wretched state is the expected, normal Christian experience, they would point to the inward groaning that Paul described as he longed for the day when his body would be redeemed (Romans 8:23–25). They also would rush us to Galatians 5:17 to prove that for now, at least, this sad state is unavoidable.[23]

"But take heart. It's not all that bad," they would add, "remember you have been justified. God sees you as righteous. And that's what really counts. So quit expecting so much out of yourself. Until you get that glorified body, you will keep right on sinning—just like Paul."

This is no small matter!

If this view of Paul's perspective is correct—*if this is the normal, to-be-expected Christian life*—we must draw two conclusions:

First, Christians are wrong in hoping for even partial victory over sin. Instead, they should anticipate *total failure*. Why? Because total failure is what Romans 7:14–25 is all about. Read those verses to see if you can find even a moment of victory. In addition, we must resign ourselves to the wretchedness he described, with our only hope being that day when we will be rescued from our physical bodies. (For additional clarification of the meaning of Romans 7:7–25, please see Appendix.)

Is this really what Paul meant? Let's listen to his answers in the verses before and after Romans 7.

> *Should we continue to sin in order that grace may abound? By no means! How can we who died to sin go on living in it?... We know that our old self was crucified with him so that the body of sin might be rendered inactive....* [24] *But thanks be to God that you, having once been slaves of sin...having been set free from sin, have become slaves of righteousness.... For the law of the Spirit of life in Christ Jesus has set you free from the law of sin and of death.... So then...if by the Spirit you put to death the deeds of the body, you will live (Romans 6:1–2, 6, 17–18; 8:2, 12–13).* [25]

Why is it in our eagerness to paint the darkest picture we can, we choose to ignore Paul's important flow of thought? Yes, our hope in the future redemption of our bodies is delicious to think about. And yes, in our flesh (7:18) there will be nothing but failure. That's all true—but I am sure Paul would have shouted out to those who so misuse Romans 7, "You are not in the flesh anymore! If you choose to limit God by depending on your own flesh-level resources to fulfill his law, you will make the same agonizing discovery I did. You will find yourself locked in as 'a captive to the law of sin.'[26] Why not see yourself as you truly are? You are not a captive to sin anymore! You have been set free. The 'law of the Spirit of life in Christ Jesus has set you free from the law of sin and of death.' You are free to 'walk' and 'live' under this greater law—the law of the Spirit. So get busy and 'walk by the Spirit.' The result will be God's moral law *actually lived out in you*" (Romans 8:2–6; cf. Galatians 5:16, NASB. Note: The negative in this verse is emphatic in the Greek text—"you will by no means fulfill the desire of the flesh").

Freedom from the Law of Sin

In light of these verses, it would be wrong to conclude that Paul understood our freedom from the law of sin as being based only upon the doctrine of justification—that God sees us "in Christ" as the one who fulfilled the requirement of the law for us. Remember the screen example used earlier?

The freedom described in Romans 8 is *not extrinsic* (the way God sees me), while all the time I am *intrinsically* the "wretched man" that Paul has just described.[27] Instead, the emphasis in the verses that follow Romans 7 underline the truth of an interior miracle that has infused a new quality of life within. It is Christ *in us* (See especially 8:9). The contrasts we find could not be sharper as we move from 7:7–24 to 8:1–10.

Bondage and death contrasted with *freedom and life.*

Clearly, this is not positional truth, but a "walking" truth.

In other words, Romans 6–8 are rooted in not one, but three marvelous saving acts of God—justification, reconciliation, and *regeneration*.[28] Only from these sources can sanctification (holiness) blossom. True, Paul's emphasis in Romans 3–5 was on justification by faith. But the goal of the book of Romans is not to declare our new status before God; it is about an entirely new dimension of life—risen life, eternal life.

God's act of justification was never intended as an end in itself. Rather, having made that *external* declaration on the basis of Christ's perfect life and his substitutionary death, God could then in perfect righteousness perform that marvelous *internal* miracle of regeneration based upon his resurrection.[29] When our old self was crucified with him and when we recognize as a fact that we are now actually alive to God, we are declaring in a most expressive way the implications of the miracle of *new birth,* new life—eternal life.[30]

A Life Free of Sin

Once we were the old self, devoid of life, subjected to futility, captive to the law of sin and death.[31] We are not that self anymore![32] If we were, sinning would be quite reasonable. We *are* the new self, part of a new humanity that pulsates with life from God, Jesus' own resurrection life.

Keeping in mind that God's definition of authentic life is *the only definition that counts,* he said "in him was life" (John 1:4). It was to be found nowhere else. What we thought was life wasn't life at all. Actually, it was a walking death. That walking death came to an end at that salvation moment when God made a marvelous interior change in you. The person you used to be was in some mysterious way crucified when Christ was crucified. In fact, you were crucified "with Christ." (See Appendix 2)

Try to imagine the radical change our Savior experienced. In his dying he had become all that sin was (2 Corinthians 5:21); but in his rising, this was exchanged for the fullness of his own resurrection life. (Read with care Romans 6:6–11.) This is what happened to you, except for one difference. At Jesus' resurrection, he also received his glorified body. We have resurrection life, but we still have our mortal bodies. Someday, we hope soon, we too will experience the transformation of our bodies. But can we use this as our excuse for present failure? Not if we believe Romans 6:12–14; 8:12–13 and Galatians 5:16. Those passages (plus, of course, 1 John) make it clear that our awareness of this present mortal state must not lower our expectation of present, righteous living.

Sinning really is completely inconsistent with who we now are.[33]

WHAT DOES GOD EXPECT OF US?

So what does God really expect of us? You probably know my answer: genuine holiness.

Is this some dreamy doctrine? I admit it sounds like it. We would all like to believe the new creation miracle described in Romans 6 *automatically* results in transformed lives. If "everything old has passed away" and "everything new has come" (2 Corinthians 5:17, which is the essence of Romans 6), then should we not expect all of those old sinful desires to be gone—forever?

"I used to be an alcoholic, now I hate the stuff!"

"I used to love money with a passion, now it's no problem at all!"

"I used to have homosexual desires, now they're gone!"

There are people who say such things have happened to them. But most of us have found many of our old sinful desires still very much around. I imagine all us have found times in our personal experience when Romans 7:14–25 (or even 7:7–25) described exactly how we felt.

Others remind us, "But remember, sin's power has been broken," as though sin is now a powerless foe. If that were so, why did the apostle warn us, "do not let sin exercise *dominion* in your mortal bodies"? (Romans 6:12, italics mine) We dare not deceive ourselves. Sin remains a powerful enemy to godliness.

Well then, is God a realist or a dreamer?

Let's ask another question. "Did Paul believe his readers could experience consistent victory in their spiritual warfare, or did he know that their Christian lives would be up and down affairs in which they would experience defeats?"[34] David Wenham, writing within a context of Romans 7, answers:

> Paul would never admit the inevitability of defeat in the Christian life. His conviction is clear that "with the temptation God will also make a way of escape" (1 Corinthians 10:13). The power of the Spirit is the power that raised Jesus from the dead and will give us newness of life in the present as well as in the future. For Paul this is the most important reality of Christian experience, and he would not subscribe to the melancholy view that Spirit and flesh are two almost equal contestants within the Christian's life. Undoubtedly Paul would have subscribed to the view that the Christian life can be a life of victory, if only we will recognize and appropriate the Spirit's power.[35]

Yet how about Paul himself? For him was it an "if only it could be" kind of dream? We find his answer in the fact that repeatedly he presented himself to others as an example of a godly man—a life worthy of being copied. (See 1 Thessalonians 1:5–6; 2:5–12)[36]

As to Paul's own experience, Wenham says:

> Paul in his letters gives remarkably little hint that he is conscious
> of sin in his own life as a believer. There are, on the contrary, more
> and clearer indications of Paul's confidence in his own moral
> uprightness (seen of course entirely as a work of grace). This and
> the lack of exhortations to his readers to confess their sins could
> be taken to indicate that the spirit of penitence resulting from con-
> sciousness of sin was not nearly as important to Paul as it has been
> for many saints of later ages.[37]

You Don't Have to Sin

No matter how heartfelt and beautiful some of our Christian traditions are,
we dare not allow them to alter God's New Covenant truth. Consider the
centuries old "General Confession" from the *Common Book of Prayer,* spoken daily, perhaps by millions around the world:

> Almighty and most merciful Father; We have erred and strayed
> from thy ways like lost sheep. We have followed too much the
> devices and desires of our own hearts. We have offended against
> thy holy laws. We have left undone those things which we ought
> to have done; And we have done those things which we ought not
> to have done; and there is no health in us. But thou, O Lord, have
> mercy upon us, miserable offenders. Spare thou those, O God,
> who confess their faults. Restore thou those who are penitent;
> According to thy promises declared unto mankind in Christ Jesus
> our Lord. And grant, O most merciful Father, for his sake; That we
> may hereafter live a godly, righteous, and sober life, To the glory of
> thy holy Name. Amen.[38]

We must ask ourselves, "Does this reflect God's expectations for his
miracle children—as those who 'have erred and strayed' as 'miserable
offenders'—to the degree that such must be our daily confession? Every
morning to pray that this day 'we may hereafter live a godly, righteous, and
sober life,' only to be assured our prayer will go unanswered, knowing the

next morning we will find ourselves once again as miserable offenders?"

"Yes," we all say, "but I do fail so often!"

But why? Has our God ordained that his resources for godliness will always be just beyond our reach? Did he give us a dream to treasure, knowing full well it was only a dream? Is this the teaching of the epistles?[39]

No matter how discouraged we may be as to the sins in our own lives, once and for all you and I must reject the idea that sin is to be accepted as the unavoidable norm. We must reject the teaching that says there's not too much we can do about it except to keep our confessions up–to–date, inhale the Spirit's power, and then, perhaps, enjoy a few seconds of cleanness before we start the miserable cycle all over again.

What *are* God's expectations? The unmistakable answer is *a life of genuine holiness*. Yes, but has anyone ever done it perfectly? And if so, how was it done? The first answer is yes! And the second answer is as clear as crystal. All this will be in our next chapter.

CHAPTER 7

God's Working Model of a Miracle Life

Though our central focus in this chapter will be on God's working model of a perfect life of holiness, we will need first to step back far enough to take another look at the remarkable difference between life under the Old Covenant and life under the New Covenant—life before Christ's resurrection and the Day of Pentecost, and life after those events.

THE DIFFERENCE BETWEEN THEN AND NOW

God did many marvelous things in and through the lives of Old Testament believers. They too were justified by faith. They too were reconciled to God. What then is so special about what God is doing now?

Some of the differences are easy to spot. For example, repeatedly, Old Testament believers had to bring their atoning sacrifices to the altar. Over the years, tens of thousands of gallons of blood were poured out before that altar. Now we look back on the cross and the blood of Christ shed once for all. Back then they needed sympathetic priests to approach God on their behalf.[1] Now "we have confidence to enter the sanctuary by the blood of Jesus." In fact, he is our great high priest (Hebrews 10:19–22; 4:14–16).

Certainly the Holy Spirit related to people in a different way in Old Covenant times. Jesus made that quite clear when he said "he abides *with* you, and he will be *in* you" (John 14:17, italics for emphasis). Yet even before Pentecost, we come across individuals who were filled with the Spirit. But in every case, they were people to whom God had given some special task to accomplish—to rule or prophesy, or even to produce the artistry for the tabernacle.[2] Such fillings were far different from the dream of those who longed for the coming of the New Covenant age—the age of the Spirit (cf. Isaiah 32:15; 59:20–21; Ezekiel 36:26–27).

There is another important difference that is often missed. It has to do with two very different ways human righteousness was to be understood.

Two Ways of Understanding Righteousness

In the Old Covenant, the most wicked people were those who saw no greater purpose in life than their own pleasure. The idea of God simply got in their way. If they knew of Jehovah, it only made their wickedness worse because it revealed their conscious rebellion.

If, in their state of independence from God, they happened to choose to be altruistic by considering the welfare of loved ones or country, society would have considered them righteous. But that was not God's evaluation. Some people seem to be born with tender hearts toward others, whether for people or animals. If you asked them why they responded with so much sensitivity, they might answer, "It makes me feel good when I do it" or "I couldn't live with myself if I didn't help." (I imagine Esau was such a man.)

If instead they attempted to keep on God's good side both out of guilt and a fear of God's anger, they also might have been viewed as something less than wicked. (Would Balaam fit here?)

But righteous? Hardly that.

A righteous person was one who, under divine conviction, responded with warmth and humility to the worthiness of God. Purely by grace, God performed that interior miracle of reconciliation—he changed their heart attitude both toward him and toward his law. Moved by love for such a God, they would set out to please him.

> He has told you, O mortal, what is good;
> and what does the LORD require of you

> *but to do justice and to love kindness,*
>> *and to walk humbly with your God?* (Micah 6:8)

To some degree this was actually possible.

There were righteous people under the Old Covenant—the Jobs and Ruths and Daniels of the Old Testament.[3] (Consider the list in Hebrews 11.) It wasn't impossible. Do you remember what God told the Israelites?

> *"Surely, this commandment that I am commanding you today is not too hard for you, nor is it too far away.... I have set before you life and death, blessings and curses. Choose life so that you and your descendants may live, loving the LORD your God, obeying him, and holding fast to him; for that means life to you and length of days, so that you may live in the land that the LORD swore to give to your ancestors, to Abraham, to Isaac, and to Jacob"[4] (Deuteronomy 30:11, 19, 20).*

Was the Pre-Christian Paul Righteous?

This type of righteousness could be well illustrated even in the life of the Apostle Paul before his revolutionary encounter with Jesus. Of his whole life he said, "as to righteousness under the law, blameless."[5] He could also say, "up to this day I have lived my life with a clear conscience before God." Of his actions in persecuting the Christians, his response was that he acted as one "zealous for God" doing the things he felt "he ought to do" as expressions of his devotion to God (Philippians 3:6; Acts 23:1; 22:3; 26:9).

Was Paul a sincerely devout man? Of course he was, though terribly misled by his own blind commitment to the prevalent Jewish concept that God never would nor could become a real man. Later, reflecting back on those pre-Jesus days, he acknowledged he was "once a blasphemer and a persecutor and a violent man." But he quickly added that he acted in ignorance (1 Timothy 1:13).[6]

Under the Old Covenant a "righteous" man was aware of how much he needed God's gracious help. (Paul may have spent time in the temple praying earnestly for God's blessing before he started on his way to persecute Christians in Damascus [cf. Galatians 1:14].) It was this very kind of person (though far more open than Paul) that the life of Jesus touched again and again.

When Jesus was a baby, it was Anna and Simeon. During his ministry it was Nathaniel and most of his other disciples—probably Nicodemus also. After his death it was Joseph of Arimathea and Cornelius. Yet it was to this kind of people, "righteous" people, that Jesus said in anticipation of the New Covenant, "You *must be born again*." New Covenant righteousness was a new proposition altogether.[7]

"God As My Helper" vs. "God As My Life"

At the risk of oversimplification, the differences between Old Covenant righteousness and New Covenant righteousness could be compared with the difference between "God as my helper" and "God as my life."

Look at it another way. In the Old Testament, God's people were characterized as his vineyard. God was the owner and protector of this vineyard, as well as the One who deserved the harvest (Isaiah 5:1–7). In anticipating the New Covenant, however, Jesus told his disciples, *"I am the vine; you are the branches"* (John 15:5). The difference is a radical one indeed.

The Search for a Better Butterfly

This fact is most important to see when we face up to the problem of sin in our lives and our concern in pleasing the Savior. If righteousness is merely a matter of avoiding bad things and performing good things, then victory may be considerably easier than we think (Job 1:1). Paul once thought so!

So often we hear "victorious life" speakers say words like these: "Because the old man has been crucified, you don't have to listen to his commands any more. His power has been broken. You don't *have* to swear or cheat. Before, you couldn't help it, but now…"

This may sound liberating. And there is some truth in the words. But it can also be quite misleading.

Let's suppose that I am a young man who has become fascinated with butterflies. Before long I become a consummate expert. My collection knows few peers. Every waking moment of my life is utterly captivated by these amazing, colorful, infinitely varied creatures. Finally I arrange my adventure of a lifetime—a trip far up the steaming reaches of the Amazon in search of a rare, exotic species. With scarcely a second thought I turn my back on the world's materialism, its air-conditioned comfort, pretty girls, soft music, new car showrooms, moonlight shopping center sales, the love of money, my physical appearance, my health, and other people's opinions of me. It's easy to leave those things behind; they never really bother me much anyway.

Really? Yes, really. With full sincerity I would tell you that I have found a highly fulfilling reason to be alive. I've found meaning. I have neither time nor interest for so many of the things that captivate other people. And so, all alone under my mosquito netting, lying in a slightly damp hammock, I fall asleep like a child, dreaming of that golden-winged insect somewhere upstream.

If you said that my life was all wrapped up in self, I would counter you with honest force of conviction. One of my greatest joys is to see delight play across the faces of the many people who discover the beauty of butterflies through my display. Mine is the quiet confidence that the world is better, richer because of what I do. I might even go one step further. Even as a non-Christian, I might insist that my efforts were bringing justifiable glory to the Creator!

For you see, a non-Christian doesn't *have* to swear or cheat, either. From this, some Christians falsely assume that some particular sin is conquered because they have found the strength not to do it. But is this unique to Christians? Of course not. All around us we see examples of non-Christians who have broken the power of swearing, stealing, or being immoral. It is quite obvious by the fact that they no longer engage in these things. Out of the simple, determined discipline of their own persons, they have pressed themselves into other patterns of thought and behavior. They lead community battles against pornography; they are disgusted with the way other people have so degraded themselves. For the general welfare of society we can be very thankful for such non-Christians. But this by no means is New Covenant righteousness! These people still are not truly alive.

How easy it is to forget that sin is not simply what we do or don't do; *sin relates to our independence from or dependence upon life from God!* As Jesus said, "apart from me you can do nothing" (John 15:5).[8]

We've all met Christians (we've met ourselves!) who admit they've had more intense struggles with sin *after* they received Christ. In many cases, they are really saying: "It isn't just the 'doing' of sinful things that bothers me, it's the 'wishing'."

It was hardly by chance that Paul selected the sin of coveting in Romans 7:8. It is a very secret sin. It can exist when by all measurements I am living that Christian "eagle scout" life. For you see, true victory over sin is only a reality when not only am I not doing the sin but (1) I honestly *do not desire* what my flesh finds tantalizing, and (2) in place of that desire, I experience a *positive life* flowing from God, manifested in holy living.

THE MODEL

What did we say? "God's purpose for us is *that we become actual extensions of his life through a dependent love relationship with him."* That sounds so right, but so impossible. If only God could give us just one flesh-and-blood example of how such a life might work.

Well, he has. John tells us that the one who abides in Jesus "ought to walk just as he walked" (1 John 2:6).

Just how did Jesus walk?

What were the mechanics?

What made his life "work"?

Did Jesus Have an Unfair Advantage?

Growing up in a Christian environment, I was taught from the beginning that Jesus was God—and he is. I was also taught that he was a human being. But somehow, in my own warped way, I thought of Jesus as some sort of a Clark Kent. Sometimes he acted as simply that—a man. But every once in a while and *wham!* he was Superman—God. Of course, underneath his business suit and behind his glasses he was always Superman in disguise. We knew that.

Though I'm embarrassed to admit it, I can remember times when I heard someone describe Jesus' horrible sufferings on the cross. Yet in my boyish logic I thought, *Well, it didn't have to hurt any more than he wanted it to, because he was God. If the pain got a bit too much, he could just pour on some deity and soothe the pain.*

I now know this is not at all what he did. Jesus was not simply God in human disguise. Yes, he was God in the fullest sense of that word.[9] Yet in so many ways the Gospels underline that he was *a full-fledged human being*.

On the next few pages we are going to focus on this one truth. You might suppose that such an emphasis would cast a shadow on the glory of our Savior's deity. Far from it! Of all the amazing facts in Scripture, there may be none that cause us more to fall to our faces in wonderment before the sacrificial passion of the Son of God toward those who would someday become his bride. We will find ourselves lost in awe as we try to grasp the mystery of his stepping out of the glory he shared with his Father into the narrow confines of our humanness.

What About Miracles?

"But, honestly," you may ask, "did the Son of God *truly* share the boundaries of our humanness? Are we not confronted time and again by expressions of his deity?"

For example, how many times have you been told that the miracles Jesus performed were proofs of his deity? He raised the dead. Only God can do that. He fed the multitude and healed the sick. Isn't this the reason the Bible records them? To show that he was God?

It would be one thing if the Bible used such miracles as proofs of his deity. The fact is, it does not.

In the Old Testament, a true prophet at times would perform miraculous signs by the power of God in order to verify that his messages were from God. The Gospels teach that this was exactly the purpose and the effect of Jesus' miracles.[10] Actually, we may be very thankful his miracles were not presented as evidences of his deity,[11] otherwise we might wonder about who Moses, Elijah, Peter, etc. were in view of the miracles they performed. In fact, Jesus said his disciples would perform greater works than he had done.[12] (Perhaps right now you are thinking, *Yes, but they never hinted that they themselves were the source of their power.* The truth is, neither did Jesus.)

All the evidence suggests that from his birth to his death, Jesus never drew upon his own divine attributes either to know or to do anything.[13]

His Resources Are Our Resources

It may also come as a surprise to us that in the Gospel written to assure us that Jesus was indeed the Son of God, we observe John bending over backward to assure us that the resources Jesus used to produce the life he lived *were exactly the same as the resources available to every believer today.*

Because this is so important to grasp, we are going to glance here and there through the Gospel of John, noting how much this truth is emphasized.

> I can do nothing on my own [lit. "from myself"] (5:30).

> My teaching is not mine but his who sent me. Anyone who resolves to do the will of God will know whether the teaching is from God or whether I am speaking on my own [lit. "from myself"] (7:16–17).

> I do nothing on my own [lit. "from myself"], but I speak these things as the Father instructed me.... You are trying to kill me, a man who has told you the truth that I heard from God (8:28, 40).

> If I am not doing the works of my Father, then do not believe me (10:37).

> And whoever sees me sees him who sent me.... For I have not spoken on my own [lit. "from myself"], but the Father who sent me has himself given me a commandment about what to say and what to speak...therefore I speak just as the Father has told me (12:45, 49, 50).[14]

Finally we come to Philip's remarkably bold request in John 14: "Lord, show us the Father, and we will be satisfied." Too hastily we have assumed that Jesus' answer, "Whoever has seen me has seen the Father," was his claim to deity as part of the Trinity. We have done the same with his words "I am in the Father and the Father is in me" (14:8–10). Why is it we ignore the fact that a few verses later the Savior said exactly the same words regarding us? "On that day you will know that I am in the Father, *and you in me, and I in you*" (14:20). (Later the same evening he prayed to his Father, "that they may all be one. As you, Father, are in me and I am in you, may they also be in us.… I in them and you in me" [17:21, 23].)

It seems there was a sadness in Jesus' response to Philip, as though his disciples had missed the obvious: "Dear disciples, my entire life has been my Father's life in me. His power, his words—not mine.[15] Didn't you understand? Total dependence on the Father is the story of my life. You have been seeing the Father all the time! And now, as I leave, I am depending on you that your life will be *my life in you just as the Father's life has been in me*. The world will be seeing me when it sees you! As the Father has sent me, so I send you!"

Everything Falls into Place

Sadly, we, as Philip, have missed the obvious. Yet once we come to rest with this truth, so many things fall into place:

- Jesus' admission that he did not know when he was returning (Matthew 24:36; Mark 13:32).
- His comment regarding asking the Father for twelve legions of angels for assistance, rather than simply ordering them himself (Matthew 26:53).
- His thanking his Father for hearing him, just before the miracle of raising Lazarus from the dead (John 11:41).
- Luke's statements that "Jesus, filled with the power of the Spirit, returned to Galilee," and "the power of the Lord was *with him* to heal," or Jesus' comment that he cast out demons "by the Spirit of God" (Luke 4:14; 5:17, italics mine; Matthew 12:28).

• Peter's explanation on the Day of Pentecost for Jesus' amazing life: "Jesus of Nazareth, *a man* attested to you by God with deeds of power, wonders, and signs *that God did through him* among you, as you yourselves know" (Acts 2:22, italics mine).

To Have Doesn't Mean to Use

Did Jesus ever, for a moment, cease to be God? Never! Did he lose his divine attributes? No!

But there is a world of difference between *possessing* divine attributes and *using* them. Let me illustrate.

Right now, I choose to close my eyes. No, I have not lost the attribute of sight. But at this point I make a choice not to use it. Through the next few minutes I might get along fairly well using my computer and moving about my very familiar office. But if I continued to keep my eyes shut for hours—for days—I would encounter the same kinds of difficulties confronting a blind person. The same weaknesses, the same inadequacies, the same need for assistance. Gradually I would begin to understand what it means to be blind. Eventually I might be able to truly sympathize with someone who is blind. Yes, always *possessing*, but not *using*.

So it was when Jesus became a human being. He made a choice that he would not—for a moment—draw upon any of his marvelous divine resources as God. He was committed to total dependence upon his Father and the Holy Spirit's power. Only then could he experience humanness—genuine humanness—with all of its frailty and inadequacy.

He would be a real baby, thinking baby thoughts, needing as much parental care as any other baby.

He would learn how to crawl, to talk, to read and write (Luke 2:40, 52).

He would live through adolescence.

He would face temptations with all their enticements (Hebrews 4:15).

He would know the joys of human friendships, the pain of weariness, loneliness, and rejection—the sting of tears.

He would be a real man.[16]

When the Bible says we ought to walk as he walked, God isn't playing games with us. He's not saying, "Yes, I want you to walk that way, but of course I don't expect too much. We both know my Son had an edge on you because he was God. He had his own personal '911' deity on call for any emergency; and of course, you don't."

What about His Authority?

"But," someone might ask, "didn't Jesus exert his authority?" Indeed he did (Mark 2:10). But he also said his authority was given to him by his Father (John 5:27; 17:2). For that matter, he in turn gave this same authority to his disciples (John 20:23). This could also be said of his glory (John 1:14). It too was glory the Father had given him, yet glory he in turn gave to his own (John 17:22).

"But Jesus had life 'in himself…just as the Father,' didn't he?" (John 5:26). That's right, but he also used the identical terminology with regard to us when he said "unless you eat the flesh of the Son of Man and drink his blood, you have no life in you [lit. "in yourselves"]" (John 6:53). In fact, right after that, he made another direct parallel regarding a radically different kind of life that would soon be theirs when he said, "Just as the living Father sent me, and *I live because of the Father, so whoever eats me will live because of me*" (John 6:57, italics mine).

> *"I in the Father; the Father in me."*
>
> *"You in me and I in you."*

Could there be more simple yet profound words than these? Dare we echo them back to him? "I in you, Lord Jesus Christ, and you—my Lord— in me."

The Umbilical Cord

There is one analogy I can think of that allows us to see into these remarkable words, "You in me and I in you": a baby in his mother's womb. Before a child is born, there is a real sense in which he is in his mother and his mother is in him. Not only does his mother provide the boundaries of his existence, but her very life is his life. Her nature is imaged in her baby's nature. Linked by an umbilical cord, he lives because she lives—totally dependent, yet a distinct person. Apart from her life, he would die.

So with us. But in that moment when God gave both life and birth to you, *he never severed the umbilical cord.* Enveloped in the Savior, identified with everything Jesus is and did—including the cross and the resurrection—you are always, ever "in him." But Jesus is also "in you." For us "to live is Christ"; our lives are extensions of his life and marked by his image. Partaking of his divine nature, yet not being "part of God"; possessing his life, yet always as a distinct person—how can I even begin to wrap my mind around that? Eternally, his life will be my life. It is this, above all else, that makes the words *eternal life* mean far more than simply existing forever. It means to possess everything that characterizes his life—his joy, his purity, his love, his intimacy, his peace. All of that and more. "Whoever has the Son has life" (1 John 5:12).

You live because he lives.

Without life from him, you have nothing worthy of being called "life," no matter what you may feel. Though you may appear to be very much alive during those times when the invisible umbilical cord is well-nigh strangled and flesh has temporarily become your sphere of existence, it is only mock life, sham existence. Tragically, those "feeling alive" surgings of sinful passions (of whatever sort) that seem to pulsate with life are not life at all.

Grasping the Implications

Dear Christian, can any of us imagine the full implications of these things? To wake up in the morning and declare to God, "Gracious Lord, *I have no life to express today except as you give me life. And thank you! You will!*"[17]

Can we begin now to grasp the import of Paul's bold declaration in Galatians and his prayer for the Ephesians?

> *I have been crucified with Christ; and it is no longer I who live, but it is Christ who lives in me. And the life I now live in the flesh I live by faith in the Son of God, who loved me and gave himself for me (Galatians 2:20).*

> *I pray that, according to the riches of his glory, he may grant that you may be strengthened in your inner being with power through his Spirit, and that Christ may dwell ["to be fully at home"] in your hearts through faith...that you may be filled with all the fullness of God (Ephesians 3:16, 17, 19).*

Can we fathom the depth of mystery wrapped up in Paul's words when, after describing Jesus as seated with the Father "at his right hand in heavenly places," he then added that the Father has "seated us with him in heavenly places"?[18] O, what a mysterious union!

What then do truly alive human beings look like? *They look like Jesus.* It is as simple and as awesome as that. Certainly there are mysteries about the Trinity we will never fathom, but it would seem as though God has gone to special lengths to encourage us to appreciate his Son as a real man, a man whose image God has purposed for us to model—"predestined to be conformed to the image of his son" (Romans 8:29). Once again we are brought back to the "image" idea with which this book began—yet we find it now lifted far above its Genesis meaning.

Earlier I said that the resources for a holy life that were available to Jesus are identical to those available to us. For him there were two resources: *total dependence on the Father* for the life he was to live, plus *the power and fullness of the Holy Spirit.*[19] The parallels with God's provisions for us are unmistakable.

Are There Any Differences?

Well then, if the resources are the same, how are we to understand the sad contrasts all of us are aware of when we compare our lives to his? There must have been differences. Yes, there were (although they do not excuse us from fulfilling the model). First, we all began our human existence "by nature" as "children of wrath," rebels against God (Ephesians 2:3). Jesus didn't. In fact, the angel Gabriel promised Mary that her baby would be "holy" (Luke 1:35).

From that beginning, Jesus possessed a built-in, irresistible commitment to do the will of God. He once said, "I always do what is pleasing to him" (John 8:29; cf. Psalm 40:7–8, Isaiah 49:1–2; 50:4–5). In addition to this, as far as we know, he was the only person who was ever given the Spirit "without measure" (John 3:34). Obviously, Jesus never needed to be born again! As a result, he never allowed his mind to collect all those sinful patterns of thought so common to people. Imagine—what would you be willing to give if you could trash from your mental computer all the clutter of dark, negative, sinful programming that has collected over the years?

But what about his natural humanness—his flesh? Did he take on the *whole* of human nature? Not only must our answer be yes, but he alone demonstrated true human nature as God intended it to be—without sin.

John's simple answer was "and the Word became flesh"[20] (John 1:14). It is important to understand that when Paul said Jesus came "in the *likeness* of sinful flesh" or was "born in human *likeness,*" (Romans 8:3; Philippians 2:7), the word "likeness" clearly means "of the same kind."[21] But could he be tempted the same way we are tempted? Emphatically, Hebrews 4:15 says yes, though he never sinned.

The description in Matthew 4:2–3 expresses pointedly the genuineness of Jesus' temptations. "He fasted forty days and forty nights, and afterwards he was famished. The tempter came and said to him, 'If you are the Son of God, command these stones to become loaves of bread.'" It would have been impossible, upon hearing that suggestion, for Jesus not to have momentarily imagined the prospect of mouth-watering, fresh bread still warm from the oven. Words by their very nature create mental images.

Did his flesh desire bread? Of course. Was it the will of God for him to fulfill that desire at that moment? No. Was the temptation real? Yes. Remember, "he was famished." In other words, his digestive system was sending frantic signals to his mind: "I want bread—now!" Jesus' flesh responded exactly the same way as your flesh would have responded.

This is important to see.

But Scripture states that he never sinned, even though there must have been that momentary acknowledgment of the temptation's enticement. Happily, the Book of James makes it clear that it is *not the momentary awareness* of a flesh enticement that is sin, but the *entertainment* of that enticement (James 1:12–15). Theologians may choose to debate whether Jesus could have sinned. Regardless of the implications of his deity, the fact of his rigid commitment always to please his Father requires that he would not sin. The Bible simply says he didn't.[22]

The Mysteries Remain

Have we removed the mysteries surrounding his being both God and man? Not at all. In fact, it is good that they remain, because they humble us. But our time of focusing on his humanness these last few minutes should cause us to fall before him in absolute wonder. To wonder at his willingness to come down and down and down—all the way from the limitless glory he shared with his Father.

Down even as far as the cross (Philippians 2:6–8).

And why?

Most of all, to save us. That Jesus received to himself the full weight of our sin—our guilt—and made it his own, and having done that, he then took on the total, crushing blow of the judgment of God for our sin—this is the heart of our Christian faith, the centerpiece of the gospel. The sub-stitutionary atonement.[23]

But also he came to provide us with God's perfect example of what he intended humanness to be.

Well then, from what we have noted, he wasn't exactly the same as we are. No, he wasn't. We were born into this world with a drivenness toward sin—self-centeredness, independence from God. Before our new birth, that drivenness was our life. "All of us once lived…in the passions of our flesh, following the desires of flesh and senses [lit. "mind"]" (Ephesians 2:3). We were driven to find some sense of meaning in a world that offered only futility. Sadly, the new birth did not erase all those dark byways and dingy back alleys of our fleshly minds.

Salvation: A Many-Splendored Thing

If salvation offered only justification and forgiveness—even reconcilia-tion—we would latch on, as our life-long cry, to the anguished words,

"Wretched man that I am! Who will rescue me from the body of this death?" (Romans 7:24)

But salvation is more than that!

Paul in Romans was careful to add "much more surely, having been reconciled, will *we be saved by his life*" (Romans 5:10; cf. 5:21). Titus 3:7 expresses the same thought: "having been justified by his grace, we might become heirs according to the hope of eternal life." God's great, external act of justification permitted him to perform that capstone, regenerating miracle of infusing life—eternal life. Not only did John say, "whoever has the Son has life," but also "from his fullness we have all received" (1 John 5:12; John 1:16). Little wonder John found it hard to imagine that one who possessed such a treasure would allow sin to mark his life.

By the miracle of regeneration God has so inwardly changed us that the cry, "O wretched man that I am! [a captive to the law of sin]. Who will rescue me from the body of this death?" is drowned out by the liberating wonder of the truth of Romans 8:2: "The law of the Spirit of life in Christ Jesus has set you free from the law of sin and death." Life for us is no longer defined by our "fleshly minds"! We are no longer "in the flesh," but "in the spirit [or Spirit]."[24]

Yes, we long for the "redemption of our bodies" (Romans 8:23; our "spiritual bodies," 1 Corinthians 15:42–49). At last there will be harmony between our "inmost self" and our flesh. But *now*, already, God's enabling power is such that "the mind set on the Spirit is life and peace." We already "have the Son." To walk as Jesus walked *is not fantasy*!

THE MASTER ARTIST

Because this issue of Jesus' life being God's workable pattern for us is so crucial, I would like to conclude these thoughts with an illustration.

Try to imagine yourself growing up in a family in which your father is a master artist, world renowned. His sketches are considered by everyone to be the ultimate in artistic perfection—so alive, so expressive. But you are not just *part* of this family, you were *born* into this family—even as you were born into the family of God.

Because of this, deep within you is a nature that loves art. You take great pleasure in artistic expression because you possess an artist's nature (even as Peter reminds us that we are partakers of the divine nature). Although your last name isn't Rembrandt or Rockwell or Dali—your last name is Christian.

Though still young, you decide the time has come to start producing your own works of art. Following your dream, you build your own little studio with a large window on the north side to catch the best light. With all the best equipment in place—easel, palette, oils and brushes, water colors, pen and ink, the best of materials on which to transfer the pictures already burning in your heart—you start.

Having watched your father so many times, you move your pen across the clean white sheet, producing your own creative lines. Again and again you make your flourishing strokes. The first sheet, the second—a dozen later. But still the sketch remains locked inside your mind as only a dream. What is on paper is pure mockery!

Maybe more practice, harder work, longer hours. But no, that isn't it. The talent simply is not there. That crucial heart-hand coordination never was and never will be!

Could there be a more tragic discovery? Like loving music yet being unable to carry a tune. What you wish the most, you cannot produce. What you do produce deserves only to be trashed. How could this be? What happened in your birthing? Where is your father's touch?

(I grew up in such a family. At least four generations of marvelous artists—a sister, an uncle, one grandmother, two great-aunts, and two great-grandparents—some highly acclaimed. But not I.)

Pulling the drapes and locking the door, you leave with shattered dreams. Tomorrow you will give it one more try and then it's over—nothing but an ugly fantasy.

The next morning you hear a knock on your studio door. There stands the master artist, your father.

"Well, son, how is it going?"

"O Father, not well at all. I am embarrassed to show you anything I have drawn. And I tried so very hard!"

Tracing the Lines

Smiling, your father pulls a sheet from a long tube—one of his own perfect sketches. "My son, I have one request to make of you for today. Will you trace my lines?"

Trace! How could he possibly say that? Where is my creativity, my originality? If I trace the lines, they won't be mine, but his. Fighting your frustration, you bite your lip, holding back the anger swelling within. With a forced smile, you agree to his request. You love and respect him too much to say no.

Alone again, you stare at his sketch. So flawless, so alive. Well, a promise is a promise. *But I must have misunderstood. Surely he meant copy and not trace. At least in copying, there would be something of myself.*

Placing your own paper next to his, you begin to copy his lines. You try your best. Again and again you try; but it's not only not the same, it's just plain awful. Here and there you try to fix it up with your own flourishes, but it only makes it worse. Now, more discouraged than ever, you turn back to your own independent sketching. They're no good, but at least they are yours.

The next day, the master artist knocks again at your door. "Well, son, how did it go?"

Tracing, Not Copying

"O my Father, not well at all. I really worked hard, as hard as I could to copy your sketch. But I simply couldn't do it. Father, why can't I do what you do?"

"Copy, you say? But I asked you to trace it. Here, before I leave, is another fresh sketch of mine I drew especially for you. But please, this time, do what I ask. You have a tracing table; use it."

"Trace it." Again I struggle with the idea. "Where is my independence? Where is *my* art?"

With his beautiful work flattened out on your tracing table, you obediently place your blank sheet on top, only to discover that the moment you cover his work you can scarcely see his lines at all. Here and there you imagine you see a fuzzy line. But then, lifting up your sheet, you discover they were not his lines at all. Without your sheet, his work is so beautiful, so three-dimensional—as though you could walk right into his scene. But to trace his lines you must momentarily cover his art and in so doing, you lose not only the masterpiece, but end up with nothing in its place except your own shabby counterfeit.

In the same way, Christians come to the Word of God, reading it in all of its perfection, seeing its purity, sensing its joy. But what happens when it comes to actually living it—tracing the lines—when my thoughts of necessity must be on what I am doing rather than on God? What then? It is as though God's artistry is covered up by my own life. Since an empty life is too embarrassing, I draw the best lines I can. Though I might fool some people, anyone who truly knows the Master Artist will not be fooled at all.

Flicking on the Light

Suddenly—"Why didn't I think of it before?"—you remember the light underneath your tracing table. A flick of the switch and there, in an instant, your father's art comes through in all of its beauty, right there through your sheet. With your pen or pencil you begin to follow those lines, captivated by what is beginning to appear on your sheet. Soon all thought of independent *It's my work!* creativity dissolves under joyous wonderment at the strokes of the master artist. The hours race by as you finish the final lines and the delicate shading. But there it is! Reproduced through your fingers, with your sketching tools on your distinctive paper—his artistry! At last, what was in your heart by birth—his nature—is being expressed in life!

Though every illustration has its weaknesses (this one fails to express adequately the value of people's individuality), probably you have already guessed by now that the light is the Holy Spirit. He alone is the one who transfers God's artistry—his Son—into human experience. By choice, you affirm to God that you are not only open, but passionately depending upon the enabling power of the Holy Spirit—you turn on the light. The sketching tools and the "distinctive paper" represent your unique individuality. Probably you have also guessed that every fresh picture is the face—the life of Jesus—in all sorts of different circumstances, different poses, different shadings; but always Jesus.

Everything has changed. By choice you repudiate any thought of willful independence. Have you lost your freedom? Not at all! You have discovered an entirely new type of freedom—freedom from self-centeredness, freedom from the sin of pride. Each day brings with it a freshness, a sense of expectation beyond your dreams. Gradually it becomes automatic to reject your own creations. Why would you think for a moment of tampering with the Master Artist's lines? Each night you fall asleep imagining what sketch he might have waiting for you in the morning to add to the pages of your life.

Reproducing the Son's Life in Our Own

There is security in possessing a pattern for anything we are making—a reason for hope that what we are doing will look and work the way it should. When it comes to New Covenant life, God takes little pleasure in our creativity, but he takes great pleasure as he sees the image of his Son in us. We have no life apart from Jesus' life. We have no power apart from the Spirit's power.

This then is the kind of life that must mark the people of the new age.

"The works that I do are my Father's works."
"The words that I speak are my Father's words."
"I live because of the Father."
"You live because of me."
"As the Father has sent me, so I send you."
"For me, to live is Christ."

The New Covenant indeed has come![25] All that remains to fulfill our eternal destiny is the completion of God's careful faceting of his spiritual diamonds and the redemption of our bodies. "For this perishable body must put on imperishability, and this mortal body must put on immortality" (1 Corinthians 15:53).

Until that day comes, we have a job to do.

As Christ was the Light of the world, so we are lights in the darkness of our world. As he was the expression of the Father's love and holiness, so we are to abide in that same love and holiness.

"As He is, so also are we in this world" (1 John 4:17, NASB).

As he was his Father's Ambassador, so are we "ambassadors for Christ" (2 Corinthians 5:20).

But why, if all this is so, does it seem so easy for me to sin? I want to depend upon God. I want the Holy Spirit's power. Why on earth if I am a holy person do I so often appear to myself and to others as the sinner I feel myself to be?

It's time now that we look even closer at the mechanics of New Covenant life.

CHAPTER 8

The Mechanics of a Miracle Life

PART I: Things I Must Believe

What is a Christian to do about sin? If this miracle of the new birth is as big as the Bible says it is, then why is it so easy to sin—and what can I do about it? If I am God's new creation—his "golden delicious" workmanship—how do I stop the crab apple suckers from blossoming? If holiness is the norm for God's newly born children, what does it take to "get normal"?

Everything we have considered so far hinges on the answers to these questions. Happily, God has not left us in the dark. There are answers. Actually there are two kinds of answers: "*things I must believe*" answers and "*things I must do*" answers. First are those things I must believe.

1. *I must make sure I am thinking rightly about God.*

A. W. Tozer said it so well:

The gravest question before the Church is always God Himself, and the most portentous fact about any man is not what he at a given moment may say or do, but what he in his deep heart conceives God to be like.... There is scarcely an error in doctrine or a failure in applying Christian ethics that cannot be traced finally back to imperfect and ignoble thoughts about God.[1]

Among many things, what you believe about God will determine:

- whether you believe in moral absolutes;
- where you place prayer in your list of priorities;
- how you will approach that most precious gift—his written Word.[2]

If you are serious about the prospect of a miracle life, there is absolutely nothing more crucial toward that end than for you to become captivated by the wonder of God himself. Expressive of my own pilgrimage in this adventure of discovering God is a book I wrote titled, *Close to His Majesty*.[3] Perhaps it will encourage you along the way.

Are you serious about living a miracle life? You will be if you are confident as to the next belief issue.

2. I must be very sure I am a Christian.

Oh, but this is an easy one to do. Do I believe Jesus died for my sins? Sure! Well, that settles it, doesn't it? It would be so nifty to say "That's it!" And it would be "it" if becoming a Christian were something we do. But it isn't; it is something God does.[4] Yes, we must receive the gift of his grace, but I'm afraid it is possible for a person to receive when God the Holy Spirit is not at that particular moment actively giving.

For example, imagine me (a respected adult authority figure) sitting down before a group of little children—four-year-olds. With animated voice and the warmest, most loving facial expressions, using the most touching four-year-old type illustrations I can dream up (maybe a good dog story), I deftly turn their thoughts around to the love of Jesus and his dying for them. Then, just at that crucial emotionally climactic moment, I ask them how many will raise their hands because they "want to ask Jesus into their hearts." How many do you think will respond? That's right—most, if not all, will raise their hands. Are they sincere? I think so. Are they saved? I am not sure at all!

How easy it is for us to mistake psychologically conditioned emotional sincerity for the convicting, enlightening work of the sovereign Holy Spirit. Or for that matter, how easy it is to assume that my level-headed agreement with irrefutable arguments concerning Jesus and the cross *does* it in the same way that believing in certain political platforms makes me a Democrat or a Republican. Could this have happened with you? How do you know you have been born again? Praise God, he doesn't leave us in the dark over an issue this crucial.

How Can We Know for Sure?

The Apostle Paul wrote, "the Spirit Himself bears witness with our spirit that we are children of God" (Romans 8:16, NASB). That sounds clear enough, but what if I don't *feel* that way? What, instead, if I am plagued with doubts?

John wrote, "By this we know that we abide in him and he in us, because he has given us of his Spirit" (1 John 4:13). But what if I don't sense his presence? John also wrote, "we know we have passed from death to life because we love one another" (3:14). Fine, but right now I'm having a hard enough time loving myself; how can I even consider loving anyone else? Then there is that one in 1 John 2:3, "By this we may be sure that we know him, if we obey his commandments." Now, that's a big help! His commandments *are my problem*. I am not keeping them even though I know I should.

Please, how can I know?

In those times when I have had my own doubts, there is one unmistakable passage that has always settled the issue for me—and I trust for you. It is this: "Therefore I want you to understand that no one...can say 'Jesus is Lord' except by the Holy Spirit" (1 Corinthians 12:3). In those darkest of times with my mind strewn with the wreckage of battered beliefs and emotions, I have forced myself to peel off all of those disturbing emotions as one might tear away slimy, wilted lettuce leaves to expose its still-crisp core.

Your Deepest Desire

"David, what is your deepest desire? What is it you desire more than anything else?" Though such deep searching has not come easily, I have always found the same answer. Yes, it is there! Covered over and lost from sight, but it is there—"Yes, I do want to follow Jesus. I do not want to walk away from him. Jesus is Lord. My Lord!" It was no passing comment when Paul closed his epistle with the words, "Let anyone be accursed who has no love for the Lord" (1 Corinthians 16:22).

With all that is going on these days regarding what has been called "the Lordship debate," I fear we have missed the heart of the matter. On one hand, the proof you are a Christian *is not* your promise to follow Christ. Who would be so brash, so self-confident as to make such a boast? Nor, on the other side, is it simply some form of "easy believism" that implies that becoming a Christian is nothing more than affirming certain facts. Rather, the proof is in that mysterious, inner working of the Holy Spirit. He *does* "bear witness" that you, by his grace alone, have indeed responded to those most earnest words, "We entreat you on behalf of Christ, *be reconciled to God*" (2 Corinthians 5:20, italics mine). "Yes, I do remember those open, loving arms of God receiving me as I received him. I saw—I see—the cross, the Savior, and I cry out, 'My Lord and my God!'"

The Unavoidable Issue

To become a Christian is to become part of the kingdom of God. It was the "kingdom of God" that Christians preached throughout the book of Acts. How could anyone assume he or she is entering the kingdom of God and at the same time rejecting the King, the rule of Christ? If Jesus is not Lord, then the new believer has no prayer to pray. Out of his humanism, he might as well call his God "Santa Claus." To whom will he speak? To God? A God before whom he will not bow?

Some people may be satisfied with an intellectual assent to the deity of Christ. They may agree that he died for them and that God loves them and has accepted them. But the moment they pray to him they are assuming a relationship. And at this point the issue of Lordship is unavoidable, unless they are simply playing a game with words.

Groping for a Pole

Every year I plant a row of pole string beans in our backyard. Soon after a seed sprouts in the damp spring soil, its tendril begins to reach upward, moving back and forth, searching, groping for something that will direct its climb. Eventually, if it finds nothing, it will collapse to the dirt. Continuing to twist and turn, it will often grab hold of itself in a desperate attempt to find some support for climbing. Ultimately it will become a tangled confusion with a pittance of the harvest it might have had.

But if it finds a pole...it will become artistry in motion. It will climb higher and higher producing lush foliage, blossoms, and long, crisp string beans.

Biblical truth concerning God—His Lordship—is that pole, the object around which the Spirit will entwine God's child. By nature he reaches upward; by the Word of God he finds direction.

But because some converts are so inadequately introduced to the relational aspects of becoming a Christian, they may for years know only the depression and frustration of attempting to reach upward, only to fall back in defeat and introspection. After a few stabs at reaching out for whatever comes along, they may out of sheer desperation attempt to climb upon themselves through legalism or self-created experience, unwittingly quenching the Spirit's work. And then one day—perhaps very suddenly—they discover from deep within a heart that beats with God's heart. And they cry "Jesus is Lord!"

Salesmanship Evangelism

You have a right to ask why I am making such a point of this.

Consider for a moment where we are in much of today's evangelism. It seems as though we are so eager not only to convert people but to give them assurance of their salvation that they end up with a self-centered, humanistic package that is really a perversion of the gospel. I am afraid that due to the guilt feelings most of us have had for not witnessing and our dread fear of the whole business, that good old American ingenuity has come to our rescue.

Loaded with our well-memorized, super salesman pitch—easy open, snap in place, instant this or that philosophy—we venture forth with our product, convinced that it beats all the other religious products on the market. Loaded with well-rehearsed answers to every possible question and a neat way to close the sale, we at last discover we have found deliverance from our guilt—our customer signed on the dotted line! And why shouldn't he sign? Hell's no fun. If Jesus had used this approach you can be sure the rich young ruler never would have gone away sorrowing, would he? (Luke 18:18–23)

(It would be wrong to conclude that this type of evangelism never produces truly regenerate people. I imagine that some of you date your salvation from such an encounter. We worship a wonderfully merciful God who sometimes brings about His regenerating miracle in spite of our methodology.)

Unless somehow our witness leads to repentance in view of the holiness of God, we have failed to provide a truly biblical, informed basis for the convicting work of the Spirit. And unless we speak of a relationship with Jesus as Savior and Lord, regeneration may not take place at all. And if it doesn't then there is no corresponding gift of the Spirit and no Spirit produced witness of assurance, "Jesus is Lord!" "Abba! Father!" Apart from the gift of the Spirit no one is regenerated no matter what a person may say he believes. "If anyone does not have the Spirit of Christ, he does not belong to Christ" (Romans 8:9). This is fundamental to new covenant conversion.

Sadly, in our sincere zeal for converts, we have made assurance an academic, nonexperiential abstraction in contrast with the repeated biblical explanations as to how assurance is realized. (1 John 4:13–18)

Security vs. Assurance

It is absolutely necessary for Christians to distinguish between security and assurance. The Bible is clear that one is secure if he is truly born again (Hebrews 10:39) even though at times his experience may provide him with no basis for assurance. But I am convinced that the personal pleasure of assurance was never given by God to gently soothe the anxieties of an individual who is at odds with the Lordship of Christ. Tragically I have encountered professing believers who were in willful rebellion against the holiness of God and knew it. Yet they would say they were not concerned too much because, after all, they had been saved and at least heaven was a certainty even though they would have to pay a price for what they had chosen to do. In such cases the shoddy teaching of the doctrine of assurance became like grease on the skids of their spiritual rebellion. The doctrine of security is an objective theological fact; the doctrine of assurance is something else!

Remember, Simon the sorcerer "believed" and was baptized just like the rest of the Samaritans. But there was something critically wrong with his belief. To him, believing in the gospel was a nifty gimmick to get what he wanted—a new act he could put together that was better than the one he had. There was no response to the convicting work of the Spirit leading to repentance and saving faith which would be manifested by his receiving the Spirit.

Who knows how many Simons are "believers" and members of our churches who are either watching out for their own skins ("Who wants to go to hell, anyway?") or who are seeking some new experience that will put some zest into life. Such sincere though crass humanism is not what regeneration is all about. And evangelism which leads to such products is not worthy of the name.

I suspect someone is saying that to hold such a view of evangelism is to insert works into the gospel of grace. But if one assumes that saving faith is a work of the Spirit and therefore not a human self-effort, why should one cry "Works!" if the same Spirit brings conviction that leads to repentance?

The Tragedy of Missing Reality

Of all the troubles humans encounter I think one is the most pitiable of all. There are diseases so dreaded that the mere mention of them causes instantaneous fear. There are physical losses such as paralysis, blindness, or deafness that are true tragedies. But one—the loss of one's sanity—is the saddest. To be unable to distinguish the real from the unreal or to be unable to function in reality even if one knew where it was, is a type of darkness only those who have been there can describe. Strangely enough, some who are truly insane are the least worried about it because they have concluded that they are the only ones who are sane.

A similar insanity with far more serious implications is epidemic in evangelicalism today. There are only two explanations the Bible gives us for the absence of an active commitment to Jesus' Lordship on the part of professing believers: either they are not true believers, or they are out of touch with reality. The first reason is expressed in 2 Corinthians 13:5.

Examine yourselves to see whether you are in the faith; test yourselves. Do you not realize that Jesus Christ is in you—unless, of course, you fail the test? (NIV)

The second reason (being out of touch with reality) can happen to any true believer whenever he loses sight either of the majesty and heart of God or of his own spiritual identity. The repeated expression "do you not know" in 1 Corinthians illustrates this.

Or do you not know that your body is a temple of the Holy Spirit within you, which you have from God, and that you are not your own? For you were bought with a price (1 Corinthians 6:19; cf. 6:2, 3, 9, 15, 16; 9:24. Also see James 4:4).

I wonder how many new Christians realize that they no longer belong to themselves?

Because it is so easy for us to forget his Lordship, all of us have found ourselves shifting so easily from real to counterfeit life. Time and again after failing in holiness we have said, "If I had only remembered, I never would have done that!" or "Sorry, Lord, I simply forgot," or "Lord, won't I ever learn?" But such forgetfulness is quite different from saying that God has given us an option. There is no option! A Christian is a person to whom Jesus is Lord whether he is always aware of it or not. Though we have the power to ignore his Lordship, and by so doing, exist (not live) outside of reality, we do not have the right! (Read 1 John again.)

Ignorance of Christ's Lordship by any Christian demonstrates that he or she is really living in a dark fantasy world, an irrational world. He desperately needs someone to point the way to where life truly happens in the real world of the kingdom of God and its Most High King.

It should come as a shock to all of us that we have so broadened the limits of Christian sanity so as to make the Lordship of Christ an option! As though I could still enjoy fellowship with God and excuse myself for giving only a partial response to the call of Romans 12:1–2. It would be like a husband saying to his wife, "I want you to know that I love you more than anyone or anything—you are the focus of all the love I have to give. Therefore, in order to show you how much I love you, I have decided to spend five nights a week with you and only two with that cute secretary at my office."

Yes, there will come times even after our commitment when we see the implications of Lordship in such fresh light that we might wonder whether we had ever truly faced Lordship before. Those are momentous times. And afterward life is never quite the same again. But that is far removed from the tragic "option" idea.

The big first question is not, "Tell me *what* to believe," but "Tell me *in whom* I must believe." Once you have been given a solid introduction to the God of Scripture in tandem with the Spirit of grace, you will be in a secure position to respond to whatever he asks you to believe. Though beliefs are foundational, salvation at its heart is the beginning of an almost too-good-to-be-true devoted love relationship between yourself and—GOD.

Yes, you can know if you are a Christian. But you must search beneath the superficial to uncover that deep, perhaps scarcely whispered witness from your spirit that you are a child of God. Is this true of you? "Examine yourselves to see whether you are living in the faith. Test yourselves. Do you not realize that Jesus Christ is in you?—unless, indeed, you fail to meet the test!" (2 Corinthians 13:5)

3. *I must be settled once and for all as to who I most deeply am and therefore where life is to be found.*

This, of course, touches the heart of this book. Like scuba divers on the floor of the sea, the apostles knew they were living in an alien environment. They were not of this world any more than Jesus was (John 17:14, 16). Life for them had to come from above—from their true home. Though to the world, they may have appeared a bit strange—like sea creatures with flapping fins, masks, and wetsuits—they knew they were aliens. Because of this, they looked at life through different eyes. Their awareness of their new identity automatically produced in them a revolutionary change as to why they were alive—as to who and what it was that gave purpose and significance to their existence.

No longer was meaning or personal worth measured by prosperity or worldly acclaim. As needs arose, Christians willingly sold their lands and houses to share with those who had less. Paul must have echoed the testimony of many when he said, "I have learned to be content with whatever I have.... In any and all circumstances I have learned the secret of being well-fed and of going hungry, of having plenty and of being in need" (Philippians 4:11, 12, cf. Acts 4:34).[5] In Hebrews 10:34 we find that remarkable statement, "you cheerfully accepted the plundering of your possessions, knowing that you yourselves possessed something better and more lasting." (How many of us are comfortable with that statement?) To whatever degree this awareness of life is missing today, to that degree holiness will be perverted.

For instance, if I wrongly assume that holiness comes in saying no to all of my desires in order to say yes to God (since I am primarily a sinner with sinful desires), then, on top of all the normally expected trials and disciplines and Satanic pressures, I will have to carry the added burden of my own self-pity. How radically opposite to this is Paul's declaration when he said, "I have suffered the loss of all things...that I may gain Christ" (Philippians 3:8). In view of the positive (*which was his desire*) he considered the loss but rubbish. He knew that to say death to the flesh was indeed saying life not only to the glory of God but also to himself as a future partaker of that glory as a joint heir with his Lord. *Christians who really know this can truly be themselves without being selfish!*

Why Is This So Hard to Do?

If this truth is so biblically reasonable, and certainly wonderful, why is it that some Christians find it so difficult to believe that their greatest worth, their truest identity, is deeper than flesh (natural mortal humaness)? I believe the most common reason is they have already found their self-worth somewhere else:

in their physical attractiveness;

in their high intelligence, even their grasp of Scripture;

in their talents, abilities, giftednesses, even in their ministry successes;

in their material possessions;

in their warm fulfilling relationships with spouse, children, friends;

in their positions of power or control over others;

in their determination to fulfill their passions, even the biblically acceptable ones, and their success in doing so;

in their spiritual disciplines;

and in the honor, admiration, respect, and acceptance they receive.

Why seek (or even be open to) any deeper self-worth or identity if these are working well enough?

Well then, how did this come about? In addition to the natural bent of *flesh* to seek worth in itself, most of us, from childhood on, have been programmed by our culture to measure our worth on a strictly *flesh* level. (Of course, there *are* many aspects of our mortal humanness that we should value.)

Because of this, it is not easy for any of us to have a wholesome respect for flesh level self-worth while at the same time rejoicing in a far deeper level. The first step is to at least admit that we have a shallow evaluation of our worth as God's spiritual masterpieces.

Not the Whole Show

But awareness of identity is scarcely the whole show. It rather enables you to go forward in your discovery of meaning. Once identity is a settled thing, your focus is no longer self, but on life right there in front of you.

Though the initial focus is on identity, the lasting focus must be on life. "And this is eternal life," Jesus said, "that they may know you, the only true God, and Jesus Christ whom you have sent" (John 17:3). John later added that if we truly know God, our active reaching out in love toward people would be the proof that our life indeed *was from God* (1 John 4:7–12). Hence, authentic life is always relational, both vertically and horizontally.

Yet if all of this is to be a working reality, I must be sure I have made that jolting discovery that my flesh—especially my inborn mental programming—is an inveterate liar. In fact, I must be prepared for frontal lobe attacks by my fleshly mind, stirred up by the devil himself, that none of the above is true. Sometimes these attacks will be so disguised they may even look spiritual. I can expect to be bombarded by proud assertions that if I really worked at it *on my own*, I could find not only significance and love, but I could even satisfy God.

We see this vividly described by Paul in Romans 7. "There was a time," Paul says, "when I thought I was alive—a good, decent, God-fearing Jew. Then I made that devastating discovery that righteousness involved more than performance, more than duty, it involved desire— 'Thou shalt not covet.' I couldn't handle that. How could I stop wanting what I wanted?" And in that moment he watched life as he knew it shrivel up and die.[6] Often we hear of the need of brokenness. This is what brokenness is all about. It is that painful, pride-shattering discovery that "in my flesh dwells no good thing." Before I will welcome with joyous enthusiasm God's entirely new perspective, I must force myself to be devastated by the lecherousness of my flesh—it "lusts against the Spirit" (Galatians 5:17).[7]

Happily, Paul saw the door swing wide open to authentic life as he wrote, "The law of the Spirit of life in Christ Jesus has set you free from the law of sin and of death.… If by the Spirit you put to death the deeds of the body, you will live" (Romans 8:2, 13). Not only had God changed his heart (reconciliation), but he also made the joyous discovery that he was now alive to an entirely new dimension of existence: life in the spirit by the Spirit (regeneration).

Another Look at an Opposing View

Since understanding the mechanics of holiness is so important, I can think of only one other way to underline what is so much on my heart, and that is to take another brief look at an opposing view that seems to be so common today.

This view appears to be built on the idea that whenever you are feeling sinful desires, you are actually encountering your fundamental nature—a sinner. In those hot, pressured times, you either follow through with those desires and *do what you want,* or you by God's strength resist them and end up *doing what you ought.*

Whenever you end up in one of those "interior cabinet meetings" by deciding to go against what you want in order to do what you ought, you discover a variety of emotional responses. On one hand, you may feel good because you know you've made some points with God by obeying his urgings. But on the other hand, you may also feel a sense of loss by your decision because you know you have missed out *on what you really wanted to do.* (Remember the illustration of watching TV?)

Yet whether or not you obey the "oughts," you still must reckon with the true nature of the kind of person you assume yourself to be— at heart, a sinful person. According to this view, the choice to go against oneself is called "dying to self" or "getting self off the throne."[8] Those holding this belief would say this is what Jesus meant when he said, "If any want to become my followers, let them deny themselves and take up their cross and follow me" (Matthew 16:24). Didn't Paul express the same thing when he wrote of "not seeking my own advantage" and of doing "nothing from selfish ambition or conceit" (1 Corinthians 10:33, Philippians 2:3)?

But self-denial may be understood either as denying selfishness and self-centeredness, or denying one's essential personhood (because of its supposed evil bent). Before we choose the latter, we need to face the fact that Jesus, too, knew "self-denial." He not only denied the desires of his flesh for food when he was tempted, but we may assume there were many other similar flesh desires he rejected because they interfered with his deepest desire to do his Father's will.[9] Certainly for him there was no "sinful self" to take "off the throne."

Fulfilling the Self We Most Deeply Are

Whether or not we realize it, the desire of our inmost self is the same as Paul's—"for me to live is Christ!" It is correct to speak of Christian self-denial within the limits of a sense of selfishness or self-centeredness, both of which are enemies of dependence. But it is also fully biblical to say that I as a Christian—a self, a person—am to do the exact opposite of denial.[10] I am to fulfill the self I most deeply am, even as our Lord Jesus fulfilled the self he was and is. Galatians 2:20 very pointedly underlines these distinctions.[11]

How very important it is for Christians to be taught quickly that when they were saved, not only were they justified, but God also performed those interior miracles that changed the focus of their selfhood from flesh to spirit. Their deepest level of self, their truest self, never desires to sin. That self is always in perfect agreement with the "oughts" of God's moral law.

Tragically, if in their early Christian years "justification by faith" was all they knew, they may struggle for years before discovering that the "oughts," which so often seemed opposed to their "wants," were not some nagging warnings of their conscience or God, but rather the longing cry of their own reconciled, regenerated selves. I fear the voices of well-meaning teachers have drowned out the voice of the Spirit who "bears witness with our spirit that we are children [born ones] of God" (Romans 8:16). (This might be a good time to turn back and reread chapter 4.)

Giving Up Prime Rib

Ready for a bit of imagination? Try to visualize yourself in the restaurant of an airline terminal, eating a thick, juicy slice of prime rib (or whatever tantalizes you the most) while waiting to depart to some far-off, exotic place. Suddenly you hear the final call for your flight. Even though you see, there on your plate, those last, choicest morsels, you push away from the table and race to claim your dream. If there was a voice saying "Just one more delicious bite," you never heard it.

Why did you push away the plate? Was it because you did not want to disappoint your rich uncle who lovingly bankrolled the trip? Was it because you were part of a very rule-conscious tour group?

Nonsense! You did it because you most deeply *wanted* to. To miss going would be to miss life.

Before our new birth, we were like a person with no reservation and no ticket in a terminal where there weren't any real flights, anyway. Only fantasy flights. So where is "life" for that person? Life for them is the terminal—the curio shop, the magazine stands, the restaurant, the bar, and perhaps a coin operated flight simulator. For that person, it would make no sense at all to shove aside the prime rib.

Do you see the point? We must stop believing that living a godly life is a sacrifice we should be willing to make for God.

Changing Our Beliefs

For many of us who have been shaped by a duty-failure-confession-for-giveness-oriented Christianity, it is so hard to change our beliefs. We slip back so easily into those old ruts. Sure, being a Christian is exciting as long as something exciting is going on. Some special music group, stirring speaker, mega rally, glowing report of evangelistic successes, TV extravaganza. But how is it away from that, in those awkward, private times when my self-image has to stand by itself—alone? There I am, faced with an impossible task of being a self-centered sinner whose purpose in life is to produce God-centered holiness. Since this is too painful to endure, I search for one of those threadbare counterfeits;

"Maybe I could give myself to intense, personal discipline—to 'walk the line.' Then at least my outward behavior would look Christian.

"Or, I could become the best salesperson for God around, crossing land and sea to make new converts.[12] There's no doubt about it. I do have a wonderful product to offer—forgiveness now and heaven when you die!

"I know! I could teach theology, the Bible. Since I can't change my nature, I can at least improve my knowledge and multiply that knowledge in my students."[13]

As a Bible college teacher, this last one hits close to home. With each fresh year, it seems, I find myself increasingly captivated by the truth God has seen fit to share with us in his Word. It is pure pleasure to anticipate the exciting discoveries my students will make while adding to their reservoir of biblical knowledge. I visualize myself as God's park ranger standing—not in front of Old Faithful in Yellowstone Park, but in front of the "Fountain of Living Water"—with my students looking right past me as they observe the majesty of God's glorious fountain.

The Divine Fountain

During their stay in Bible college, they will analyze the fountain with great care—its freshness, its flow, its purity, its clarity, its beauty. They will write papers on the fountain, pass exams on the fountain, preach sermons on the fountain. Together we will even have times of worship before the fountain. Maybe, eventually, they will find their own "Christian park ranger position," traveling to the ends of the world, spreading the good news about "the fountain of living water."

But God's fountain was never meant simply to be a "look at it," "talk about it" fountain, but a "drink from it" fountain. One day in the temple, Jesus "cried out, 'Let anyone who is thirsty come to me, and let the one who believes in me drink.'" To the Samaritan woman by the well, he said, "Everyone who drinks of this water will be thirsty again, but those who drink of the water that I will give them will never be thirsty. The water that I will give will become in them a spring of water gushing up to eternal life" (John 7:37; 4:13, 14). Our Bibles end with the words "Whoever is thirsty, let him come; and whoever wishes, let him take the free gift of the water of life" (Revelation 22:17, NIV).[14]

Pride and its counterpart, shame,[15] dissolve when we discover that God did not save us first to use us, to get us to perform. No, he saved us to love us, to keep on giving himself to us!

There is not much space for pride when you are bending low enough to drink from the spring of Living Water. The new birth begins there. The Christian life stays there.

Yes, we must know the truth. But truth has a goal. That goal is *drinking in life*. The new birth is the beginning of that life. How it grows as we continually drink in Christ's risen life will be measured by the outflow of a life full of meaning—significance—love.

Actually *receiving* (drinking) says it all.

We were saved by receiving God's love—his self-giving (John 1:12).

We then respond to God's love by fulfilling his command to love him by *giving ourselves to him.* How? By lifting up to him our lives as empty dishes so that he may fulfill his heart's desire by continuing to pour his love—himself—into us.

The result? His life, his love spills out and splashes on everyone around—from *our lives!* They become the visible expression of our receiving God's infinite self-giving. (See diagram below.)

GOD
**GIVES HIMSELF
TO ME**
(He Loves Me)

GOD
**CONTINUES TO
GIVE HIMSELF
TO ME**
(He Loves Me)

I
**RECEIVE
HIS SELF
GIVING**

I
**GIVE MYSELF
TO HIM
(I Love Him)**
I also continue to
receive his
self giving

I
**GIVE MYSEL
TO OTHERS
(I Love Ther**

His love has no limit;
His grace has no measure;
His pow'r has no boundary known unto men.
For out of His infinite riches in Jesus,
He giveth, and giveth, and giveth again.[16]

4. I must be convinced that God's expectation for his children is that they do not sin.

Even though we confronted this truth in chapter 6, I admit I still find myself hesitating to type that statement. It simply sounds too radical. We are so used to assuming that sinning is normal—that we are always failing God in one way or another. As we noted earlier, not only did John in his First Epistle repeatedly deny such an idea, but New Covenant truth in general denies it. John stated,

> I am writing these things to you so that you may not sin. But if anyone does sin, we have an advocate with the Father, Jesus Christ, the righteous.
>
> Those who have been born of God do not sin, because God's seed abides in them, they cannot sin, because they have been born of God (1 John 2:1; 3:9).

Though John allowed that sin was possible for a child of God, to sin would be nothing short of temporary insanity. The Apostle Paul expressed the same perspective to the Christians at Corinth when he said, "Come to a sober and right mind, and sin no more; for some people have no knowledge of God. I say this to your shame" (1 Corinthians 15:34).[17]

Rather than assuming that some measure of sin was to be expected, the epistles as a whole—whether written to correct or to encourage—share in common the belief that sin is both abnormal and irrational behavior for a child of God. (Among the many examples, see Romans 8:12–13; Galatians 5:16, 21; Ephesians 4–6; Colossians 3–4; Titus 2:11–14; Hebrews 12:14; James 3:10–12; 1 Peter 2:11, 21–25; 4:1–4; 2 Peter 1:3–9).[18]

When Does a Temptation become a Sin?

Closely related to this is the importance of being able to identify when sin is actually taking place. Too readily we Christians have assumed we have already blown it the moment we discover an evil thought registering itself in our consciousness. (Remember, there are a myriad such thought patterns already programmed in our brains.) As we noted earlier, it is so humiliating to admit to myself, much more to anyone else, that my flesh—the mind of my flesh operating independently from God—is just plain lecherous. I hate to admit how often thoughts have burst into my consciousness that are just plain sick. I would blush to make a list—but you know them, too. My first reaction to that awareness is both shock and dismay. "How could I ever think something that bad?"

In the past, my automatic assumption was that since I was already conscious of the thought, I already had messed up. If this was so, what difference did it make whether I let the thought linger for a while? *What's the use of fighting it when I have already lost?* If such thoughts came during my devotional times, which so often happened, they ruined any prospect of happy fellowship with God. Even if I confessed my sin, it seemed as though no time went by before the whole cycle would recur. I had no difficulty agreeing with one writer who said that "we resonate with confession."[19] Sadly, I had failed to distinguish a temptation from a sin.[20]

This is a classic example of calling something a sin even though we are directly contradicting Scripture. James 1:14–15 is quite specific in separating *the existence of a sinful thought* from *the entertaining of a sinful thought.* What an important distinction! We have not sinned until we make the choice to entertain an evil thought.[21]

This is a most encouraging truth. When we recognize the myriad megabytes of uncensored trash filed away in the computers of our minds, how thankful we may be that God does not measure our personal holiness by evaluating the contents of our brains. (This paragraph is worth reading again!)

If in that moment of awareness, I repudiate the right of that thought to contaminate my consciousness and immediately affirm righteous thoughts, *I have not sinned.*[22] I have not sinned any more than if I instantly reject something I have seen or heard which, if given a chance, would stir my fleshly passions. Rather than those thought patterns arising from who we most deeply are,[23] they find their source in what Paul calls "the law of sin which dwells *in my members*" (Romans 7:23, italics mine).

Is Personal Failure Always Sin?

There is another false assumption I have made regarding sin. I have assumed that personal failure was always a sin. Of course, sometimes it is. But failure as a result of poor judgment or poor memory, for example, may not have any sinful overtones. So many decisions we make and actions we take are not related to moral issues at all. They are simply matters of judgment. I am embarrassed to admit how much precious time I have wasted grieving over these kinds of failure as being not simply failures, but sins before God. To put it simply, just because something may be stupid does not necessarily mean it is sinful.

Of course, if I fail to seek the counsel of those who are wiser because I am too proud, or if I forgot to do something because I was wrapped up in my own self-centeredness, I must admit to sin. But I must call the sin "pride" or "self-centeredness," rather than poor judgment or forgetfulness.

How encouraging it is to find Romans 14:1–6 in the Bible. Even in issues in which a lack of spiritual maturity might result in opposing opinions, God encourages us to remember that he looks at our motives and not only welcomes us, but makes us stand accepted before him, even if our judgment is not the best.[24] What a relief!

5. *I must be convinced a miracle life is impossible without the Holy Spirit's power.*

This is so easy to say. Who needs to be convinced? We all know it is true even if our lives are saying the opposite. Sadly, the fact that we know a truth so well may cause us to place it in some dusty back room of our consciousness. To do so frees us up to give our attention to far more interesting matters—the hottest religious controversy, the newest prophetic fad, the latest moral crusade. We pride ourselves that we are living on the cutting edge of the church. Could God be saying to us, "You foolish Galatians! Who has bewitched you?… Are you so foolish? Having started with the Spirit, are you now ending with the flesh? Did you experience so much for nothing?—if it really was for nothing" (Galatians 3:1, 3–4).

Carport Christianity

You've seen, perhaps, the children's books where an automobile takes on human characteristics? The smiling grill, the blinking headlights…get the idea? We're thinking of a car as a person. This happens to be a Christian car. His reason for existing is to glorify God. Remember, a receiver, responder, and displayer of the life—the love of God. How does he do this? By moving. He was created to move.

Of course, this car can do many other things as well. There are windshield wipers to swish, a horn to honk, CDs to blast, lights to blink—all sorts of interesting gadgets and tiny motors ready to adjust your seat and lower your windows. In fact, with all those fascinating things to toy with (and the manuals to read!) one might get so wrapped up he misses the main purpose of the car—which is *to move*.

Though all of these accessories get their power from the battery, the battery is not the core of the car at all. The core is the engine.

For the Christian, the engine is the inmost self, the deepest level of selfhood. The battery is the will. Sadly, it is possible for a Christian to become so involved in all the varied potentialities of his flesh—his mortal being—that he may begin to think that life is right there, in the accessories. With radio blaring, horn honking, wipers swishing, lights blinking, he may have everyone believing he is a productive Christian. But where is he? Still in the carport. He has not moved at all.

On the other hand, this Christian might honestly realize the reason for which God saved him. Therefore he exerts his will to roll forward. (At this point his will would be the actions he takes, expressive of his deep, truly godly desires. See Romans 7:18, 22.) Of course, he finds it very difficult. He presses on the starter with the gears meshed and—ah!—that good ol' battery comes through. The car lurches forward. (At least some cars used to do this!) How far? About two inches. Somehow he knows that moving must involve something more significant than this. An inch here, a lurch there. And anyway, the battery is bound to wear down.

Hmmm. Well, it's back to the turn signals or the CD—something that isn't quite so hard on the battery.

Maybe someday he'll get the hang of this moving idea. But then, none of the other cars around him seem to be moving, so why should he? Everyone else seems satisfied with their electronic gadgets and accessories. No one seems to disapprove of their lifestyle. Maybe this moving idea is something you are to take by faith. One thing for sure—the scenery hasn't changed a bit.

Distinctive Honks and Fine-Focused Fog Lights

Ah, thank goodness for the books and seminars that specialize on personality types and individual gifts. This Christian can now focus on his personhood—the distinctive honk of his horn or the fidelity of his stereo. He finds his identity as a "pre-programmed seat adjustment" person in contrast with someone else who happens to be a unique "4-wheel drive" or "variable, intermittent-wiper" person. And, of course, that makes each one very special and of unique worth.

Yet, even with all this, the whole thing is depressing because the battery (his will) keeps running down and he has to find someone to charge it up again. Happily, there always seems to be some new thing going on in town that provides the necessary jump to keep him going.

Of course, all these variables between individual cars opens a very disturbing potential: He may start comparing himself with someone else and either become depressed or jealous (or both) if he senses he is not nearly the car the other is. Or he may become very proud because he decides it is just the opposite. No matter how he feels, it always hurts when some new model comes out.

"Oh God, I Want to Move!"

And then one day he stops and thinks, really thinks. Just what am I doing? Something inside me—way down deep—is crying out for action. Real action—moving action! Who am I? What is my identity? I am a person created by God as a receiver, responder, and displayer of the life of Jesus in the world. I was created to move! "Oh God, I want to move!"

Quickly he turns to his Bible and begins to read with diligent study. *Maybe*, he thinks, *if I knew more of what this book says, that would make me move.* So with his will he sets his alarm to go off half an hour earlier in the morning. With his will he rejects the urge to tap the snooze button on his alarm. With his will he opens the Bible, reads the verses—even takes notes and memorizes a verse or two. He closes with a prayer and his day begins.

But is he moving?

We all know that our simple wills *cannot produce holiness*, any more than a battery can make a car go. No, he isn't moving.

"Well, what next? I've tried Bible study and prayer, maybe if I volunteered to take an evangelism class or opened my home for a group Bible study? Maybe…"

What then *can* produce holiness? What does it take to get the car moving? How about the fuel tank? Can we, with all respect and reverence, make the fuel the power, by the Spirit, of the risen life of Jesus? *Finally our illustration begins to fit.* How does a car move? In layman's terms, I think it happens like this: Drawing initially on the resources of my battery, I press down the clutch pedal (or shift into Park), turn the ignition key to the On position and, holding it there, turn the engine over. In so doing, fuel is drawn into the fuel injector where it is prepared to join a spark from the battery. A series of inner explosions begin, the gears are meshed…I move.

Ignition!

Consider the similarities in our lives as Christians. A Christian's will in itself *does not* produce holiness. But it does initiate the circumstances in which holiness can be realized. That most important act of drawing *in the fuel* with the ignition key to On and the gears disengaged parallels an essential spiritual event: one's conscious openness, dependency, and expectation of receiving the necessary risen-life energy by the Holy Spirit. *That openness to him and his supernatural empowering must be an attitude of the mind, not simply a passing thought.* I resolve to say yes to *anything* he might wish to do in and through my life—he is sovereign. It is then that I find myself moving into an entirely new dimension of living. The scenery is changing. I *am* moving. Jesus is being seen through me!

My will does in fact set the alarm to go off. And that same will continues to function as I open my Bible and read words and sentences using my intellect. But I find that I cannot credit my will (battery) with the adequate power to move, even though it is fundamentally part of the power system because it is wired to the engine (my inmost self). The credit goes to God the Holy Spirit. He, "the Spirit of Christ," is my life! He is my strength (Romans 8:9; Philippians 1:19).

Why Is It So Easy to Sin?

This all sounds so wonderful. But still we wonder, "Paul, John—God! Is a life of victory possible?"

Their answer is "Yes!"

"But is it reasonable?"

Their answer is still "Yes!"

"Then please, why—even though I believe these things—why does sinning seem to come so easily? And what can be done about it?" With these weighty questions, we now turn to our next chapter.

CHAPTER 9

The Mechanics
of a Miracle
Life

PART II: THINGS I MUST DO

Passivity—even spiritual passivity—will never produce holiness, nor, for that matter, will our passionate pleading with God. Happily, he has laid out for us both those things we must *believe* (chapter 8), plus a variety of things we must *do*. With those two questions, "Why is it so easy to sin?" and "What can I do about it?" still before us, it is time we look at four crucial action steps directly linked to those things we must believe.

1. *I must clear away the clutter in my life by drinking in God's forgiveness and freedom from guilt.*

I will never forget a night long ago out under the stars when I discovered forgiveness as I had never known it before. I had always believed Jesus' death on the cross had paid for my sins. But this particular night those words from Isaiah 53, "the Lord has laid on him the iniquity of us all" and "he bore the sins of many" came alive. Yes, Jesus took the punishment I deserved, I knew that. But he did more than that. *He actually took my sins and made them his own!* He "became" my sin (2 Corinthians 5:21).

It is one thing to imagine myself standing before a judge, condemned to pay an impossible debt for sins committed, then watch as someone volunteers to pay my debt in full. The judgment is gone, I am free—but not free. Why? Because my guilt remains. I still *did those evil deeds* and I will have the weight of that guilt pressing down upon me as long as I live!

It is quite another thing to grasp the truth that God's kind of forgiveness *removes the guilt as well as the debt*. This is simply amazing. That night, one by one, as I verbalized dozens of specific sins I had committed, I handed each one to Jesus, affirming they were no longer mine, but his. Symbolically I acted out what actually happened ages ago at the cross. Over and over I repeated these words, "This sin *which was mine became his.*"

So hard to believe? Yes, but that night *I believed.*

Yet it was more than the dozens of sins I could remember. It was more than all the sins I ever had or ever will commit.

Somehow on the cross, Jesus became *what I had been—a sinner.*

I—*I* had been crucified with Christ.

Is Jesus still taking the punishment I deserved?

No. He finished it.

But does he still bear the guilt he took from me when he made it his own?

No. He finished that, too!

But how? God says, "The death he died, he died to sin, once for all; but the life that he lives, he lives to God" (Romans 6:10). When Christ arose, he not only completed the punishment, but he also left the guilt behind.

What about me? The same? Yes, the same. I, too, am risen with Christ. *As new and clean and guilt-free as my risen Christ!* That is Romans 6.[1]

Christian, have you quenched your thirst for cleanness by taking huge gulps of both God's total forgiveness and deliverance from guilt? Then to top it off, why not add a few big swallows of his patience, his faithfulness, and his steadfast love? Remember, too, that this thirst-quenching fountain is always there, for every sin—those past and those that may yet take place.

Acting on What You Don't Feel

I suppose the act of accepting this marvelous gift from God could lead one into a casual attitude toward sin, were it not for the fact that such an attitude would mock the love relationship which exists between ourselves and God. Remember, even deeper than our thirst for forgiveness is our thirst for purity and transparency in that relationship.

But to believe what you may not be able to feel is so hard to do! Imagine being a pilot, who, after great effort, has obtained an instrument rating. Up there alone, high in the sky, you suddenly find yourself enveloped in a huge cloud with every visual point of reference gone. Before long, you begin to feel a terrifying sensation—your plane is going into a steep, curving dive out of control! Though the instruments tell you that you are straight and level, momentarily you find yourself unable to resist moving the stick in response to your feelings. What must you do? You know! You forcibly repudiate how you feel. You place full confidence in the instruments…and you make it!

We must do that with Scripture. It is true the temptations you may be feeling are totally real. The sins you irresponsibly permit to happen are equally real. But what God has said is an overriding reality. You must, as an act of trust, drink in his forgiveness.

Though as a child I could have quoted John 3:16 and 1 John 1:9 in my sleep, I still pictured God as a very sober Sovereign who loved me with sad love. I assumed whenever he looked my way he observed with great disappointment. Why? Because he had reason to be disappointed. Wasn't I always failing him in some way?

I find it just about impossible to rejoice in anyone who I know is unhappy with me. How long can you smile at God if he is not smiling back? So what happens? With no genuine joy, we search for some other kind of response to him. We turn to worship, awe, humbleness—even thanksgiving. But most of all, we pour out our confession. We may even talk about his love, but love without joy is like the sun hidden behind the clouds.

Yes, God loves me, but does he rejoice in me? He rejoiced when he saved me (Luke 15:6, 9, 32), but does he rejoice now? How important it is to discover we worship a God whose dominant emotion is joy[2] and who deeply wishes us to respond to him with joy. Though momentarily we may grieve the Spirit, Jesus said, "I have said these things to you so that my joy may be in you, and that your joy may be complete" (John 15:11).[3]

Whenever we have confessed some sin and received God's forgiveness, we face a crucial choice. We may either spend the next five minutes (or however long we want) groveling in the awfulness of what we did, meandering through our miseries, castigating ourselves for being such dumb jerks: "Won't I ever learn? How could God ever put up with me?" Or, after we pause long enough to identify where it was we lost our bearings— where we lost our perspective and opened the door to sin[4]—we can turn our eyes upward and gaze into the face of our most marvelous, forgiving, gracious, smiling God: "What a God! What a Savior! The slate is clean. I see the sunshine of your joy shining on my path. O, thank you, Father! Your arms are open wide and I run into your embrace."[5]

It is time now for us to confront those two questions that ended our last chapter. As we discover God's answers to the first one, "Why does sinning seem to come so easily?" we will also find his answers to our second question, "And what can we do about it?" These will be expressed in three additional action steps.

2. *I must actively participate in the renewing of my mind.*

One of the most common answers to the question, "Why is there so much sin in the lives of Christians?" is, "Well, the devil sure is busy these days." Yes, he always has been busy and we must reckon with his devious ways. But if we use the devil as an escape-hatch explanation, we will miss the heart of the answer.

I believe the most powerful force behind sin is the misuse of the most precious gift God has given us—our ability to think. In fact, I am convinced the overall reason believers sin is because they have allowed themselves to lose sight of where authentic life, significance, and love are to be found. *They have forgotten who they are and who God is and the relational implications of both.* During those forgetful moments, their flesh rushes in to fill up the vacuum none of us can endure.

Therefore, the starting point for "what I must do" is simply, *I must think about what I believe.* I must repeatedly hold each marvelous truth out in front of me—turning it around in my mind to see it in all of its wonder. I know of no better way to do this than while praying, while meditating before the face of God and affirming to him the glories of what I am seeing.

"To live is to think and to think is to do." We noted this back in chapter 2. Our choices and ultimately our emotions flow from this one source. Perhaps there are times during our sleep when thinking stops, but other than that, we are *always* thinking. And always behind our thinking is that inescapable drivenness to make some sense out of our existence. We simply cannot handle emptiness, meaninglessness. For every conscious moment of my life I must have a reason for existing.[6]

Either we will fill it with life from God—the flow of love from the Father, which in turn flows out to others—or we will fill it with "all that is in the world—the desire of the flesh, the desire of the eyes, the pride in riches [arrogant display[7]]" (1 John 2:16). Either we fill it or we die—if not physically, at least we die inside.

The Gift of Imagination

Inseparable from thinking is a marvelous quality we call imagination—that ability to form mental pictures or images, not simply of things, but of ideas. It is imagination that enables us to conceive beyond the limits of what actually is (creativity); or for that matter, beyond what ever could be (fantasy). Without imagination, language would almost cease to exist. Not only do we use numerous figures of speech, but most individual words are worthless unless they are in some way imaged in our minds. Imagination is *that* important. Rightly used it allows "streets of pure gold" and "gates of pearls" (each gate *one* pearl?) to become more than words (Revelation 21:21). We actually see them. How good of God to give us such a gift![8]

Yet wrongly used it can turn our lives into despair and remorse. It is in the misuse of imagination that most sin takes place. In fact, *sin* becomes an empty word without imagination. It was imagination which got the human race into the mess it is in. Eve imagined before she ever took one bite. Only because of this ability could the love of money be "the root of all evil." Virtually every battle we will ever fight with sin will be won or lost on the turf of our imaginations.

Strange, isn't it? Something so precious, so enriching and enjoyable can also be so self-destructive. This is especially true of fantasy, where we move into the world of make-believe, where imagination reigns supreme. Stepping into that world—the world that Disney, Spielberg, and Lucas like to capture—can either renew us so that our real world is reentered with fresh gusto, or it can so captivate us that our real world becomes ever more unfulfilling, depressing. For a Christian, fantasy as a refreshing diversion is healthy; as a substitute for life it is sick.

Because this is no minor issue, let's take a closer look at fantasies that are sick. We have all had them. With artistic flair and creativity we have dreamed into life our own secret world of tingling, pungent relationships, adventures, intimacies, possessions, and emotions that far surpass Dorothy's as she stepped out of black-and-white Kansas and into full-color Munchkinland. But instead of clicking our magic shoes, homesick for reality, we step back into the real world, disillusioned to find it is just as we left it, drab and boring.

None of us should blame a non-Christian for this type of fantasy. Reality *is* dark. Life without God is futile, meaningless, a "striving after the wind." It is quite understandable for a lost world to creatively manufacture one fantasy on top of another. Billions of dollars are smartly invested every year on pictures, books, TV, music, drugs, lotteries, and casinos in order to sell temporary escape from dead-end street reality.

But for us it should be totally different. For us, reality is limited only by the infinite imagination of a God who always functions in the real world. Certainly, the manna in the wilderness for forty years did seem at times a bit bland in place of the leeks and garlic back in Egypt, back in the slave days. But that was all right—they were on their way to a land flowing with milk and honey. And it was perfectly okay to dream about that! That was reality. But to sneak out my cherished book of *Twenty Best Leek and Garlic Dishes* from behind my tent flap and then, one by one, to turn those picture pages of Egyptian gourmet delicacies while the manna simmered in the pot—that was not okay. It was sick. (And don't forget, those forty years were never God's intention in the first place.)

The trouble is, too many of us who are Christians do not see ourselves as all that different. Because we don't, we have become fair game for the world's fantasy mongers. In the process, all too often we somehow find the resources actually *to go back to Egypt,* to transform our fantasies into reality as gross perversions of the reality our loving Father had waiting for us just around the next bend.

Is Holiness Getting Harder?

Some of us can remember long years ago when we were challenged to live lives "separated from the world." Remember those all-too-legalistic lists of Do's and Don'ts? No, I would not wish their return. But somehow we need to be jolted—shaken—into a fresh awareness that a large share of the things that claim the imaginations of the world are not simply a waste of time. They are diabolically destructive to New Covenant life and holiness.

Is a truly godly life more difficult to live now than in the past? If we say yes, someone is bound to remind us of other morally monstrous pages of history.

But the answer *is* yes. Our "pure minds" (2 Peter 3:1) are more at risk now than ever in the history of the world. Never before has human imagination been so exploited, so bombarded, as in our present mechanized, media-mad electronic age. Without realizing the consequences, we are now not only racing along the "information/imagination highway," we are also racing down the twisting street of increasingly sick fantasy that dead ends in the dehumanizing impact of virtual reality.

Could there be a greater paradox than to be part of an "advanced" society that proclaims so loudly its repulsion of demented human behavior (which in other times and places was taken in stride, often as forms of entertainment such as town square hangings and burnings at the stake, plus all sorts of dehumanizing practices, the more brutal, the better), but in its place, rents the videos and privately fantasizes the same brutalities (or worse) while maintaining a respectable public conscience?[9]

Even within evangelicalism we are seeing truth being bartered away for whatever stirs the heart[10] and increases the numbers. Flashy ideas peddled by shortsighted Christian entrepreneurs sparkle, sputter, and die only to be outdone by a new show next season. In the process, personal piety, nurtured in those very private contemplative times with God, has been replaced by deafening decibels of mass enthusiasm. And our precious gift of imagination continues to be tossed about at the whim of jugglers who have unknowingly learned their skills from the master deceiver himself.

If I am committed to holiness, I must face up to the fact that I am surrounded by an incessant bombardment from both the world and the prince of this world. They are calling out to me in sounds and shapes and ideas that precisely conform to the desires of my insatiable flesh. Already, countless automatic, sinful, chain-reaction thought patterns have been stored away in my brain, ready for instant recall. I hope it is not too late for Christians to welcome the radical, personal disciplines that will enable the church to start behaving as strangers in Vanity Fair.

The Key: Renewing the Mind

Because of all of this, it comes as no surprise when we are informed by the Apostle Paul that if a believer is ever to know a transformed life, *there must be a renewing of the mind* (Romans 12:2).[11]

We should thank James for telling us that genuine faith doesn't just sit there, it takes action. Therefore, *I must participate in the renewing of my mind by removing myself from the circumstances that not only will add more trash to my memory bank, but will make temptations increasingly accessible*.[12] Sometimes it will be as simple as:

- changing channels or turning off the TV,
- putting down what I am reading,
- ceasing to look in a particular direction.

But most of the time it requires something much more difficult. I must force myself to change the direction my thoughts are moving. I must repudiate my brain's usurped authority to continue down a particular path of thought.

> So I do not run aimlessly, nor do I box as though beating the air; but I punish my body and enslave it, so that after proclaiming to others I myself should not be disqualified (1 Corinthians 9:26–27).
>
> For just as you once presented your members as slaves to impurity and to greater and greater iniquity, so now present your members as slaves to righteousness for sanctification (Romans 6:19).

What part of Paul's body did he discipline the most? What member did he make his slave? Not his hand or foot or eye, but his body's control center: his brain, his mind. I fear we have been so accustomed to giving in to our thoughts, we are not sure that controlling them is possible.

Many years ago I subscribed to *Mother Earth News*. What's so bad about that? Nothing. But for me, it became my *Leeks and Garlic Picture Book*. You see, I grew up on a ranch way out in the country and I loved every moment of it. Today we live in the middle of a large city. In fact, right in front of us, two major freeways bisect.

Though I made a small space for a garden, I knew that having a few animals, raising chickens, and living that simple "back to nature" life was no longer an option. So instead, I nurtured my fantasies. With the arrival of each new magazine, I found myself slipping into my dream world, planning, building, even smelling the life I would never live. Was that okay? No! Bit by bit I became less content with our city lot and its tiny garden. My fantasy bred discontent like rabbits. Soon it spread a dull gray over everything I did. It even interfered with my prayer times. Too easily my mind slid into my *Mother Earth* dream world right in the middle of my worship.

Something had to go; I was miserable in between. Was I hopelessly trapped? No. I simply had to do that hardest of tasks. I had to take charge of my thoughts. Canceling the subscription was the easy part.

Of course, during those times when something such as our job requires our total concentration, imagination is not difficult to control. There simply is no room. But what about all those times when concentration is not demanded? When imagination fills the emptiness? We *will* think. But what will we think *about?* Our answer to that will determine so much.

Tough Decisions

Does this mean there is no place for escapist times? A good book, a movie? I haven't the slightest doubt God is pleased to program into our lives an ample supply of lazy afternoons and evenings of doing nothing more than sitting on the porch and watching the sky until the last of the sun's rays fade away and the first evening star glimmers its way into existence. I imagine he delights even in a few vacation trips out of which dreams are made.

But we must ask ourselves, "Will these thoughts I entertain refresh me for the real world, or will they only add to my reservoir of the 'if onlys,' the 'might have beens,' and the 'what ifs' of my imagination?"

Each of us is different. Perhaps you are the type who can happily be engrossed in some gripping story and then in a moment switch back into the real world with no carryover at all. I envy you! Instead, I find myself, though back in the real world, yet still living other peoples' lives—hours later—inwardly shedding their tears and grasping at their dreams. It is strange how my very active imagination can at times be my best friend or my worst enemy! Paul's expressive words, "Taking every thought captive to the obedience of Christ" are words I must live by if I am to live in the real world.

Let's face it. Fantasy is a little secret room you can enter at a moment's notice. You are the god of that room. You create whatever you wish. From the swish of a skirt you can create that forbidden weekend. In a moment of rejection you can step into a churning stadium with yourself the center of attention. From one word, *Maserati*, you can conjure up your own Grand Prix, complete with all the sounds and tingling suspense, right up to passing under the checkered flag. Fantasy is amazing!

Cheryl Forbes, in her book *Imagination*, states that "Neurophysiologists have discovered that the brain responds to these mental images as if the activity were actually happening. There is no difference in the brain wave whether an athlete is swinging a bat or only seeing an image of himself doing so."[13] Little wonder that Jesus equated entertaining sinful thoughts with sinful action.

A life of personal holiness will always be an illusion apart from a disciplined mind and a godly use of the gift of imagination. Without this discipline, I might someday hear myself praying,

"Please, God, don't ask me to give up my fantasy room. No one can reject me in that room, Lord. I'm not lonely there. I'm not bored there. Strange, but sometimes I don't want to come out of my fantasy room. My real world isn't going the way I hoped it would. I can control my fantasy world; my real world I can't. I'm the god of my fantasy world. And you are the God of the real world. And sometimes I think that I'm a better god than you."

Yet the renewal of our minds is far more than simply exercising brain power. A crucial "how" of holiness is inseparable from knowing the truth of God's Word, but it must be more than simply quantitative information. It must involve a *participant, relational* type of knowledge, which in the Bible is inseparable from the power of its Author. Instead of simply telling us to "memorize the Bible," Paul prayed,

> that the God of our Lord Jesus Christ, the Father of glory, may give to you a spirit of wisdom and revelation as you come to know him, so that, with the eyes of your heart enlightened, you may know what is the hope to which he has called you, what are the riches of his glorious inheritance among the saints, and what is the immeasurable greatness of his power for us who believe, according to the working of his great power (Ephesians 1:17–19).

The fact that this requires supernatural enablement leads us to our most crucial third action step.

3. *I must repeatedly affirm my total dependence upon the Holy Spirit to enable me to express the power of Jesus' risen life.*

Why is it so easy to sin? Obviously, our flesh still has its bent toward sin.

That's no surprise. It came equipped with its own built-in drivenness to fill up its own emptiness by seeking out its own meaning, significance, and love—and to do so independently from God. But still, if we are new creations, why do we as Christians find it so much easier to sin than to practice holiness? The answer leads us to this third action step.

Not only did our flesh come well equipped to *try* to satisfy its own desires; it also came equipped to actually *fulfill* (at least in some measure) the desires it feels. Normally, one's will is followed by action. I will to move my arm and it moves. I will to bite my tongue and "ouch!" In the same way, I will to tell a lie and there it is. I just do it. If, with my fleshly mind, I desire recognition, I can make it happen (if I know the right stings to pull). If I seek to fulfill some lustful desire, I can make that happen, too, if no more than in my fantasies. In other words, both the desire and the power to sin are resident in my flesh.

But to *move*—to produce holiness, to produce love—requires dependence upon a power source distinct from my will. It involves dependence upon the power of another *person*, the Holy Spirit. (Remember our illustration of the light underneath the tracing table?)

Though both the desire and the power for holiness (the Holy Spirit) are within, God has purposed that *the release of that power* comes only as a result of a life of active dependence upon him, the Source of our life.[14]

When you were born again, God could have at the same moment poured into you a reservoir full of spiritual power you could draw upon at will to last you until you died. He did not do that. Why? Why did God make it more difficult to produce holiness than to produce sin? Just so we could say "I fought a good fight"?

No. He did it by design.

Remember, God did not save us simply to use us. He did not save us to get such and such quantity of holiness produced. *He saved us for love— for a dependent love relationship with him* in the context of living and loving both with our brothers and sisters in Christ and the world outside. Once God calls us home, we will never walk by faith again. It is here and now alone that we have the challenge to "fly by the instruments." As children of the light, he greatly values our trusting him in the dark. It is in this context as we are confronted by our own total flesh inadequacy that we cry out, *"Lord, I cannot live apart from your life!* I have no life unless you pour your life into me. I have jettisoned all back-up systems. I will live because of you, or I will die" (See John 6:57; Romans 8:6, 13).

We simply cannot escape the fact that the Christian life is strictly supernatural, nor should we want it any other way. And that life, above all else, is marked by supernatural love.

I believe the most scathing exposure of how much *apparent holiness* can be done apart from that first fruit of the Spirit—love—is found in 1 Corinthians 13:1–3. Those verses (read them if you don't remember) undercut virtually every other traditional measurement of Christian success:

- spiritual gifts;[15]
- biblical and theological knowledge and the abilities to express them;
- dramatic exercises of faith;
- personal sacrifice, including all that I have given up for Jesus, even to the sacrificing of my body as I burn out for Jesus.

THE MOST IMPORTANT PRAYER IN THE BIBLE

Because of the deception of flesh-produced righteousness, it is worth our time to look at one of the most amazing, comprehensive prayers in all the Bible—*the most important prayer I know to pray!* It is found in Ephesians 3:14–21 (NIV). Let's spread these verses out so that we can take a good look at them.

> For this reason
> I kneel before the Father,
> from whom his whole family
> in heaven and on earth
> derives its name.
> I pray that out of his glorious riches
> he may strengthen you with power
> through his Spirit

in your inner being,

so that Christ may dwell[16] in your hearts

through faith.

And I pray that you, being rooted and established in love,

may have power, together with all the saints

to grasp how wide

and long

and high

and deep

is the love of Christ,

and to know this love

that surpasses knowledge—

that you may be filled to the measure of all the fullness of God.

Now to him who is able to do

immeasurably more

than all we ask or imagine,

according to his power that is at work within us,

to him be glory in the church and

in Christ Jesus throughout all generations,

for ever and ever!

Amen.

Yes! The kind of love God wants to give us is supernatural, beyond anything we could imagine.[17] It involves "all the fullness of God." Our automatic response should be, "Paul—no! That's an impossible dream."

"It is not!" Paul responds. "Our God is the God of the impossible—able to accomplish abundantly far more than all we can ask or imagine." And how? By the Spirit's power "at work within us."

Christian, are you listening? Are you allowing yourself to be stretched as you never have been stretched before? Remember, it is not only for yourself, but it is "with all the saints." Remember, too, the end in view is not self-centered. The end is the glory of God. The glory of God "in the church and in Christ Jesus…for ever and ever."

(At this point, if space allowed, I would add another action step: *I must actively participate in a local body of God's miracle children.* God has no interest in "lone ranger" saints. Ephesians 4–5 and Colossians 3–4 express so well the necessity of believers functioning within a local body.)

Oh, what an open door! Walk through it! And then keep on walking in moment-by-moment, total dependence upon his enablement.

Holiness as Sanctified Stress

"Moment by moment"—that is so easy to say but impossible to do. Life with all of its demands simply will not allow me to consciously do that. Of course, God knows this is so. Happily, even though moment-by-moment dependence is our prayer, its fulfillment does not require our constant attention. In other words, *God has not asked us to exchange one kind of stress—the stress of the world—for another kind—the stress of holiness.* (This is so important to see.)

How dreadful our lives would be if we believed God expected us to seek his will and his enablement prior to every decision we make. Life is saturated with decision making. Some decisions are major; most are minor. But we never can tell when a minor decision actually turns out to be radically life changing.

I remember one completely flip—and by all measurements, insignificant—decision I made forty plus years ago, which to my surprise resulted in spending an afternoon with a young woman who is now my wife. I have no doubt God was actively participating in that "incidental," deciding moment.

When Paul urged us to pray without ceasing, I am sure he had in mind our living in the context of an ongoing walk with God, resting in his supernatural, personal involvement right in the midst of the multitudes of activities and demands that surround us. In such times, instead of my prayer having a formal beginning and ending, it is rather snatches of an ongoing conversation sprinkled through the day—a silent "I need you" here, a "take this burden, Lord" there. But most of all are those whispered "thank-yous" by the dozens that pass between my Friend and me.[18] Rather than thinking of those long spaces when duties require my total concentration as interruptions, I am sure God wishes me to assume our praying relationship has not been interrupted at all. They are simply silent times we both accept as being all right.

This reality points to another crucial truth that is fundamental to a life of continual dependence.

Building on a disciplined pattern of regular times given over to nurturing our ongoing friendship with God in prayer, we begin each day affirming both our desire and expectation that the hours awaiting us will be filled with the life of Jesus. Having done that, *God expects us to assume he is answering our prayer until we have good reason to believe otherwise*. In other words, God does not want us to live on pins and needles, worrying as to whether it is happening. Of course, the moment we are aware of entertaining sinful motives, thoughts, or actions, we must quickly drink in his cleansing and then realign ourselves with *life* (1 John 1:7).

A Context for Holiness

Though by all means, the life that is now ours to live is supernatural, there are a variety of things, which in themselves initially may not be supernatural, yet are necessary in creating the context in which the life of Jesus is both fully received and displayed. As I take these actions, I place myself in a position where miracles happen.

- I drink in the truth of God's Word.
- I maintain regular times of prayer, where only God and the angels (and myself) are aware of the significance of what is taking place. During those times, in addition to my prayer list—in fact, before I touch it—I must practice the discipline of drinking at the fountain. I must take great gulps of God's faithfulness, forgiveness, power, patience, love. I must relish the flavor of his sovereign kingdom reign as I bow low before his majesty. (Of course, true prayer, by its very nature, is supernatural.)
- I get busy with tasks I know God wants me to do. This may involve simply working hard at the job I am paid to do. The work you do does matter to God. (See Galatians 6:10; Ephesians 6:5–9.)
- I physically remove myself from a particular circumstance where

fulfilling some temptation is fostered. I don't take that second look.

- I place myself in people-loving circumstances with my friends, my church, my spouse, my children, the unsaved—some circumstance in which Jesus' life, his love, is dispensed to someone else. Oh, how much God's people need encouragement! By the way, unless you are a hermit, *you are already* in those kinds of circumstances.
- I write that letter, make that call. I reach out, trusting that the "touch" is the actual extension of the hand of the Savior himself.
- I reject, as illegal aliens, any thoughts that would become sin if entertained. I directly repudiate their right to exist in my conscious thoughts. (Here again, as in prayer, though I "will" this action, I am assuming the Holy Spirit's powerful participation in my act of willing.)
- I involve myself in doing one of the "whatsoevers" of Philippians 4:8. That opens the door to all sorts of options![19]

As this happens, emptiness is replaced by fullness, even though at first I may be most conscious of my complaining flesh. But since flesh is not what I most deeply am, I reject its enticing cries. The result? Fullness in regard to my true identity—God's new creation, his "by birth" child.[20]

Not only will I not be doing whatever sins had earlier tempted me, but I will increasingly realize that *I really don't want to do them*. That other sin—that most secret one, covetousness—is also gone. That which my deepest level of selfhood truly desired all along—holiness—is now my conscious, dominant desire (Philippians 1:20–21; 3:8–11).

Dear Christian, if you have taken God's interior miracle seriously, *you must make your mind your slave*. Are you ready to confront those vile intruders, calling them what they are?

"Wicked thought, you are both an alien and an enemy of who I most deeply am. I hereby repudiate your right to exist. Be gone! I will give you no space. I hereby choose to think of:

whatever is true,
whatever is honorable,
whatever is just,

whatever is pure,
whatever is pleasing,
whatever is commendable,
anything worthy of praise" (Philippians 4:8).

Right now as I try to picture you reading, are you seeing this as the liberating truth that it is? It is not too late to start making your body—that fleshy mind of yours—your slave. Yes, it will be a tough discipline; mental discipline is the toughest one of all. But the Spirit is eager to respond to your choice (Romans 8:13). The question is, will you do it?

Strangely enough, I have found that my own need of responding to this truth is greatest during those times when my life is least structured—when the pressures are off. When I flop down in my recliner and flip on the TV; when I window-shop at the neighborhood mall; those are the most dangerous times. What is it about us that so easily corrupts rest into restlessness and well-deserved vacations into struggles with guilt and boredom?

What is it? Simply that none of us were ever made to endure a state of meaninglessness very long. How often we sin simply out of boredom!

Making Dependence Our Lifestyle

I'm afraid sometimes we Christians deceive ourselves into thinking we are handling this problem fairly well by packing our spare time so full of one thing or another—especially if we are either witnessing or reading our Bibles—that we're not even aware we have completely lost touch with authentic life. The answer is not in busyness, but in making *dependence* our lifestyle.

It still embarrasses me to think about it, but I remember a lazy vacation afternoon quite a few years ago when I went with our children to our motel swimming pool. All was well until a couple of very attractive women joined us. Having nothing else to do, I found myself staring—discreetly, of course. Time and again I determined not to look, only to look again (that law "in the members of my body" was working overtime!). In my determination I went so far as to think through the fact that I was indeed God's new creation; that I was not "in the flesh." But somehow even this was not enough to override the desires that I felt.

I remember thinking as we left the pool, *David, that pool is out for you.* (At first this seemed the right action step to take.) But it hurt because it meant cutting my children out of what for them would be just plain fun. Not only that, but to depend only on that one action step would just about require my becoming a hermit!

Then I asked, "Could Jesus have been at that pool?" Sure he could have. But he would have had some positive reason for being there. What was mine? Though I heard no voice from heaven, I knew what the answer was. It involved one expression of this action step: *to place myself in a people-loving circumstance in dependence upon the Spirit's power.* What people? Those two children I loved so much.

That was it! I now had a reason for going to that pool that was in full harmony with who I was. "Thank you, Father, for an answer to the vacuum my flesh had been so eager to satisfy!"

Sure enough, the next time we went, it worked. I simply wrapped my life around those two very special children. The problem was gone because *life* had filled the vacuum.

I'm sure this same principle is equally effective whenever we find ourselves momentarily free from things that demand our attention. I remember one time becoming impatient with a friend who kept me waiting at a restaurant. What right did he have to mess up my schedule? After a few minutes of steaming inside I was stopped short by the question, "David, what is the most important thing in your life right now?"

"Oh, I guess, as usual, it would be to express the fruit of the Spirit—to be that container for the fragrance of Christ."

"Well then, in regard to life, is this delay really a frustration for you? Remember, *patience* is part of the fruit he produces."

"When you put it that way, I guess I really don't have any reason for being upset."

"Wake up to it, David—you're free! Free to simply wait and in waiting know that you are fulfilling life."

Oh, that felt so good to be free! And in that atmosphere of freedom it was amazing to discover how readily the Holy Spirit filled those minutes with significance. To my surprise, I became aware of people all around me who needed to be loved.

Making the Spirit an Active Participant

Only God knows whether right around the next bend awaiting us is a surprise attack in spiritual warfare, a sudden open door for introducing someone to Jesus, or maybe simply one of those serendipity times of sheer pleasure from a God "who richly provides us with everything for our enjoyment" (1 Timothy 6:17). But he *does know* and that is enough.

Still, the Spirit must be an active participant. Otherwise, we will fall prey to those extremely subtle counterfeits of righteousness that can unknowingly slip in to fill the void.

It is so hard to keep in mind that eternally significant living is not found in simply rejecting sinful things, nor is it found in coming up with wholesome alternatives; it is found *only* as God's life is actually received and displayed through us as a prism receives light and, in turn, produces the varied colors of the rainbow.

Jesus' life was not holy simply because he was an honest carpenter or a boy who respected his parents. He was holy because as he said, "I can do nothing from myself.... I live because of the Father."

Christianity is not simply living that ideal "eagle scout" life; it is *dependent resurrection life.*[21]

Across all of the lists of spiritual disciplines you have seen should be written in large bold letters "The discipline of dependence." Of all disciplines, this is the crucial one.

It is not simply memorizing the manual. It is in actually living as a *receiver* and *responder* and *displayer* of the love of God. This, above all else, is life.

No matter how we look at it, we can't get away from the fact that spiritual life is exactly that: *spiritual*. And as such it is mysterious and beyond the reach of the human will alone. It *is* supernatural.

Even when one comes across the numerous commands in the epistles concerning behavior, we must understand that the simple response to the command to be loving does not in itself produce the "fruit of the Spirit." I may not only *know* that I should love someone who appears to be unlovable; I may actually *want* to love them. In fact, I may push myself to perform a loving act, yet still miss expressing the fruit of the Spirit (non-Christians can do that).

It is at this point that the simplest and yet most mysterious of all statements must be seen in sharp focus: "you in me, and I in you" (John 14:20). Mysterious? Yes. Complicated? No. Such a life is available equally to every child of God apart from all those intellectual, professional, giftedness yardsticks we wrongly use to measure a Christian's worth.

Only out of the Spirit-empowered motives of one's inmost self, death is declared upon all other motives. And as one single will arises to God, unconditionally open to his Lordship, the Spirit of life places his royal impress upon our words and actions and the divine dimension of resurrection life occurs—Jesus is seen in human flesh, our flesh![22]

The Icing on the Cake

One of the encouraging discoveries we make as we become more acquainted with the Bible is its marvelous balance. God, the infinite Lover, is not exclusively utilitarian in his self-giving, as though he loves us only so that his love may flow out to others. Often he blesses simply because he delights in the pure pleasures of his children. Paul caught this happy thought when he wrote, "God...richly provides us with everything for our enjoyment" (1 Timothy 6:17). God's love does not always have ulterior motives! Think of all those clean flesh-level pleasures that come to us as love gifts with no strings attached:

- a nice home
- a delicious meal
- a beautiful sunset
- a good bed...my own pillow!

No, these are not *life*, no matter how nice they are. If we have them, we shouldn't feel guilty. Instead, we say "Thank you!" If we don't have them, it's all right. Contentment is still ours as long as we don't begin to think they *were* life.

4. I must welcome the trial times of my life as evidences of my Father's love.

Since you have come this far with me, the last thing I need to do is prove to you the importance of this action step, this attitudinal choice each of us must make. You know it is true.

Over the years as I have taken my evening walks with God, I used to feel a sense of sadness when autumn came as I watched the lush green leaves turn brown, wither and fall to the ground, exposing tangled, bare black branches silhouetted against the sky. I knew it would be months before I would see any life again. Then one night after a rain, as I passed beneath a street light, I peered up into one of those "dead" trees to discover hundreds of sparkling concentric circles—shimmering halos—of light, transforming bare, wet twigs and branches into captivating beauty. No tangle; no ugliness; only wonder! I could hardly wait for my next evening walk!

Eventually spring arrived. But with the first appearance of new leaves, those concentric circles disappeared, and I knew I would not see them again until fall came.

Grace and Glory in Our Trials

Perhaps right now you are experiencing some shattered dream, some fear or sense of loneliness, loss, pain, or grief. If only you might find grace to look up *through* to see the glory! That's the way it is with trial times. Once we see the glory, we are never the same again. (Please take the time to read 1 Peter 1:6–9.)

From a somewhat different perspective, let me tell you about an object I keep in the top drawer of my desk. I have used it so often over the years as an illustration that it is not only badly chipped, it has produced several holes in my pockets from carrying it around. It's a small glass prism (my humble substitute for a diamond). Without light, it really isn't much at all. But with sunlight, Oh! Suddenly you see all the shades of the rainbow dancing across the wall, splashing colors upon whatever it touches.

Who is a Christian? In terms of deep, spiritual personhood, *he or she is God's uniquely designed prism, his ultimate spiritual masterpiece. Created clean as a flawless diamond, progressively being faceted as a receiver, responder, and displayer of the otherwise invisible glories of the infinite God into limitless, visible colors—the rainbow of his own attributes—so that all creation might see GOD.*

That is wonderfully true! And it is simply amazing. Our lives are the means by which the invisible God becomes visible to a world that will not see him any other way. Our inmost being, the prism; our flesh, the wall upon which the colors are seen. Could there be any greater purpose, any greater significance for being alive than this?

But for this to happen, the Master Diamond Cutter must progressively transform that flawless product of his birthing by cutting multiple facets upon its surface. The trials of our faith *are* this painful cutting process. There is no other way if we are to display "his holiness…the peaceful fruit of righteousness" (Hebrews 12:10, 11).

Can we trust our Diamond Cutter never to make a cut too deep?[23] Remember, his intentions for us are not only for time, but forever. "Those who are wise shall shine like the brightness of the sky, and those who lead many to righteousness, like the stars for ever and ever" (Daniel 12:3).

With such an important destiny, do you actually believe that God would mishandle so precious a treasure as you are to him? You and everyone else but God may be surprised beyond words some day. Surprised at the multiple facets of your eternal being as they splash the beauty of God throughout the ramparts of heaven—displayed through your resurrected spiritual body.

CHAPTER 10

The Goal of God's Miracle Children

You and I worship a fabulously creative God. We began this book with this truth. He tells us that creation—the entire universe—bears witness to his "invisible qualities—his eternal power and divine nature" (Romans 1:20, NIV). And indeed, we agree it does, no matter in which direction we might look:

Up into the vastness of the heavens with its myriad forms of gaseous nebula, stars, galaxies, black holes, dark matter, quasars, and who knows beyond that.

Or down into the infinitesimal smallness of sub-atomic structures that only tantalize us with their unsolved mysteries.

Or all around us, the mysterious electromagnetic world we are just beginning to uncover and use.

Or that more touchable world of birds singing a thousand different songs, of reptiles, mammals, and fishes with fantastic varieties of shape, size, and color that boggle our minds. Of a myriad different butterflies, along with the tens of thousands of distinctly different insects. Spiders weaving masterpieces sparkling in the morning dew. Each kind of tree and plant with its own distinctive shape of branch, leaf, bloom, and fragrance. And all of it flowing from the unbelievably inventive mind of God!

Indeed, we worship a God who is so fantastically inventive as to paint the colors and shape the forms of myriad flower petals and endless sunsets, plus mixing in the fragrances, tastes, and sounds that surround us (Genesis 1:31; 2:9; Psalm 19:1–6; 65:5–13).

Yet when we stand back and attempt to evaluate the flow of human history—its tragedy and tears, its confusion and cruelty, its seemingly endless cycles—it appears to fall far short of expressing the creative touch of a truly wise, powerful, and good God. So much appears haphazard, full of apparent mindless, cruel happenings—city slums, homeless children, battlefields by the thousands, broad fields of white crosses, and mounds piled deep with the unknown wretches of the world.

In addition, the Bible asks us to believe that, sprinkled about this paradoxical world, are a variety of supernatural aliens whose true home is heaven and who bear witness to a God of love and grace (Matthew 7:13–14; Luke 12:32; Philippians 3:20).

How does this harmonize with the marvelous creativity of the God we see elsewhere in his universe? Does it not sound much more like the feeble efforts of a less-than-sovereign God, trying his best to reclaim something good from his botched-up Edenic plan?

It's strange, yet often true, that some of God's most beautiful masterpieces of creativity arise out of the very opposites of those masterpieces. From the dead and decaying marshlands, the lilies grow. From rotting fir needles and slimy leaves, trilliums sprout and bloom. And so it is that out of the darkness and gross evil of a justly cursed humanity, God has chosen to produce the crowning product of his new creation—his most captivating creation—a Bride for his Son (Ephesians 5:25–27; Revelation 19:6–8).

Think again of God's creativity in the universe. Try, for example, to hold carefully in your mind the image of a perfect rose. Imagine all those wellnigh incomprehensible, scarcely understood chemical, electrical, submicroscopic DNA and RNA processes that brought that *one* rose blossom into existence. Yet this creative God of ours produces *a myriad roses*, mostly hidden away in the wildernesses of the world only God sees.

If this is so, is it not the ultimate of human folly to assume that such a

God who demonstrates his perfections in billions of momentary blossoms would approach the ultimate, eternally existing exhibition of his creativity—the church, the people of God—with haphazard weakness? Is it not far more reasonable to believe this remarkable God has at least an equal masterfulness of perfection in mind as he creates a Bride for his Son?

Should we not assume this strange process, which has now spread over thousands of years of gathering together "a people for his name," is guided by a God who is acting with matchless wisdom and purpose? Though we remain humbled by the mysteries that harmonize God's sovereign will and human choice, we dare not miss his joy over every lost sheep that is found—here and around the world—each one adding a special touch to the ultimate beauty of the Bride.

Is it not much wiser for us to assume that we are simply too close—like microscopic bugs walking across the surface of a rose petal—to see the grand design? Like the proverbial

> Inch worm, inch worm, measuring the marigolds,
> Why don't you stop and see how beautiful they are?

Or better still, too close—like single threads woven among countless other threads over thousands of years—to see a tapestry being created with absolute perfection? Indeed, someday all creation will gasp before the glory of the unveiling of the saints! (Romans 8:18–21) Even now, his church, his new creation, as yet physically unredeemed, continues to display itself like the late winter blossoms on some trees—unexpected, not yet overly beautiful, but still the harbinger of spring.

"Not yet overly beautiful" surely is an understatement when one considers with embarrassment the mottled history of the church. Though here and there among its dark pages are sparkling examples of God's individual miracles, the overall history of the church has been more a display of his patience and grace than of the church's grand successes.

This should surprise us were it not for the fact that his Bride, rather than being the goal of history, is actually exhibit A of God's true goal—his own glory. What is his glory? *The displayed splendor of all of his attributes.*

I confess that the first time I realized the goal of everything was the glory of God, my response was, "That sounds too self-centered." The more I thought, the more disturbed I became. *I don't like people who are self-centered. It isn't right to be self-centered.* Then I made a simple discovery.

Imagine a living room with a concert grand piano as the centerpiece. With great expectations, all eyes focus on one person who happens to be a master pianist. Yet repeatedly she refuses our invitations to play. "No! I will not do it. All it would do is glorify myself. I would become the center of attention. No, I will not play."

Momentarily we are taken by her humility, but not for long. Instead we become disgusted, angry, that such a gifted person would keep those gifts to herself. They deserve to be heard! We might become so bold as to say "Well, if that's the way you feel about it, forget it. Be selfish, if you want. Keep your gifts locked inside. We don't like you anyway."

The same could be said of an artist who will not paint, an inventor who will not create, a wise judge who will not take his seat in court, a lover who keeps to himself.

Why then should we be so surprised that God, the possessor of limitless qualities of infinite perfection, should so choose to display them? What rightness could there be if the possessor of absolute love and grace, patience and justice, power and wisdom never allowed them to be seen?

This then is the reasonableness behind that great statement: "His eternal purpose according to the counsel of his will, for his own glory, he hath foreordained whatsoever comes to pass."[1]

How then do we handle this captivating mystery? How are we to respond to such a God?

We should find much security and joy in the fact that his plan of creating a Bride for his Son was in his mind from eternity past—"just as he chose us in Christ before the foundation of the world to be holy and blameless before him in love" (Ephesians 1:4). He has also told us this masterpiece of his creativity is "according to the purpose of him who accomplishes all things according to his counsel and will" (Ephesians 1:11). Clearly, this captivating mystery of the Bride was no midcourse correction after his first plan in the Garden of Eden went awry. In fact, with purpose it included the cross and the resurrection, as God unfolded his own wisdom and power (1 Corinthians 1:18–24).

When at last the moment of all moments arrives and the Son lifts up the kingdom to his Father, when at last every dazzling facet of the diamond of God's own Being is fully revealed—marvel of marvels, we will be there, standing "in the presence of his glory with rejoicing" (Jude 24). No longer knowing in part, but "then [we] will know fully, even as [we] have been fully known" (1 Corinthians 13:12). *We will be there.* Only then will we experience in its fullness that to be alive for the first time is to be alive forever.

OUR BIRTHRIGHT

Having exchanged the mortality and oft morbidity of our unredeemed flesh for the inexpressible glory of the image of the man of heaven, *we will be there.* Dare we imagine the true nature of our resurrection bodies that will be as radically transformed as a plant is from the seed from which it came? We do know "we will be like him, for we will see him as he is" (1 John 3:2; cf. 1 Corinthians 15:37, 47–48).

With uninhibited freedom—all flesh/spirit conflicts removed—*we will be there,* unendingly fulfilling the destiny for which we were made as the receivers, the responders, and the displayers of God's love (Philippians 3:12–14).

Have all our questions about the miracles of grace been answered? Far from it. Mysteries remain that stir our curiosity. But until then we must rest easy, knowing that when at last all creation beholds the Bride, you and I will be there lifting our transformed voices with emotional energies beyond our dreams, shouting "from him and through him and to him are all things. To him be the glory forever, Amen" (Romans 11:36).

A Summary of the Practical Values of a Biblical Perspective on New Covenant Life

1. This perspective delivers me from the frustration of believing that if I am to do the will of God and live for him, I must go against myself and all I desire in life. True, I must go against my flesh, but I am never called upon to go against my authentic personhood, myself as God's newly created child.

2. It allows me to have a positive, wholesome sense of self worth and yet protects me from pride due to the fact that the fundamental nature of my true personhood is one of absolute dependence upon life which flows from God. It delivers me from the morbidity of some of the "crucified life" approaches to spirituality.

3. It protects me from a variety of extremes, such as believing that my flesh in itself is essentially evil, or that I am really two persons—a good one and a bad one—or that my ultimate deliverance is when at last "self" is forever eliminated (when I get to heaven) as though somehow being a "self" is bad.

4. It liberates the biblical concept of Christian liberty. If my basic nature is righteous even as Christ is righteous, then I am totally free to fulfill life. I am truly free to do what I want to do! As Paul says, "for me to live is Christ." Because of this a delightfully positive tone is added to the entire picture of the Christian life.

5. Through understanding why I sin, I can retrace my way back to the cause and really do something about it.

6. Since by the new birth all the "equipment" is present for a God-oriented, meaningful life, it directs my attention to the fundamental necessity of the energizing power of the Holy Spirit. Ephesians 3:14–21 becomes overwhelmingly significant.

7. It opens the door to a much fuller appreciation of every believer I meet realizing that he, too, whether it is outwardly apparent or not, is God's inner workmanship, his pure creation. Since there is no evidence that would lead us to think that there are varying degrees of quality or value in God's individual creations, it allows me to show the fullest respect for *every* child of God.

8. It frees me from a warped emphasis on the values of various aspects of my mortality. I am not less of a person if I am not married, if I cannot walk, or if my mental faculties are not in the best shape.

9. It encourages me to enlarge my concept of my spirit (used here as a synonym for "inner man") so as to see myself fundamentally as a spiritual being, regardless of what might happen to my physical brain or any other part of my mortality.

10. It brings new sense into Paul's statement "my spirit prays" (1 Corinthians 14:14–15; cf. 14:2, 4, 28). Regardless of one's particular view concerning present-day tongues speaking, at least the *concept* of private praying in tongues can be understood as being a means by which one's spirit, the deepest level of his personhood, may offer praise to God. The resulting edification occurs, then, apart from the management by one's mortal brain of the nature of that praise.

11. In a simple manner it replaces the very complicated approaches to spirituality which are often marketed today. In so doing it corresponds to the obvious simplicity of operation of the first generation believers.

12. It enables me to appreciate by direct parallel how the earthly life of my Lord Jesus can be an actual working example for me.

13. It frees me from having to believe in the well meant "double talk" of so many popular explanations of Romans 6 which teach that victory comes only when a dead man is being controlled, or that by some mysterious exercise of faith a positional truth becomes actual, but only as long as you are believing it to be so. (I am referring here to the view that "reckoning" makes the crucifixion of the old man a reality.) It therefore allows a variety of Scripture passages to speak with fresh authority rather than being bridled by the well meant rationalizations of some Bible teachers.

14. It encourages me to greatly value the facetting process which God is undertaking in my life. And even though it is painful at times, I can truly rejoice because I know that the process only increases the potential of meaning, of glorifying God—which is ultimate meaning—both in time and eternity.

15. It tremendously heightens my vision of the prospects of manifesting holiness.

16. It increases my appreciation of the continuity between my life here on earth and my life in heaven. Since the Bible does not teach that there will be any change in my authentic personhood between the moment I die and my arrival in heaven, it then logically underlines the sacredness of my present union with Christ. Naturally it also causes me to joyfully anticipate the time I will receive a redeemed body to match my presently redeemed spirit.

Suggestions Toward an
Understanding of Romans 6–8

Fundamental to one's understanding of any portion of Scripture is an appreciation of its historical setting. Because of this, though our goal will be to grasp the personal implications of Romans 6–8 for God's people today, our first step must be to attempt to see it through Paul's eyes and those of his original readers.

Of first importance is that both Paul and a significant portion of his audience had been nurtured in Old Covenant Jewish beliefs that centered on pleasing God through obedience to the Mosaic Law. This nurturing had produced a variety of responses, two of which appear repeatedly in the Gospels. The first was seen in those who responded to both the Scriptures and the teachings of their rabbis with sincere, humble, obedient faith in the love and mercy of God. Theirs was the response expressed in Micah 6:8, "to do justice, to love kindness [more literally, "loyal devotion"], and to walk humbly with your God." In Luke 1–2 we find Zechariah and Elizabeth, Mary and Joseph, Simeon and Anna; later on, most of the disciples, the seventy sent out to preach the good news of the kingdom, and, at the end, Joseph of Arimathea, "a good and righteous man." All these, when introduced to their Messiah, responded in deep gratitude and love.

We may assume prior to the resurrection, though they must have been baffled by the deity claims of Jesus, they did not allow this paradox to override their simple trust.[1] Even after the resurrection, the perspective of the two men on the road to Emmaus illustrates that, though certainly "saved" individuals, having heard and believed much he had taught, they still viewed him as "a prophet mighty in deed and word before God" (Luke 24:19). Up to that point there was not even a glimmer of understanding of the substitutionary significance of Jesus' death or the implications of his resurrection.[2]

There was also a second type of response illustrated by the hypocritical, proud, wholly works-oriented Jews, as most vividly evident in the scribes and Pharisees Jesus condemned in Matthew 23. Most of them, we may assume, never responded positively to Jesus, even in the years after his passion, resurrection, and the coming of the Spirit. (See Acts 22–23.)

Though we automatically tend to place the Apostle Paul in the latter group, there is some justification for his belonging to the first group, but as one who had not been introduced to Jesus until that day on the Damascus Road (see first part of chapter 7). One might go so far as to argue that in many ways Paul could be compared with an Old Testament Ezra or Amos, with one crucial difference: the fact that his zeal for God was misdirected due to his own admitted ignorance regarding Jesus ("not in accordance with knowledge," Romans 10:2, NASB).[3]

Though Paul had both Jewish groups in mind as he wrote the Book of Romans (Romans 2:7–10), his prime audience was the first group, which needed to be grounded in New Covenant truth. (Romans 2:1–6, 17–24, initially describes the second group.) Since Paul's primary purpose for his lengthy epistle was to expound the wonder of the gospel (Romans 1:16–17), were it not for this unique historical context, it would be hard to justify the large amount of space he gave to the gospel's relation to the Mosaic Law.

It takes some tough thinking to set aside momentarily our modern context in order to imagine the radical adjustments that were required of believing Jews during this unique covenantal "crossover" period of history (from Old Covenant to New Covenant) in which the Book of Romans was written.

Their first adjustment (which his audience had already made) involved their being introduced to Jesus as their Messiah.[4] For the few who were part of that first circle of his disciples, this was not overly difficult. Jesus had provided them with a solid information base on which to build their trust—his words and his works. (Can we imagine what would have transpired if Paul had been among Jesus' initial disciples? Certainly he would have been another "son of thunder"!) This jolting truth was the focus of Peter's first two sermons in Acts. The one whom they had crucified was "both Lord and Christ [Messiah]."[5]

Closely related to this first adjustment was their discovery of their Messiah, Jesus, as God's agent for their *justification before him* (deliverance from his wrath) and their *reconciliation to him*. The Messiah was their Passover Lamb![6] Although this truth was not foreign to the church at Rome, there must have been some measure of misunderstanding so as to require the detailed arguments regarding the doctrine of justification found in Romans 3–5.

But the external act of justification plus the resulting internal miracle of a heart change toward God and his law (reconciliation) were not ends in themselves. There was a *third* most wonderful adjustment to be made. It had to do with the second internal miracle, the infusion of Jesus' life (regeneration) and the mechanics of that life now that they were in a right relationship with him. An initial clue to this is found in Romans 5:10. Having described their being saved from God's wrath by being "justified by his blood," he added, "For if while we were enemies, we were reconciled to God through the death of his Son, *much more surely*, having been reconciled, *will we be saved by his life*" (italics mine).[7]

Both for their present life of practical righteousness and their ultimate salvation, God was now saving them "by his life" through the Holy Spirit. It is this third issue that becomes central in Romans 6–8. Since regeneration is a divine begetting of a new kind of life, these chapters are actually Paul's enlargement on the truth of John 3:3–8 and 1 John 3:1–9.[8] To put it another way, holiness of life (sanctification), in simplest terms, is the outgrowth of the new birth. A new life has come into being; this is how it grows.[9]

I suggest the following steps in Paul's progression of thought:

(1) **Romans 6:1–7:6**[10] Newness of life results from one's identification with Christ not only in his death, but most especially in his resurrection. (See also Colossians 3:1–4.)

(2) **Romans 7:7–25** The crucial nature of this new life source (Romans 6:1–7:6) must be seen over against its absence under an Old Covenant mindset if Paul's Jewish audience is to understand.

(3) **Romans 8:1–17** The Holy Spirit is one's enabler to fulfill God's moral absolutes *in life now* while still in an unredeemed body. (See also Galatians 3:1–3; 5:16–25.)

(4) **Romans 8:18–39** Future bodily resurrection is the ultimate life answer both to present suffering and to the necessity of putting "to death the deeds of the body."

Romans 8:25–39 provides the closing doxology.

Without attempting a verse-by-verse analysis of these four sections, several issues must be considered if one is to appreciate Paul's progression of thought and its relevance for us.

(Note: Though the NIV represents excellent scholarship and care in many areas, its perceived necessity of rendering "flesh" by "sin nature" or other similar terminology, plus its occasional unjustified efforts at clarifying the text—as seen, for example in Romans 8:5–9—cause me to recommend the NRSV, NASB, or NKJV as more faithfully expressing in English the meaning of the Greek text for these chapters in Romans.)

(1) **Romans 6:1–7:6** Newness of life results from one's identification with Christ not only in his death, but most especially in his resurrection. (See also Colossians 3:1–4.)

Keeping in mind this section follows directly Paul's emphasis on the truth of justification by faith, one might assume his references to our death to sin, our being united with Jesus in his death and burial, the crucifixion of "our old self" (6:1–4), might be nothing more than restatements of the justification "screen" idea (see chapter 3), expressing God's legal reckoning. In other words, if this is the way God sees us in view of his taking the entire record of our sin and ascribing it to his Son, and also taking the entire record of his Son's righteousness and ascribing it to us; then we should set about to live up to this status. This we should do, not because there has been any change in us, but rather because this is the way our record in heaven reads. Of course, according to this view, we will have to wait until our future resurrection when our status at last becomes our actual state of being.

Though several scholars hold this point of view,[11] I believe it is inadequate in explaining Paul's emphasis in the passage on newness of life:

"so we too might walk in newness of life."
"consider yourselves dead to sin and alive to God."

"those who have been brought from death to life."
*"so that we are slaves not under the old written code but in the new life
of the Spirit." (6:4, 11, 13; 7:6, and probably also 6:5 and 8)*

It appears rather that Paul was affirming an actual, direct parallel
between what happened to Jesus and what has happened to every regenerate person. According to 2 Corinthians 5:21, the dying of Jesus took on
profound significance because he, the sinless one, became personally fully
identified with—joined to—sin. "He became sin." Yet in his resurrection,
he experienced complete newness of life (6:4), as one who was "freed from
sin" (6:7). Having "died to sin, once for all," he therefore now "lives to God"
(6:10).

We too were once in that state of sin.

We too have newness of life as those who are also freed from sin.

We too now live to God as those who share in the same kind of resurrection life that is also his.

There is nothing in the passage to suggest that though this was actual
for Christ, it is only positional for us. The pattern—what was true of him
is true of us—is consistent throughout, with but one obvious exception.
*Christ rose with a glorified resurrection body; we still remain with unredeemed
bodies.* I believe it is the failure to understand this most important exception that has brought about much of the controversy over this passage.

Paul, well aware his immediate audience would spot this exception,
confronted it head-on in 6:6, 12–14 and 19. Understanding his comments
is fundamental to appreciating the entire section, chapters 6–8. We will
look especially at 6:6, the meaning of which determines much that follows.

*We know that our old self [man] was crucified with him so that the body
of sin might be destroyed [rendered inactive], and we might no longer be
enslaved to sin.*

Working from the end to the beginning, "might be destroyed" should
most certainly be understood as "might be made ineffective or inactive."[12]
By correctly removing the "destroyed" idea, the expression "body of sin"
may be taken at its face value as referring to one's physical body "as condi-

tioned and controlled by sin."[13] Clearly, as we have noted earlier, the thinking faculties of our body, rather than simply the senses and appendages, are the focal point for the problem of sin.[14] "Something marvelous has happened," Paul says, "so that our bodies would be inactive as expressers of sin."

What then has happened? "Our old self [man] has been crucified." Who is that? Could it be the most obvious choice is the correct meaning? In some sense, the person I used to be has been crucified. By all means I still have the same body/thought mechanisms—my body is not yet redeemed. Nevertheless, I am no longer an "in the flesh" kind of person. I am alive in the Spirit; I am an "alive to God" kind of person! Newness of life is mine to live (8:2, 9; 6:4, 11; 7:6). Certainly *the kind of life* one possesses above all else determines the kind of person one is—one's true identity.

Though the expression "old man" ("old self," NRSV, NIV, NASB) has been understood by some as conveying a corporate idea ("old humanity" or "Israel under the law"[15]), the truth remains that the "old humanity" (or as a Jew, "Israel under the law,") was made up of individual people. What was true corporately was also true personally to the degree that I, as Christ, have died to sin. Though, *not as Christ*, I still await a resurrection body, it is nevertheless now possible for my "body of sin" to no longer be active in producing sin. In fact, such is the expected effect of my having both died with Christ and also having been raised with him as one who is "alive from the dead" to the degree that my members ("my body") are to be "instruments of righteousness" (Romans 6:13).[16]

This is a momentous truth because it of necessity involves a fundamental interior change in an individual's essential being. One kind of life has been superseded by another. What we were—persons whose life was "in the flesh"—has died ("our old self"). In that dying, we "died to sin" and became "alive to God." Could we find any better clarification of new birth?[17] It was to this "fundamental interior change" that John wrote, "Everyone who does what is right is righteous, *just as he is righteous*.... They cannot sin, because they have been born of God" (1 John 3:7, 9, italics mine).[18] John's words were getting at essentially the same truth found in Paul's words, "What then are we to say? Should we continue in sin in order that grace may abound? By no means! How can we who died to sin go on living in it?" (Romans 6:1–2)

Regarding this section, it should also be noted that though Paul urged, "do not let sin exercise dominion in your mortal bodies"; "no longer present your members to sin as instruments of wickedness"; and "sin will have no dominion over you" (6:12–14); he has said nothing up to this point about the power necessary to accomplish this. This fact underlines the interrelatedness of chapters 6–8.

(2) **Romans 7:7–25** The crucial nature of this new life source (Romans 6:1–7:6) must be seen over against its absence under an old covenant mindset if Paul's Jewish audience is to understand.

The conclusions we draw as to Paul's perspective in this section must be consistent both with the historical circumstance described above and three obvious facts:

1. *The passage is a description, not of partial defeat, but of total defeat.* This is the opposite of Paul's expectations as found in many of his letters, including specific passages such as Romans 8:13; Galatians 5:16–23 (cf. 1 John 3:7–10). Therefore, this cannot be a description of the normal Christian life. Note also, Paul considered his own life of holiness as being worthy of being imitated. (See 1 Corinthians 4:11–16; Philippians 3:17; 1 Thessalonians 1:5–6.)

2. *Though not perceiving himself as a two-parallel-natured individual (Paul recognized his "inmost self" as his essential selfhood), in his day-by-day existence he confessed that his flesh alone was where he lived in personal wretchedness.*

3. *The state of bondage described specifically in 7:14, 23 and broadly in the entire passage is directly opposite to the release from bondage seen in 8:2–6, and earlier in 6:18, 22 and 7:6.* Therefore, any explanation of this passage must explain this contradiction.

As we now consider the first two facts, the third will be obvious (and therefore not listed), especially as we turn to Romans 8.

1. *The passage is a description of total defeat.*
Who was Paul describing? To approach this question as though it were an

issue of whether the "I" in the passage refers to a "saved" or "unsaved" individual or to try to distinguish between 7:7–13 (unsaved) and 7:14–25 (saved), is to miss the historical context from which Paul wrote. I believe Walter Russell may be getting at the central issue when he states:

> *he is probably describing neither a Christian nor a non-Christian.*
> *Rather, he is describing the pious Israelite during the Mosaic law era who*
> *struggled with the convicting and condemning work of the Torah because*
> *he or she was still in the flesh, that is, in a body distinguished by cir-*
> *cumcision and restrained by Torah, yet still under sin's dominion and not*
> *indwelt by God's Spirit (7:14). This condition led to a unique state of*
> *wretchedness for the believing Israelite.... This wretchedness is now*
> *removed only in Christ Jesus (8:1) through his death, burial and resur-*
> *rection (6:3–11; 8:2–11).[19]*

We may assume from this that he (and they) were sincere, "pious," Old Covenant believers and therefore saved individuals, though hardly Christian. (Cf. Micah 6:8.) As such, they would have been justified even as Abraham and, as David, they would have experienced some measure of God's grace in changing their heart attitudes toward him (reconciliation). Inwardly they delighted in God's law (7:22, cf. Psalm 5:11; 18:1; 19:7–10).

Therefore he (and they) were still, as Russell states, "in the flesh" (7:5), "of the flesh" (7:14),[20] knowing nothing yet of the transforming miracle of Romans 6:3–11[21] and the freedom and power resource described in Romans 8:2–11.

Though the first person "I" might not be autobiographical, I would think it is quite reasonable that this indeed may also have been Paul's personal experience prior to the Damascus Road, or at least prior to God's revelation to him of the truth of Romans 6 and 8.[22]

Significant in Paul's description of Old Covenant defeat was his discovery of the killing effect of the law's attitudinal demands. It was as though for the first time he saw God's moral absolutes as requiring attitudes, not simply actions. He could avoid bearing false witness, stealing, committing adultery, etc. In fact, he had considered himself to be "blameless!" (Philippians 3:6) But he could not avoid the law's attitudinal demand—"You shall not covet." No matter how hard he might try, God's attitudinal demands devastated him.[23] This, most of all, proved to Paul both the sinfulness of sin and the total impossibility of life as God demanded (Romans 7:7–13). Instead of finding life in his commitment to please God, he found death and hopelessness.

This inward attitude probably is what Paul had in view when he refers to the desires of his "inmost self" in 7:22. This was also his dominant mental attitude, as he states "with my mind I am a slave to the law of God" (7:25, cf. v. 23). Yet in spite of this attitudinal change, he recognized he lacked the life-power enablement to fulfill that positive attitude; in fact, just the opposite, sin, marked his behavior.

2. *Though not perceiving of himself as a two-parallel-natured individual (Paul recognized his "inmost self" as his essential selfhood), in his day-by-day existence he confessed that his flesh alone was where he lived in personal wretchedness.*
Statements such as "I do the very thing I hate" (7:15), cannot be understood as supporting the idea that a believer (Old or New Covenant) is a person possessing two parallel but opposing "I's" or natures or dispositions due to the radical force of 7:17, 18, "it is no longer I that do it, but sin that dwells within me, that is, in my flesh" (repeated in 7:20).

Though on one hand Paul acknowledged personal responsibility for sins produced, he affirmed that he in his "inmost being" was not the source, but rather it was his flesh and the "law of sin" operating there—in the members of his body. It is difficult to imagine how Paul could have been more specific in identifying the mechanics of personal sin. Since, in the context, the only sin he mentioned, coveting, is exclusively a "mental" sin involving no physical action outside the brain, it is quite clear that "members" included more than just from the neck down. Though he perceived of himself as having two levels to his selfhood—two levels of "mind"—only that "inmost" level deserved the full force of "I."[24] Consider the following admittedly less than perfect analogy.

Imagine I have a huge, powerful dog that is very close to me—part of my life. Though he is beneficial to me, he has a proneness to bite people, which I seem unable to control. Nevertheless, I am responsible. The failure is not in my wishing people would be bitten; I do not. Rather, I am unable to control his actions. Therefore, in a broad sense, one might say, "You bit that person because it was your dog and you let him do it!" Whereas in a narrow sense, though I apologize and take full responsibility for my failure in causing the evil done by my lack of control, I disassociate myself from the actual thought and action that produced the biting. I did not wish the biting to happen. (Obviously, this analogy is far removed from the "white dog/black dog" illustration of two parallel, equal natures in which the one I say "sic 'em" to, wins.)

This then was the wretchedness in which pious, God-fearing Old Covenant believers found themselves—"sold into slavery under sin," as seen throughout the section from 7:9 through 24. It so happens, it is also the same depressive state of a New Covenant believer who has not yet comprehended the miraculous nature of Christ being his life by the Holy Spirit. By including this section, Paul has both established the radical nature of the truth shared in 6:2–7:6 and created a profound need for the truth that follows in chapter 8, which is anticipated in his parenthetical expression, "Thanks be to God through Jesus Christ our Lord!" (7:25)

(3) **Romans 8:1–17** The Holy Spirit is one's enabler to fulfill God's moral absolutes in life now while still in an unredeemed body. (See also Galatians 3:1–3; 5:16–25.)

As one reads straight through chapter 7 into chapter 8, the brilliance, freedom, and joy of the latter is impossible to miss. Yes, our ultimate deliverance awaits the redemption of our bodies; but "life and peace" are ours *now*.

Here, as in Romans 6, Paul's reference to our being "in Christ" (8:1) has been understood by some as teaching nothing beyond the truth of justification.[25] According to this view, Christ has fulfilled righteousness for us, having also condemned sin. Therefore, though our status from God's judicial perspective is fully acceptable, we are intrinsically unchanged and essentially sinful.[26]

Once again this view must be rejected in light of the positive descriptions declaring we are no longer "in the flesh" (8:9) because "Christ is in you" (8:10). We are indeed more than justified.

Perhaps the most striking difference we encounter moving from chapter 7 to 8 is found in the occurrences of the word *law*. Chapter 7 ends with the paradox of being in one's flesh, an active and productive "slave to the law of sin," while at the same time in one's inmost mind, a completely ineffective slave to the law of God (7:25, cf. 21–23). Chapter 8 declares it is not merely *possible* to be set free from this "law of sin," rather, "the law of the Spirit of life in Christ Jesus *has set you free* from the law of sin and death" (8:2, italics mine). Yet if people assume they are still in bondage, they will behave in light of this illusion and fail to use the resources that freedom from the law of sin brings. The result of this failure will be much the same as the "death" Paul described in Romans 7:9–11, cf. 8:6, 13.[27]

When we hear the word *law*, our first thought is that it tells us what we can or cannot do. I suggest a more comprehensive understanding of this word as illustrated by the "law of gravity" or the "law of centrifugal force." Understood this way, *law* is simply *the way something works,* unless some other law intervenes. God's moral law is, first of all, an expression of the way "he works." This law is nothing short of absolute perfection and is seen in all descriptions of God in the Bible. God's moral law for human beings (expressed in many of the commandments in the Bible) is actually a description of the way human beings "work" if they are to relate properly to such a God. Only then are they able to fulfill the reason for which God made them.

But in Genesis 3:1–19, God allowed another law to come into force—the law of sin (Romans 7:22–23). It overrode the initial way human beings were meant to operate in the paradise of Eden. Because of this, following the Fall, God revealed his law through Moses to show his covenant people how they were "to work" if they were to be right with God in a world in which this alien "law of sin" was also in operation. Happily, it included a temporary means of gaining forgiveness.

Of course this was before the cross, the resurrection, and the coming of the Spirit. Only in the New Covenant age—our times!—has God brought about our being set free from this "law of sin and death." Yet to appreciate our freedom requires an active dependence upon the Spirit's enablement in putting "to death the deeds of the body" (8:13) as we oper-ate under the new and higher "law of the Spirit of life" (8:2).

Therefore, for us as regenerated children of God, "to live" is more than being aware that our deepest desires are in harmony with the law of God (7:22). It is also more than simply the Spirit dispensing the power to help us do what God's moral law requires. Authentic living requires the actual fulfill-ment of those desires in our behavior by the Spirit's *reproducing in us the actual extension of the life of Jesus*. In light of this, 8:10 needs special comment.

> But if Christ is in you, your body is dead because of sin, yet your spirit is alive [life] because of righteousness (8:10, NIV, cf. NASB).

In light of my earlier comments regarding *body* and *flesh* in chapter 5, I believe Paul's point in Romans 8:10 is essentially the same as his declara-tion in Galatians 5:24, "Those who belong to Jesus Christ have crucified the flesh with its passions and desires." Both express a crucial truth: as regenerated people, our flesh, our bodies, especially their passions and desires, *are dead to us as being where life is to be found*. This is true whether or not we realize it.

Both passages describe entities that are nevertheless very much alive. Unless one reads into Romans 8:10 that our bodies are dead in the sense that physical death awaits us all or that the "principle of death" is present in all of us,[28] it seems more reasonable to make a direct connection between "the body is dead" and "this body of death" (7:24). The thought is: There are no "righteous" resources in my flesh, my body. *Therefore it is truly dead* as being the facilitator of the life God expects me to live. Of course, before I was born again, my flesh—my body—was where "life" was. It was nowhere else.

I believe Galatians 5:24 expresses the identical truth. A Christian's flesh is, in one sense, very much alive, otherwise we would not be warned against gratifying the desires of the flesh or told our flesh is in opposition to the Spirit (Galatians 5:16–17). Yet it is most certainly *also* dead as being a facilitator of the life God expects me to live. I believe it is with the same thought that later (Galatians 6:14) Paul stated, "the world has been cruci-fied to me, and I to the world." The world is truly dead to me as being where life is, even as I am dead to the world in this same sense.[29]

In joyous contrast, Paul adds, "the spirit is alive [life] because of right-eousness" (Romans 8:10, NASB, cf. NIV). Though we should be less than dogmatic as to whether Paul was referring to the human spirit or to the Holy Spirit or to both,[30] his statement finds a direct parallel in Jesus' words in John 6:63, "It is the spirit [or Spirit] that gives life; the flesh is useless. The words that I have spoken to you are spirit and life." What words?

> *"I am the living bread that came down from heaven. Whoever eats this bread will live forever; and the bread that I will give for the life of the world is my flesh.… Those who eat my flesh and drink my blood abide in me, and I in them. Just as the living Father sent me, and I live because of the Father, so whoever eats me will live because of me" (John 6:51, 56–57).*

Standing on the edge of mystery, we reach out to grasp the wonder of possessing Jesus' life because of the righteousness of his accomplished work. We, as spirit (John 3:6; cf. Romans 8:16), by the Spirit *live* because Christ "is our life" (Colossians 3:4), even as he lived by the Spirit because the Father was his life.

(4) **Romans 8:18–39** Future bodily resurrection is the ultimate life answer both to present suffering and to the necessity of putting "to death the deeds of the body."

Though the majesty of this closing section deserves major attention, I believe the truth conveyed may be grasped without extended comment. I prefer rather to pause once again, on the edge of mystery, as we read Paul's climactic words:

> *For those whom he foreknew he also predestined to be conformed to the image of his Son, in order that he might be the firstborn within a large family. And those whom he predestined he also called; and those whom he called he also justified; and those whom he justified he also glorified (Romans 8:29–30).*

Though Paul wrote earlier of future glory (8:17, 21), to whatever degree God's New Covenant people are conforming to "the image of his

Son," to that degree the glorification is already in process. Perhaps, in part, this is the reason Paul chose to write "he also glorified" rather than "he will glorify," though the past tense serves to underscore the absolute certainty of future glorification.

Without question, the glorification began in that moment of new birth, a new creation. As Norman Douty writes, "As regeneration is glorification in the bud, so glorification is regeneration in the flower."[31] It continues as God progressively "facets" his precious spiritual diamonds. As his workmanship "we are being transformed into the same image [the glory of the Lord] from one degree of glory to another" (2 Corinthians 3:18; cf. Colossians 3:10) even as he "predestined us to be conformed to the image of his Son" (Romans 8:29). Already "the light of the knowledge of the glory of God in the face of Jesus Christ" is to be found in these "clay jars" (2 Corinthians 4:5–7).

Yet with overflowing joy, we still dream of "the ages to come" when God will show us "the immeasurable riches of his grace in kindness toward us in Christ Jesus" (Ephesians 2:7). The best is yet to come!

Notes

1. For several reasons I have chosen to use the New Revised Standard Version of the Bible for most quotations. It follows a similar translation methodology as the American Standard Bible (1901) and the New American Standard Bible (1963), while going a step further in expressing the truth in contemporary English, including dropping pronouns such as *thee* and *thou* and their corresponding archaic verbs. As a rule, the NRSV has also been more successful than the New International Version in avoiding the temptation to clarify the text beyond what was available to the original readers. For example, where the NIV has *sin nature*, the NRSV has maintained the direct English equivalent for the Greek word for *flesh*. By so doing, the NRSV allows the present reader the same opportunity to determine its meaning as the original audience. If the Holy Spirit had intended *sin nature*, the corresponding Greek words were readily available.

2. See 1 Cor. 15:45–48. Note also that Adam and Eve never tasted of the Tree of Life.

3. Some people believe the term *living being* in Gen. 2:7 refers to man's eternal soul, but a study of the use of the word in other contexts rules this out—unless one is willing to say that every fish, bird, and animal also has an eternal soul. By contrast, note the following statement: "Actually, the description of man as a 'living being' in Gen. 2:7 shows his likeness to other living beings rather than his differences from them." (A. Berkeley Mickelson and Alvera M. Mickelson, *Understanding Scripture, How to Read and Study the Bible,* [Peabody, Mass.: Hendrickson Pub. Co., 1992], 110.) Regarding God's breathing into man causing him to be a living soul, Bernard Ramm comments, "The spiration of God is not to be interpreted as a breathing of a soul into man (as in Roman Catholic exegesis of Gen. 2:7) but as that which makes man an animate being." (Ramm, *Them He Glorified,* [Grand Rapids: Wm. B. Eerdmans Pub. Co., 1963], 93). With a few possible exceptions, the same is true of the Greek word *psyche* as used in the New Testament. For that matter, animals are referred to as souls in the New Testament as well as the Old Testament. See

Rev. 8:8 and 16:3. Later (chapter 5) we will consider the use of the word *soul* as descriptive of one's existence after death. The emphasis in our present chapter is on mortal humanness.

4. The following are representative of the extensive literature dealing with the expression "the image of God": Ronald B. Allen, *The Majesty of Man* (Portland, Ore.: Multnomah Press, 1984); Ray S. Anderson, *On Being Human, Essays in Theological Anthropology* (Grand Rapids: Eerdmans, 1982); G. C. Berkouwer, *Man: The Image of God* (Grand Rapids: Eerdmans, 1962); *Christian Perspectives on Being Human: A Multidisciplinary Approach to Integration,* ed. J. P. Mooreland and David M. Ciocchi (Grand Rapids: Baker Book House, 1993); Anthony A. Hoekema, *Created in God's Image* (Grand Rapids: Eerdmans, 1986); Philip E. Hughes, *The True Image: The Origin and Destiny of Man in Christ* (Grand Rapids: Eerdmans); Ranald Macaulay and Jerram Barrs, *Being Human: The Nature of Spiritual Experience* (Downers Grove, Ill.: InterVarsity Press, 1978); H. D. McDonald, *The Christian View of Man* (Westchester, Ill.: Crossway Books, 1981).

5. Though the words *image* and *likeness* have a shade of difference in meaning, for our purposes, I think it is best to accept the view of many scholars that these two words are getting at essentially the same idea. See Hoekema, *Created in God's Image,* 13; also Robert L. Saucy, "The Theology of Human Nature," *Christian Perspectives On Being Human*, ed. Mooreland and Ciocchi, (Grand Rapids: Baker Book House, 1993), 22.

6. The verse does not say that it takes *both* maleness and femaleness to equal the image of God, nor does the text require that "image" involves person-to-person relationships, although both of these ideas have been made focal points by several scholars. If those ideas are part of the "image" idea, then one must assume God expects us to be experts at reading between the lines.

7. The expression "image of God" is used of human beings after the Fall (see Gen. 9:6 and James 3:9). This supports the conclusion that every human being possesses this quality, including the unsaved. Though it is commonly assumed the image was in some way damaged in the Fall, nothing in the Bible suggests this idea. (Later we will focus on a marvelous new use of "image of God" when we turn to New Covenant passages related to the "image of Christ.")

8.   Erickson defines "image" as "the powers of personality that make man, like God, a being capable of interacting with other persons, of thinking and reflecting and of willing freely." (Millard J. Erickson, *Christian Theology,* vol. 2 [Grand Rapids: Baker Book House, 1984], 513.) Rather than include the reasoning that led him to this conclusion, I recommend his overall discussion (pp. 495–515).

9.   Though at first glance such a view seems quite weak because we know God is essentially spirit, yet a psycho-physical parallel would appear to be in view when Seth is described as being in Adam's "own likeness, according to his image" (Gen. 5:3). Most of the visual appearances of God to people were in human form. Jesus, speaking of the Father, said, "you have never heard his voice or seen his form" (John 5:37). See also Gen. 18; 32:30; Ex. 33:19–23; Isa. 6; Ezek. 1:26–28; Rev. 4:3; 5:7. The last two references are especially significant because the person in view is clearly God the Father, as is so in John 5:37. See Eichrodt for his arguments against this view. (Walther Eichrodt, *Theology of the Old Testament,* vol. 2 [Philadelphia: Westminster Press], 122–31.)

10.   Gen. 1:26. Centuries later in Ps. 8, which the Old Testament scholar, Franz Delitzsch, described as "a lyric echo" of Gen. 1:27–28 (an enlargement of Gen. 1:26), King David wrestled with the same question confronting us, "What is man?" His answer was the same—not *what he is,* but *what he does.*

> *When I consider your heavens,*
> *the work of your fingers,*
> *the moon and the stars,*
> *which you have set in place,*
> *what is man that you are mindful of him,*
> *the son of man that you care for him?*
> *You made him a little lower than the heavenly beings*
> *and crowned him with glory and honor.*
> *You made him ruler over the works of your hands,*
> *you put everything under his feet:*
> *all the flocks and herds,*
> *and the beasts of the fields,*
> *the birds of the air,*

and the fish of the sea,

all that swim the paths of the sea. (Ps. 8:6–8, NIV)

In David's mind, rulership over the creatures of this planet was what it meant for man to be "crowned with glory and honor" (Ps. 8:5). Because of this, Hans Wolff states, "It is precisely in his function as ruler that he is God's image." Wolff goes on to say, "In the ancient East the setting up of the king's statue was the equivalent to the proclamation of his dominion over the sphere in which the statue was erected (cf. Dan. 3:1, 5f.). When in the thirteenth century B.C. the pharaoh Rameses II had his image hewn out of rock at the mouth of the *nahr el-kelb,* on the Mediterranean north of Beirut, the image meant that he was the ruler of this area. Accordingly man is set in the midst of creation as God's statue. He is evidence that God is the Lord of creation; but as God's steward he also exerts his rule, fulfilling his task not in arbitrary despotism but as a responsible agent. His rule and his duty to rule are not autonomous; they are copies." (Hans Walter Wolff, *Anthropology of the Old Testament* [Philadelphia: Fortress Press, 1974], 160–61.)

The "image of God" usage in 1 Cor. 11:7 also appears to point to the rulership, stewardship idea as a limited imaging of God's sovereignty. "For a man ought not to have his head covered, since he is the image and glory of God; but the woman is the glory of man." From this we conclude that God has ordained a chain of authority in which adult male members of a local body of believers, rather than the female members, are to bear the weight of leadership under Christ.

Regardless, I believe Erickson's arguments favoring a substantive view (qualities of personality) over a functional view of "image of God" are strong enough to outweigh the functional view argued by Wolff as illustrated by 1 Cor. 11:7. See Erickson, *Christian Theology,* 2: 496–517. It is also difficult to see anything but a substantive view in Gen. 5:3 in which Seth is described as being in the "image and likeness" of his father, Adam. This probably was another way of saying that he possessed those special human qualities that, as with his father, distinguished him from animals.

11. I believe it would be difficult to underestimate the importance of the gift of complex language in identifying the meaning of "image of God." It is foundational to all uniquely human relationships. It also seems impossible for

human beings to fulfill the greatest commandment, "You shall love the Lord your God with all your heart, and with all your soul and *with all your mind*," (Matt. 22:37, italics mine) without this remarkable divine/human quality.

12. Indeed, Adam and Eve *were* God-conscious. But this fact says much more about God's self-revelation than it does about the necessity of some sort of nonmaterial essence about them. Balaam's donkey, in fact, was more God-conscious (or at least angel conscious) than Balaam!

13. Boivin describes this as developing during the medieval period. (Michael J. Boivin, "The Hebraic Model of the Person: Toward a Unified Psychological Science Among Christian Helping Professions," *Journal of Psychology and Theology* 19:158.) Building on the fact that God is spirit, I used to assume that being in the image of God meant being spirit. Not only does 1 Cor. 15:45 argue against that view, but as we observed, none of the Genesis passages suggest it. See Franz Delitzsch, *Commentary on Genesis* (Edinburgh: T. and T. Clark, 1888), p. 49 as representative of this view. This is not to suggest there was nothing about human beings as originally created that transcended the physical. Rather, it is to say the Bible does not explain either original or unregenerate human behavior prior to death by using nonphysical terminology, satanic influence excepted. (Regarding the human spirit as being part of original creation, see note 33, chapter 5.)

14. One of the leading Christian scholars grappling with this mystery is John MacKay who writes, "I confess that to me the two-way relationship between brain activity and conscious experience seems really too close to justify taking metaphors in terms of 'clothing' or 'tents' as proving that the soul is an invisible 'substance' *inhabiting* the body. The data rather suggest that man is at one and the same time (i) a body, (ii) a 'living soul' or conscious being (the Hebrew word *nephesh*, also used of lower animals) and (iii) a spiritual being, in the sense that he can be called to account by God, can come to know God, and can enjoy the gift of eternal life with God." (John M. MacKay, *Human Science and Human Dignity* [Downers Grove, Ill.: InterVarsity Press, 1979], 33–34.) To this I would add that only by the miracle of regeneration, the word *spiritual* takes on that final quality he mentions—eternal life. This will be a central issue later in this book.

15. "In looking for those areas where humans differ from animals, I find

that the brain is certainly rich with discovery. Both dualists and materialists agree that we are somehow up there behind our eyes, inside our head. Since we are so different from animals, it is inside the brain where the major differences must reside." (p. 145)

"The areas of human brain that distinguish it from the animal brain are the following. First, the human brain has a massive enlargement of the frontal lobes. Second, the human brain has a massive enlargement of areas collectively known as association cortex. Third, the human brain shows some remarkable hemispheric specialization in speech, manual dexterity, and other functions. Fourth, the human brain has a unique area devoted to the production and perception of speech—the frontal lobes.

"Approximately one-half of the volume of our cerebral cortex consists of the frontal cortex. This brain area includes the premotor and motor cortex as well as the mysterious prefrontal areas immediately behind the forehead and eyes. It is this latter area that most people have in mind when they speak of the frontal lobes. Since the prefrontal cortex barely exists in laboratory rats and mice, it has been difficult to study. In cats and dogs the prefrontal cortex makes up 3.5 and 7 percent of the cerebral cortex respectively. In chimpanzees prefrontal cortex makes up 17 percent of the cerebral cortex. Our own prefrontal cortex is most impressive—at 29 percent—almost a third of the entire cerebral cortex." (p. 149)

"Our responses to the environment are affected by our anticipations of the future. We are able to focus on both the past and future as twin supports to lift our self-awareness out of present time. We are thus able to move back and forth from past memories through present ideals to future goals. We can imagine that which does not yet exist or that which will never exist. Our huge memory capacity is utilized by frontal-lobe mechanisms as a type of non-genetic inheritance to shape our future decisions. The frontal lobes are able to hold on to the past memory traces as it moves us into the future. Man is the only creature on earth who lives as if his brain has allowed him to transcend the physical. And that is what it is to be human." (p. 152)

(Referring to the distinction of left-brain, right-brain, Cosgrove notes that in contrast with humans, this distinction is minimal in animals.) "Animals with no lateralization of brain functions can have none of the advantages in thinking and experience that combine rational and intuitive modes of processing can offer. Great ideas and constructions, in both science and art, must proceed with both sides of the ladder of knowing each assisting the other. Animal experiences cannot reverberate these two epistemologies back and forth in the brain. Nor does the animal brain possess the dominant characteristic of language, which the body human bestows on the left hemisphere. Language provides the symbolic frames for merging reason and holistic experience into thought." (p. 163)

"The unique purposes of these brain distinctions for the body human are enormous. They give meaning to the array of sensory input—through association, through symbolic labels of language, and through left and right hemispheric differences. We are able to operate in a world of meaning, contacting other persons, sharing experiences and knowledge, building of culture, and standing of memories, while reaching toward plans, goals, and aspirations unique to human nature. The brain of the body human makes all this possible." (p. 166) The above quotations are from Mark P. Cosgrove, *The Amazing Body Human, God's Design for Personhood* (Grand Rapids: Baker Book House, 1987).

Closely related are the following comments by Michael J. Boivin: "What sets us above the physical aspect of our nature is not a proposed ethereal aspect to what we are, as a dualistic approach would have us believe. It is, instead, relational aspects, as defined by our sophisticated social nature, and a capacity to know and have social interaction with God (Gen. 1:26, 2:15–17, NIV). Furthermore, the neurological, cognitive and behavioral traits necessary for human relationships (with God and with each other) are amenable to empirical investigation. Human social behaviors are far more easily observed within an empirical framework, and this does not violate the creative wonder of God." (Michael J. Boivin, "The Hebraic Model of the Person: Toward a Unified Psychological Science," *Journal of Psychology and Theology* 19:163.) See also Donald M. MacKay, *Human Science and Human Dignity* (Downers Grove, Ill.: InterVarsity Press, 1979); and *Brains, Machines and Persons* (Grand Rapids: Wm. B. Eerdmans Pub. Co., 1980), especially MacKay's chapter 6, "Man in the Image of God?" in which he explains why his view is not physical determinism. Two Christian scholars (John Yates in his article "The Origin of the Soul:

New Light on an Old Question," *Evangelical Quarterly* [1989]:121–40; and Vern A. Hannah in his article, "Death, Immortality and Resurrection: A Response to John Yates, 'The Origin of the Soul,'" *Evangelical Quarterly* [1990:241–51]) present similar evidence and conclude that it is fully agreeable with Scripture. Another significant contribution is Clifford Williams's article, "The Irrelevance of Nonmaterial Minds," *Christian Scholar's Review* 12 (1983). In view of the controversial nature of these issues, I appreciate the evident integrity of these scholars.

16. For a similar definition of "image of God" see Erickson, *Christian Theology*, 2:513.

17. Not only is this love relationship intent suggested by Gen. 3:8, but the first and greatest commandment is meaningless apart from this being fundamental in God's original purpose for human beings.

18. Though there are a few references to resurrection and ultimate immortality in the Old Testament, the truth of the worth of a human life in its eternal implications is fully developed only in the New Testament. Laird Harris comments, "On the relatively few occasions that the OT does express positive hope regarding the hereafter (e.g., Job. 19:26; Ps. 17:15; 49:15; 73:24; Isa. 26:19; 53:10–12; Dan. 12:2, 13), it is couched in terms that imply resurrection, not immortality.... From the Genesis account it seems that man was not created either immortal or mortal (see Gen. 2:17; 3:22), but with the possibility of becoming either, depending on his responsiveness to God. He was created *for* immortality rather than *with* immortality." (Harris, "Immortality," *New Dictionary of Theology* [Downers Grove, Ill.: InterVarsity Press, 1988], 332.) Apparently then, the Bible does not describe human beings as inherently immortal, but rather it is due to divine edict that immortality is imparted. Technically, only the saved will experience immortality "through the appearing of our Savior Christ Jesus, who abolished death and brought life and immortality to light through the gospel" (2 Tim. 1:10). The ultimate continuing state of the lost is of such a dark nature, that rather than being described as a state of "life," it is described as "the second death."

19. Regarding Adam's original state, Peter Toon states, "it is surely correct to hold that as created by God, Adam and Eve not only had physical perfection, but also were indwelt by the Holy Spirit. If this is so, then it is also the

case that when they chose to disobey God (and thereby experienced spiritual death), they lost the presence of the Spirit from their souls" (p. 55). Later he adds, "By his apostasy Adam drove the Holy Spirit from his soul and the souls of his descendants. Thus detached from his primeval ties by the forfeiture of the Spirit, man follows the natural rather than the spiritual, the human rather than the divine'" (p. 127, quoting Scottish reformer, George Smeaton.) Though Toon has produced a most helpful book, on this issue, *I know of no biblical support for his view.* We must confess we know precious little as to the spiritual state of Adam and Eve before the Fall. (Peter Toon, *Born Again: A Biblical and Theological Study of Regeneration* [Grand Rapids: Baker Book House, 1987]).

20. By using the word *mortal*, the NRSV gets closer to the intent of a common Hebrew word for man used here (meaning "of the ground"). For example, see Ps. 90:3 and Ps. 103:15.

21. Though some would use Eccles. 3:11 ("He has also set eternity in their heart," NASB) to support Solomon's belief in innate human immortality, it is more reasonable to assume he was expressing the truth that God "has put a sense of past and future into their minds, yet they cannot find out what God has done from the beginning to the end" (NRSV). At issue is the Hebrew word *olam*, which allows for a variety of meanings. Within human beings is a longing to understand—to see the big picture—the ultimate end by which one's present futility might make some sense. See Carl Schultz, "Ecclesiastes," *Evangelical Commentary on the Bible* (Grand Rapids: Baker Book House, 1989), 439.

22. See Ps. 104:29 for another example of "spirit" with reference to animals. See also Gen. 7:22. In these, "spirit" (*ruach*) expresses nothing more than the life-force which God instills into a physical creature. Julius Scott mentions that the NT word *spirit* (*pneuma*) can also refer simply to physical life as in Rev. 11:11; 13:15, though he adds that Paul did not seem to use it that way. See Julius J. Scott, "Life and Death," *Dictionary of Paul and His Epistles*, ed. Gerald F. Hawthorne, Ralph Martin, Daniel G. Reid (Downers Grove, Ill.: InterVarsity Press, 1993). We will consider this issue in chapter 5.

23. "Instinct" is the translation of the Greek word *phusikos*, which simply means "by nature," "native ability." The same word as a noun is used to describe the unsaved who "*by nature* are children of wrath." It would be reading far too much into Peter's brief comment regarding "unreasoning animals" to conclude

that animals never think. Anyone who has lived around animals would be quick to bear witness to all sorts of thinking processes they have observed.

24. This is not to suggest that physicalness is bad. Quite the opposite. Our eternal destiny in Christ is inseparable from our physical destiny. The truth of bodily resurrection is a major theme of Christian hope. Even now, in our present physical state, there is great value for our flesh as the "earthen vessel" in which "the light of the knowledge of the glory of God in the face of Jesus Christ" is to be seen. Nevertheless *flesh* as most often used in Scripture has a frail earthiness about it that must not be missed. Regarding it, Donald Guthrie states, "the term came to denote the natural man in his earthly origin.… Because this sense of creatureliness is strong, *sarx* [Greek word for "flesh"] came naturally to represent man in his weakness." (Donald Guthrie, *New Testament Theology* [Downers Grove, Ill.: InterVarsity Press, 1981]). James Stewart states "in the majority of passages it stands for human nature on its material side. It includes all that is peculiar to human nature in its corporeal embodiment." (James S. Stewart, *A Man In Christ: The Vital Elements of St. Paul's Religion* [New York: Harper and Bros., n.d.], 102.) I will be making extended comments regarding the significance of the word *flesh* in chapter 5.

25. This personal translation is true to the Greek text. The NASB renders it "that no *man* should boast," while the NIV and NRSV state "so that no *one* may boast." The word *flesh* says something we dare not miss; it points to the earthiness of man as he is in himself.

26. We may assume every generation, including the present, has had its beautiful exceptions in people such as Newton and Kepler who were most careful to give God all the glory. But far more often this has not been the case. See Erich Sauer, *The King of the Earth* (Grand Rapids: Eerdmans, 1962), 88–90.

27. To enhance the image idea, there are those who use the marvelous fact that God loves us as the basis for measuring our worth. We are worth enough for Christ to die for us. But this is scarcely the thought behind Rom. 5:7–8. Rather the focus is on the amazing measure of God's love that he would bend *so low* as to love us! Paul's point was, *if we had been worth something— something good or valuable*—someone might have considered us worthy of sacrificing his life. But we weren't! It was the worth of the Lover, not the loved, that amazed the apostle.

CHAPTER 2

1. Sin as rebellion is the direct result of becoming the determiner of what is right and wrong for myself. In other words, self-sovereignty is rebellion. In light of this, Paul stated "the power of sin is the law" (1 Cor. 15:56). God's law confronts me as a threat to my own sovereignty. See Renald Showers, *The New Nature* (Neptune, N. J.: Loizeaux Brothers, 1986), 87. In spite of this, communication with God continued after the Fall. Not only did God speak to that first couple, but later to their son, Cain, and from time to time to others who, even then, chose to remain in their state of rebellious independence.

2. The following statements by G. C. Berkouwer serve to underline the inseparable relationship between sin and independence: "Exegetes have said that this thread of the story [a reference to the story of the Fall] is not concerned with purely intellectual knowledge of good and evil but with *deciding for oneself what good and evil are.* In that view the tempter seduces man to self determination and autonomy, which could then be exchanged for his own creaturely and dependent 'listening' to the commandment of God.... 'Knowledge of good and evil' signifies that a man knows himself to be independent and defines and decides *what* is good and *what* is evil for him [quoting Kuyper, *De Gemeene Gratie, I.,* 198].... In contrast to God's commandment and justice, he now substitutes his own decision of his own sovereignty and prerogative to choose. In the act of sinning he makes this 'knowledge' his own. Thus he chooses his *own* judgment on what pleases himself. Furthermore, in his 'emancipation' he receives precisely what he desired. Therefore Genesis 3:22 is such a 'dreadfully serious' text. 'Man has taken leave of the relation of dependence. He has refused to obey and has willed himself independent.' [quoting Von Rad, *Genesis,* 78].... In desiring to be 'like God' man thrusts himself into a dismal and self-defeating privation. In doing so he forfeits the glory of his creaturehood." (G. C. Berkouwer, *Sin* [Grand Rapids: Wm. B. Eerdmans Pub. Co., 1971], 259–61.) See also D. Martin Lloyd-Jones, *Romans, the Law and Its Functions, Exposition of Chapter 7:1–8:4* (Grand Rapids: Zondervan, 1974), 125, in which he emphasizes the inseparable relationship between sin and independence. Some helpful related thoughts may be found in Richard E. Howard, *Newness of Life* (Grand Rapids: Baker Book House, 1975), 42–43.

3. A necessary corrective to Descartes's "I think; therefore I am."

4. See chapter 5 for extended comments regarding the word *flesh*.

5. See 1 Sam. 12:20–21, NASB, "but serve the Lord with all your heart. And you must not turn aside, for then you would go after futile things which cannot profit or deliver, because they are futile." Also 2 Kings 17:15, NASB, "they rejected His statutes…and they followed vanity and became vain;" (the same word for futility or vanity as is found in Ecclesiastes).

6. It is in this sense, I believe, that the following familiar expressions of the sinfulness of man can best be understood: "There is no one who does good, not even one." "All our righteous deeds are like a filthy garment." "Since all have sinned and fall short of the glory of God;" (Ps. 14:3; Isa. 64:6; Rom. 3:23). In view of the relative lack of literature from an evangelical point of view concerning the issue of meaning, it is important to see that the Bible is anything but silent. Both the Hebrew word *habal* and the Greek word *mataios* usually convey the idea of emptiness or futility.

Richard Trench described the Greek understanding of this word as follows: "*Mataios,* as observed already, will express the aimlessness, the leading to no object or end, the vanity, of all which has not Him, who is the only true object and end of any intelligent creature, for its scope" (p. 181). Elaborating on the background of this word form, he added, "*Mataiotes* is a word altogether strange to profane Greek; one, too, which the old heathen world, had it possessed it, could never have imparted that depth of meaning which in Scripture it has obtained. For indeed that heathen world was itself too deeply and hopelessly sunken in 'vanity' to be fully alive to the fact that it was sunken in it at all; was committed so far as to have lost all power to pronounce that judgment upon itself which this word pronounced upon it." (Richard Chenevix Trench, *Synonyms of the New Testament* [Grand Rapids: Eerdmans, 1948], 182). See also Vine's comparison of *kenos* with *mataios.* W. E. Vine, *An Expository Dictionary of New Testament Words* (Old Tappan, N.J.: Fleming H. Revell Company, 1966), 2:25. Also, Colin Brown, ed., *The New International Dictionary of New Testament Theology*, 3 vols. (Grand Rapids: Zondervan Publishing House, 1975), 1:549–53.

7. "Rebellion" and "perversion" are more precise renderings of the words *transgressions* and *iniquities.* See Gleason L. Archer, *In the Shadow of the Cross*

(Grand Rapids: Zondervan Publishing House, 1957), 13–14.

8. "In fact, pride—a preoccupation with one's own wisdom, accomplishments, power, abilities, reputation, or possessions—is idolatry." Dennis B. Plies, "To Will to Be Himself Is Man's True Vocation—Kierkegaard," *Faculty Dialogue* (Winter 1993-94):108.

9. Victor Frankl, who as far as I know was not a believer, observed that the "will to meaning" is "man's most valuable asset…not only in gaining and keeping mental health, in achieving happiness, or even self-realization, but also it alone can enable man to realize the ultimate values and possibilities of which his life is capable." (Quoted by A. J. Ungersma, *The Search for Meaning, A New Approach in Psychotherapy and Pastoral Psychology* [Philadelphia: Westminster Press, 1961], 23.)

10. "The process (of the fall of Adam) was not, I conceive, comparable to mere deterioration as it may now occur in a human individual; it was a loss of status as a species. What condition was transmitted by heredity to all later generations, for it was not simply what biologists call an acquired variation. It was the emergence of a new kind of man; a new species, never made by God, *had sinned its way into existence…*. It was a radical alteration of his constitution." (C. S. Lewis, *The Problem of Pain* [New York: Macmillan, 1948], 70–71.)

CHAPTER 3

1. "Biblical" is put in quotes because I follow this with a crucial omission in my quotation of Rom. 7:18, the words, "in my flesh." In light of Paul's later use of "flesh" as distinct from "mind" (v. 25), it becomes obvious that this phrase in verse 18 was added purposely as not being inclusive of Paul's "inmost self" (v. 22).

2. Though this statement is true, it would be foolish for us to assume that God is not also able at any point to see Christians in terms of their behavior. Obviously he is aware of everything about people, including the sins Christians commit. Justification has to do with God's *judicial* evaluation of Christians; not of his *overall* evaluation. Some have pressed that expressive statement, "I will remember their sins and their lawless deeds no more," to mean that God actually cannot remember sins that he has forgiven. Since God

has placed in Scripture many descriptions of sins that he has forgiven, this would mean that God is not aware of what he has said in his own Word! For God to "remember" something is a figure of speech, meaning the issue remains a factor in God's evaluations and actions.

3. See Peter Toon for an excellent brief survey of the perspective of Luther, who, though acknowledging the necessity of regeneration, nevertheless made it a subtopic under justification. (Peter Toon, *Born Again: A Biblical and Theological Study of Regeneration* [Grand Rapids: Baker Book House, 1987], 101–103.) See also L. Berkhof, *Systematic Theology* (Grand Rapids: Wm. B. Eerdmans Pub. Co., 1953), 466.

4. Knudsen, after describing the failure at times in church history to distinguish between justification and regeneration, defines the differences as follows: "Regeneration is a renewal of man in his heart, a renovation in the deepest sense of his existence. As such it differs from justification. The latter is a judicial declaration that the sinner is righteous on the basis of the righteousness of Christ which has been imputed to him." (R. D. Knudsen, "Regeneration," *Zondervan Pictorial Encyclopedia of the Bible*, Vol. V, [Grand Rapids: Zondervan Publishing House], 56.) See also Berkhof, *Systematic Theology*, 513; and Millard J. Erickson, "Justification is a forensic act imputing the righteousness of Christ to the believer; it is not an actual infusing of holiness into the individual. It is a matter of declaring the person righteous, as a judge does in acquitting the accused. It is not a matter of making the person righteous or altering his or her spiritual condition." (*Christian Theology*, vol. 3 [Grand Rapids: Baker Book House, 1985], 956.) R. K. Johnston describes this divine act of imputation as having to do with "'our alien righteousness,' with being reckoned *as if* we were righteous." ("Imputation," *Evangelical Dictionary of Theology*, ed. Walter A. Elwell [Grand Rapids: Baker Book House, 1984], 555.)

5. Erickson, *Christian Theology*, 3: 959.

6. Berkhof states, "It is not sufficient that the sinner stands righteous before God [justified]; he must also be holy in his inmost life" (*Systematic Theology*, 536). In God's plan of salvation, the end in view was never to get people justified. His goal was to impart to them eternal life, life corresponding to the quality of life that Jesus possessed in his resurrection—free from sin, sin he so

recently had taken to himself. Therefore justification is the underlying foundation, the fundamental necessity for God to perform those necessary internal miracles by which actual holiness could come about. Clearly, internal holiness is the hallmark of eternal life.

7.   In order to support the view that God will change our essential nature when we die, some argue from Hebrews 12:22–24. Among those described as present in the heavenly Jerusalem, one group mentioned is "the spirits of righteous men made perfect." This statement, it is argued, proves that the human spirit is perfected at death. Such a conclusion ignores that the individuals— "the spirits"—represent Old Covenant believers since New Covenant believers have already been mentioned—"the assembly of the firstborn who are enrolled in heaven." Prior to the institution of the New Covenant age, the sacrifices could not "perfect the conscience of the worshipper" (9:9). Though they were commended for their faith, "they did not receive what was promised, since God had provided something better so that they would not, apart from us, be made perfect" (11:39, 40). Clearly, this passage has nothing to do with the perfecting of a New Covenant believer's "spirit" after death, but rather the "perfecting" of Old Covenant believers through Christ's New Covenant work.

Others argue from Paul's statement that since he had not yet "already been made perfect" (Phil. 3:12), Paul therefore believed it would only be at his death that God would change his essential nature from being sinful to being holy. To counter this, one needs but to observe the context. Paul's subject is spiritual maturity rather than the quality of his essential nature. See additional thoughts regarding this in chapter 6.

8.   Some have chosen to base such a belief on the dramatic post-salvation descriptions found in the Book of Acts. Yet in every case, with one possible exception, the experience (the baptism of the Holy Spirit) marked the momentous event when Old Covenant believers were being ushered into the New Covenant age. This was true of the disciples (Acts 2:1–4, cf. 11:15; 15:7–11), of Cornelius (Acts 10:44–47), of the followers of John the Baptist (Acts 19:1–6), and perhaps, of Paul himself. In other words, they were already "saved," in an Old Covenant sense. They had already been both justified and reconciled to God. Concerning the "possible exception," the Samaritans (Acts 8:12–17), we are hard-pressed to determine the nature of their response or

lack of response to the grace God had already provided for them under the Old Covenant. Probably they were not already part of the believing Old Covenant people of God. If so, could the delay in receiving the Spirit after their response to the message concerning the Savior have been to allow an apostolic confirmation that indeed the New Covenant age had been opened to Samaritans? Following that unique transition period, whenever a person is truly born again, Scripture teaches that an individual is immediately the possessor of "all the rights and privileges" of being a New Covenant child of God (1 Cor. 12:13).

9.   For an excellent, brief clarification regarding reconciliation see R. E. O. White, "Reconciliation," *Evangelical Dictionary of Theology,* ed. Walter Q. Elwell (Grand Rapids: Baker Book House, 1984), 917–18.

10.   William Childs Robinson, "Reconciliation," *Baker's Dictionary of Theology,* ed. Everett F. Harrison (Grand Rapids: Baker Book House, 1960), 438. More accurately, reconciliation produces in a person a *desire to obey*. It does not in itself provide the enablement to obey.

11.   Old Testament believers also received both God's judicial act of justification (see Rom. 3:21–25) and his interior miracle of reconciliation in anticipation of the work of the cross. As an example, God called Abraham "my friend" (2 Chron. 20:7; Is. 41:8). Certainly David took great delight in both God and his law. (Among the many examples, see Ps. 5:11; 18:1; 19:7–10.)

12.   The expression "born again" can also be understood to mean "born from above." Since Jesus did not correct Nicodemus's assumption that it meant "again" (John 3:4), we may assume that meaning is appropriate. See Erickson, *Christian Theology,* 3:943. Since both "again" and "from above" are true, some have wondered if Jesus may have had in mind both ideas. See Leon Morris, *The Gospel According to John* (Grand Rapids: Eerdmans, 1971), 212, n. 13.

13.   Toon comments, "The divine begetting causes new life. What happens to the believer is an inner resurrection in anticipation of bodily resurrection that will occur at the parousia. It is passing from death to life." After referring to John 5:24 and 8:51, he adds, "That this new life is from God through the work of the Son and the Spirit is made clear in John 5:21 and 6:63 where the apostle uses the words *zoopooiein,* which means 'to give life' or 'to make alive'." (Toon, *Born Again: A Biblical and Theological Study of Regeneration*, 32.)

14. Morris, *The Gospel According to John,* 218. Parallel are Donald Guthrie's comments referring to John 3: "The words of Jesus implied something so radical that it cannot be effected by man's own efforts…. It requires a supernatural activity to transform a man into a new creature….

"The new birth involves a person's exchanging his old nature for a new nature, an acceptance of a new kind of origin, an entry into a new relationship with God."

Referring to 1 John 4:7 and a new knowledge of God, he says, "This suggests that new birth leads to an entirely new appraisal of the 'world', a deliverance from its normal pull." (Donald Guthrie, *New Testament Theology,* [Downers Grove, Ill.: InterVarsity Press, 1981], 585–86.)

Regarding John 3, Toon states, "When born the baby is of the same human nature and flesh as the parents. Consider now being begotten by God or birth from above. This is the work of the Holy Spirit, and thus what is created is new spiritual life in the soul, a nonphysical, nonfleshly reality." (Toon, *Born Again,* 140.) (In light of the more common NT use of "spirit" as referring to that "nonfleshly reality," see note 17.)

15. Though the immediate context of the expression, "a life-giving Spirit," looks forward to our future "spiritual bodies," (cf. Rom. 8:11), Paul was well aware of the pre-bodily resurrection truth of John 3:6 and the sharp contrast between the "soulishness" of the unregenerate and the "spiritualness" of the regenerate (1 Cor. 2:14–15). In other words, Christ is a "life-giving Spirit," both in our spiritual resurrection (Rom. 6), and in our yet future bodily resurrection.

16. Renald Showers states: "The reception of the new nature [referring to regeneration] produces a radical change in him, but it does not change his inherent kind of being. He is called a 'new man' (Col. 3:10), but he is still a man. The reception of the new nature does not produce a metaphysical change in a person." (Renald Showers, *The New Nature* [Neptune, N. J.: Loizeaux Bros., 1986], 19.) The author rightly goes to considerable length to deny that the new birth results in a product who is no longer metaphysically human (see pages 49, 51, 67). But he casts an undeserved shadow on the miracle when he attempts to clarify his use of "metaphysical." He states, "He is the same person metaphysically after the new birth as before the new birth. He continues to

have the same personal name, background, parents, place of employment, and residence" (p. 74). But it is more than that. Though remaining human, regenerate people indeed *have* an additional new parentage because they are a product of divine birthing (and, for that matter, a new residence also).

Cannot we allow God the right to perform a miracle that transcends our "metaphysical" classifications without jeopardizing our creatureliness or his uniqueness as deity? See Leon Morris's comments regarding Nicodemus's response: "Can physical birth be repeated? Since this lesser miracle is quite impossible, how can we envisage a much greater miracle, *the remaking of man's essential being. Regeneration is a sheer impossibility!"* (*Gospel According to John*, 218, italics mine).

17. This is a most important statement, yet easily misunderstood. Both humanness and physicalness are good, not bad. In fact our ultimate state will involve both, though it is probable that DNA factors will be irrelevant in our glorified bodies. "Spirit" then, refers to a level within our overall being that by regeneration has been infused with life. Morris quotes G. Appleton (*John's Witness to Jesus*, London, 1955, 29), "There are two levels of existence; the one is the sphere of flesh and the other of spirit. On each level like produces like. A man can only pass from the lower order, the realm of flesh, into the higher order, the realm of spirit, by being born again" (Morris, *Gospel According to John*, 219). See chapter 5 for additional thoughts regarding the concept of "spirit."

18. Arthur C. Custance, "Man in Adam and in Christ," in *Doorway Papers*, 3 vols. (Grand Rapids: Zondervan, 1975), 3:343–44. Obviously he is using the word *species* in a broad rather than in a strict biological sense, as also used by C. S. Lewis with reference to the Fall of man (see note 10, chapter 2).

19. Our theological systems were originally built, I would imagine, as a sort of scaffolding around the truth of God. Not to support it, and certainly not to build it, but rather in order to get up close to it and observe its marvelous structure. Too easily, the scaffolding has replaced the building as the point of focus.

20. Apart from what happened in Acts 2, there is good reason for assuming the disciples' lives would have continued much the same as before that event. Though they were aware of the Great Commission and the prospect of Jesus' return, the transformation of their lives awaited the events of Pentecost. Cf. John 21:2.

21. Though Peter took this expression from Lev. 25:23, he used it in a distinctly new way. Under the Old Covenant, the Promised Land was owned by God. Therefore the Israelites were to remember they were but tenants—"aliens and sojourners." By contrast, in the New Covenant age, Peter understood Jesus' words, "not of the world," to mean that believers were aliens in a new sense.

22. Knudson states, "When one speaks of the radicality of the new birth, he can only mean that this birth affects the root (*radix*) of human existence." Later he adds, "Regeneration is presented in Scriptures as involving a real change in the believer.... The radicality and definiteness of this change are expressed in marked contrasts: that between lust and holiness, darkness and light (1 Pet. 2:9), death and resurrection to a new life (1 Pet. 3:21, 24). Beforehand, one is not a citizen but a stranger to the kingdom of God; afterwards, he is a citizen of the kingdom (Col. 1:13) and a member of God's household." (Robert D. Knudsen, "The Nature of Regeneration," *Christian Faith and Modern Theology*, ed. Carl F. H. Henry [Grand Rapids: Baker Book House, 1974], 308, 316–17.)

23. Two of the more commonly used terms in Christian literature are *sin nature* (or old nature) and *new nature*. Showers defines *nature* as a "disposition." According to him a Christian has two dispositions. (Showers, *The New Nature*, 15–19 and so throughout the book.) Though the first listed dictionary definition of the word *nature* involves the essential character of a thing, as is seen in its use in Eph. 2:3, Showers has chosen a secondary meaning that enables him to describe Christians as having two natures. Apparently Dwight Pentecost, following the primary meaning, concludes that a Christian's sin nature is his essential nature. (J. Dwight Pentecost, *Pattern for Maturity* [Chicago: Moody Press, 1966], 100.) Cullmann, describes *flesh* in "sin nature" terminology as a "transcendent power," and as "the power of death" that "seizes the outer and inner man together." (Oscar Cullmann, "Immortality of the Soul or Resurrection of the Dead, the Witness of the New Testament," *Immortality and Resurrection,"* ed. Krister Stendall [New York: Macmillan], 25.) Such a statement comes close to making flesh some sort of sin nature "substance" distinct from the individual. Though *flesh* is often used in an ethical sense, I know of no biblical basis for removing from this word its fundamental material or physical base.

Regarding the term *sin nature*, Russell comments, "the focus is upon the fact that the New Testament *never* speaks of a person possessing a sin nature nor of a Christian possessing a new nature. In other words, the writers of the New Testament never use the most common and obvious term for 'nature' (*phusis*) to refer to a sin nature or a new nature." (Walt Russell, "The Apostle Paul's View of the 'Sin Nature'/'New Nature' Struggle," *Christian Perspectives on Being Human, A Multidisciplinary Approach to Integration*, ed. J. P. Moreland and James Porter, [Grand Rapids: Baker Book House, 1993], 208.) In his conclusion he adds, "Rather than a divided self, distraught over an internal battle between flesh and Spirit, Paul pictures a new self, emboldened by the liberating work of the Holy Spirit and in vibrant community with others of like identity." (p. 226)

In view of the normal meaning of the word *nature* as referring to one's essential character, one's essence, I believe it is confusing to refer to Christians as having both a sin nature and a new nature. On the other hand, as we will emphasize in chapters 4 and 5, it is fitting to describe a Christian as being a "new natured" person (their essential nature), while still possessing a most serious fleshly propensity toward sin (but not as being their essential nature). Some may choose to call that fleshly propensity one's "sin nature," yet maintain it as distinct from one's essential nature. Other than the problem of misunderstanding, I see nothing wrong with this usage.

24. John Stott writes, "The mention of 'born of him' leads John to an outburst of wonder at God's love in making us His *sons*, or better 'children' (*tekna*, derived from *tekein*, 'to beget'), the allusion being to the divine nature we have received through being begotten of God rather than our filial status." (John R. W. Stott, *The Epistles of John* [Grand Rapids: Wm. B. Eerdmans, 1964], 118.)

This truth is further underlined in 1 John 3:9 where John states that "God's seed abides them." The "by birth" idea is also the context of John 1:12–13. Though Berkhof says "Believers are first children of God by adoption," the Bible teaches the exact reverse as also expressed by Walvoord, "one must be born 'of God' (John 1:13) in order to become a child of God." (John F. Walvoord, *The Holy Spirit* [Wheaton: Van Kampen Press, 1954], 131.) Sadly, in some theological writings the marvelous truth of being a child of God "by birth" has been overshadowed by an emphasis on the adoption concept. See J. I. Packer, *Keep In Step with the Spirit,* (Old Tappan, New Jersey: Fleming H. Revell, 1984), 49, 56, 104; and Robert P. Meye, "Spirituality," *Dictionary of Paul and His Epistles,* ed. Gerald F. Hawthrone, Ralph Martin, Daniel G. Reid, (Downers Grove, Ill.: InterVarsity Press, 1993), 910. Both link the word *children* to adoption, whereas the Bible consistently links the status of sonship with adoption. Rom. 8:15–21 ties the two together, but always birth precedes adoption. As Toon states, "We become *tekna* by regeneration and *huios* [sons] by adoption." (Toon, *Born Again,* 25.) Actually, in the only passage in which Paul elaborated on the meaning of "adoption" (Gal. 4:1–6), it involved a point in time for a child when heirship was made official—the prior birth into the family is already assumed. Common usage of this term today never conveys this idea. (The adoption illustration in this passage, though similar to its use in Rom. 8:23, is distinct from its use in Rom. 8:15.)

25. It is quite popular these days to use the statement "God loves me and accepts me as I am." I would imagine this means different things to different people. To some it's simply another way of expressing the thought of the invitation hymn, "Just As I Am." As such, it communicates the truth that an unsaved person has nothing to offer God toward his own salvation. He comes to God as the sinner that he is, casting himself upon God's grace. To someone else this expression may point to the fact that since we as Christians are waiting for "the redemption of our bodies" (Rom. 8:23), God does indeed accept our mortality as it presently is, including all its weaknesses (Rom. 8:26). Even more than *acceptance* is the tremendous encouragement that Jesus *fully understands* because he once shared in our flesh weaknesses even to the degree of "being tempted in all things as we are" (Heb. 4:15, NIV). More than *understands,* he *empathizes!* But beyond these ideas this statement may lead one to several erroneous impressions:

(a) If God "accepts me as I am" then there is no need for regeneration. Yet being a holy God, he can accept me into his holy family only because he has made a radical change in me, "as God's chosen people, *holy* and dearly loved" (Col. 3:12, italics mine). Salvation means that I will never again be what I was before. By contrast, to use this statement with the idea that the "I am" is the sinner that I am, is to reduce salvation to the idea that God accepts me because he has forgiven and justified me. *His own pure character demands more than that* (1 John 1:3–6; Eph. 5:8).

(b) Most people, I would imagine, assume that to say "God loves me" means that he finds me (and everybody else) "lovable." By all means he loves them with *agape* love, which involves an act of the will on the part of the one who chooses to give himself to another for their welfare *totally apart from* their being lovable. *Phileo* love, which involves one's natural affectionate response to a delightful object, is never used of God's love for people except toward his responsive followers. (The one apparent exception is Revelation 3:19, "I reprove and discipline those whom I love [phileo].") The context justifies the conclusion that these Christians were not so much rebellious as they were ignorant and deceived. They thought all was well. Cf. John 16:27 *(phileo)* and Mark 10:21 *(agapao)*.

26. Though some may use the expression "your position in Christ" as expressing an internal, rather than a positional, external truth, it is also commonly used as referring to justification (an external truth). Because of this I believe this expression confuses rather than clarifies and is better left unused unless it is explained. The same may be said of "this is who you are in Christ." What are we getting at when we say this—justification or regeneration? At least in Rom. 6:11, 23 Paul connects "in Christ" with God's interior miracle of imparting within us Jesus' risen life. Due to the intertwining of "in Christ" and "Christ in you," which we find in his writings (Rom. 8:1, 10; cf. 2 Cor. 5:17; 13:5; Col. 2:27–28), it may be best to assume that more often he used "in Christ" to include all that is part of the grace of God in the saving work of Christ. He may also have used it as an abbreviation for the fuller expression used by Jesus, "you in me and I in you." See also the contexts in which "in Christ" is found in Eph. 2:4–10. For examples of a correct use of the phrase "that is my position in Christ" with regard to Rom. 6, see D. Martin Lloyd-Jones, *Romans, The New Man, Exposition of Chapter 6* (Grand Rapids: Zondervan, 1972), 118, 119, 262. For an extended consideration of the expression, "in Christ," see Donald Guthrie, *New Testament Theology* (Downers Grove, Ill.: InterVarsity Press, 1981), 647–53.

27. The following words of Jesus would appear not only to contradict this

statement but also 1 John 3:7: "If you then, who are evil, know how to give good gifts to your children, how much more will the heavenly Father give the Holy Spirit to those who ask him!" (Luke 11:13) Perhaps Jesus was speaking in broad terms as referring to people in general. Perhaps, in light of the fact the Spirit had not yet been given (cf. John 7:39), he was describing Old Covenant individuals who had not experienced the life-transforming work of the Spirit that John in his epistle assumes of his readers (cf. 1 John 4:13). As a lesser possibility, Jesus may have referred to those who were evil in a similar sense to Rom. 7:21–23.

28. Erickson states, "Mankind has a twofold problem as a result of sin and the Fall. On the one hand, there is a basic corruption of human nature; our moral character has been polluted through sin. This aspect of the curse is nullified by regeneration, which reverses the direction and general tendencies of human nature. The other problem remains however: our guilt or liability to punishment for having failed to fulfill God's expectations. It is to this problem that justification relates" (p. 954). Later he states, "The union with Christ which brings justification also brings the new life." Clearly his reference to new life points to regeneration. (Erickson, *Christian Theology*, 3: 960.) John Wesley wrote, "Though it be allowed that justification and the new birth are, in point of time, inseparable from each other, yet they are easily distinguished, as not being the same, but things of widely different nature. Justification implies only a relative, the new birth, a real change. God in justifying does something *for* us; in begetting us again, he does the work *in* us. The former changes our outward relation to God, so that of enemies we became children; by the latter, our inmost souls are changed, so that of sinners we become saints." (Quoted favorably by Alister E. McGrath, *Justification By Faith, What It Means to Us Today* [Grand Rapids: Zondervan Pub. House., 1988], 65.) See also McGrath, *Iustitia Dei, A History of the Christian Doctrine of Justification*, vol. 1 (Cambridge University Press), Section 5, especially the final paragraph, p. 51.

John Stott, after underlining the true meaning of justification that involves God conferring upon us a "righteous status," then says, "If 'just' is used to signify 'made new, made alive'...this would be a misuse of the word 'just', however, for what is being described now is not justification, but regeneration." (p. 185)

Later he adds, "It would be entirely mistaken to make the equation 'salvation equals justification'. 'Salvation' is the comprehensive word, but has many facets which are illustrated by different pictures, of which justification is only one. Redemption, as we have seen, is another, and bears witness to our radical deliverance from sin as well as guilt. Another is recreation, so that "if anyone is in Christ, he is a new creation" (2 Cor. 5:17). Yet another is regeneration or new birth, which is the inward work of the Holy Spirit, who then remains as a gracious indwelling presence, transforming the believer into the image of Christ, which is the process of sanctification. All these belong together. Regeneration is not an aspect of justification, but both are aspects of salvation, and neither can take the place of the other. Indeed, the great affirmation 'he saved us' is broken down into its component parts, which are 'the washing of rebirth and renewal by the Holy Spirit' on the one hand and being 'justified by his grace' on the other (Titus 3:5–7). The justifying work of the Son and the regenerating work of the Spirit cannot be separated" (p. 188).

"Once we hold fast that the work of the Son for us and the work of the Spirit in us, that is to say, justification and regeneration, are inseparable twins, it is quite safe to go on insisting that justification is an external, legal declaration that the sinner has been put right with God, forgiven and reinstated." p. 189 (John R. W. Stott, *The Cross of Christ* [Downers Grove, Ill.: InterVarsity Press, 1986].)

Some classify regeneration under "sanctification," which may cloud its uniqueness due to the common practice of describing sanctification as being either "positional" (based on the truth of justification); "experiential" (having to do with Christian growth); and "ultimate" (realized after death). By such classification, the intrinsic new birth miracle is bypassed.

29. Perhaps this illustration doesn't "ring a bell" with you at all. Well then, think of one that does. Think of some sinful thing you want to do, but for Jesus' sake you don't, even though you continue to want to do it.

30. 2 Pet. 1:4; Rom. 6:11; 1 Pet. 2:11.

31. Jesus' righteous life and his substitutionary death are the basis for God's act of justifying a sinner. Nothing else was needed for God to make such a pronouncement. Since Christ perfectly accomplished the task given him by the Father, it was then quite right for Paul to say "he was raised because of our justification," Rom. 4:25, NASB). Except to confirm the adequacy of Christ's

saving work and the Father's full approval, his resurrection in itself was not part of the basis upon which justification rested.

On the other hand, *his resurrection was fundamental to regeneration* because regeneration is the imparting of Christ's risen life to an individual. New birth is inseparable from being "made alive together with Christ" (Eph. 2:5) when before, we were dead. The same is expressed in Col. 2:13, "when we were dead…God made us alive together with him." Therefore new birth and spiritual resurrection are essentially the same thing. (Compare Rom. 5:9 with 1 Pet. 1:3.)

Having made these distinctions, it is of value to remember that we prefer truth to be dispensed in neat, well-defined packages. We thrive on categories and precise definitions. Things are easier to file that way! Since God does not always bend to our wishes, we must admit that we may at times make sharper distinctions between particular words than God intended.

32. This paragraph parallels the logical sequence between Rom. 3–5 and 6–8. As already stated, the goal of the book of Romans is not justification by faith, but newness of life—eternal life—to the glory of God.

CHAPTER 4

1. Adam Ford, *Universe, God, Science and the Human Person* (Mystic, Conn.: Twenty-third Publications, 1987), 58, 127–28.

2. Ibid., 127–28.

3. Without any doubt, this promise anticipated the New Covenant age. Nevertheless this promise of a new heart does not allow us to assume that Jer. 17:9 ("The heart is devious above all else; it is perverse—who can understand it?") is descriptive of every human being before the coming of this age. Within the Jeremiah context, the "heart" God had in view was the stubborn, evil heart of wicked Judah. See 16:12, and especially 17:1. Certainly that was not Jeremiah's heart. See 12:3; 15:16; 16:19; 17:12–16; 20:12. Yes, Judah's heart was desperately sick as described in 17:5–6. But note the sharp contrast in the verses that follow in 17:7–8. Though Hebrews 11:39–40 acknowledged that Old Testament believers missed the full blessings of the New Covenant age, God still did special works of grace in individual lives to the degree that some could be spoken of as having pure hearts. See Ps. 24:4; 73:1, 13. Though we

may question their possession of the risen life of Christ (a New Covenant reality), those godly Old Covenant believers most certainly had experienced the inward miracle of reconciliation—a changed heart attitude toward God.

4. Saint Chrysostom, *Nicene and Post-Nicene Fathers of the Christian Church,* vol. 12, ed. Philip Schaff (Grand Rapids: Wm. B. Eerdmans Pub. Co., 1979), 319, 320.

5. See Richard B. Gaffin Jr., "'Life-giving Spirit': Probing the Center of Paul's Pneumatology," *Journal of the Evangelical Theological Society* (Dec. 1998): 573–89.

6. The contrast expressed in 1 Cor. 15:45 makes it difficult to justify Erickson's statement, "the new birth is the restoration of human nature to what it originally was intended to be and what in fact it was before sin entered the human race at the time of the fall." (Millard J. Erickson, *Introducing Christian Doctrine,* ed. L. Arnold Hustad [Grand Rapids: Baker Book House, 1992], 301.) See also his *Christian Theology,* vol. 3 (Grand Rapids: Baker Book House, 1985), 944.

7. Johannas Behm, "Kainos," *Theological Dictionary of the New Testament,* vol. 3, ed. Gerhard Kittel (Grand Rapids: Wm. B. Eerdmans Pub. Co., 1965), 449. Though he comments, "Christ himself is the new man…the initiator of the new creation of the last time," he then adds, "For the individual the new man is both a gift and a task." Clearly the individual believer is part of the new creation.

Commenting on the difference between the Old Covenant and the New Covenant, Ronald Mayers states, "There is one final aspect that indicates *why* the indwelling of the Holy Spirit during the 'new age,' the 'last days,' is discontinuous with the experience of the people of God in the Old Testament. The giving of the Holy Spirit is the 'downpayment,' the earnest money, that the *last days have really begun.* This is the Messianic era! This is how Peter in Acts 2 interprets Joel's prophecy in regard to the Holy Spirit. Paul likewise affirms this not only in 2 Corinthians 1:22 and 5:5, but more fully in Ephesians 1:13, 14." (Ronald Mayers, *Evangelical Perspectives* [University Press of America, 1987], 110.)

8. Millard J. Erickson, *Christian Theology,* 3:168 (Grand Rapids: Baker Book House, 1985), 960. Quotation from J. A. Ziesler, *The Meaning of Right-*

eousness in Paul (Cambridge: Cambridge University Press, 1972), 168.

9. J. Knox Chamblin, *Paul and the Self, Apostolic Teaching for Personal Wholeness* (Grand Rapids: Baker Book House, 1993), 85. Note also the following from *Baker Encyclopedia of the Bible*: "Ultimately, the contrast in this passage [1 Cor. 15:42–49] is between two successive world orders, creation and its consummation (new creation), each beginning with an Adam....

"The controlling emphasis is on the unity between the resurrection of Christ and believers (cf. 1 Cor 15:12–20; Col. 1:18). In the NT proclamation the resurrection of Christ is the great redemptive counterpart to creation (Rom. 4:17). According to the NT, the new creation is a present reality, dating from the resurrection of Christ.... Where the Spirit is at work as the gift of the glorified Christ, the new creation is present.

"The new creation is the eschatological fulfillment promised and anticipated in the OT. As such it has already been inaugurated and realized by the work of Christ (the last Adam), particularly his death and resurrection, and will be consummated at his return. The interval in between receives its fundamental character from the coexistence of the two creations; the new has begun, while concurrently the old continues to pass away (1 Cor. 7:31)...the new creation is the longed for 'age to come'...because Christ died and was raised again (2 Cor. 5:15), anyone in Christ is already a participant in the new creation order (v 17)." He then adds the NEB rendering of 2 Cor. 5:17, "When anyone is united to Christ, there is a new world; the old order is gone, and a new order has already begun." ("New Creation, New Creature," *Baker Encyclopedia of the Bible,* vol. 2, ed. Walter A. Elwell [Grand Rapids: Baker Book House, 1988], 1545–46.) See also I. H. Marshall's chapter 12, "The Hope of a New Age: The Kingdom of God in the New Testament," in *Jesus the Savior, Studies in New Testament Theology* (Downers Grove, Ill.: InterVarsity Press, 1990), 213–38. Danker went so far as to title his commentary on Luke *Jesus and the New Age.* (Frederick W. Danker, [Philadelphia: Fortress Press, 1988].) He concludes as follows: "Jesus had thought the unthinkable, dared the unbearable, and achieved the impossible. We only await the end of the end time, for with Jesus, the Great Benefactor, came the New Age" (p. 402).

10. F. Godet, *A Commentary on the Gospel of Luke,* vol. 1 (Edinburgh: T. & T. Clark, n.d.), 350–51. Geldenhuys comments, "But although he, as the last

envoy of the Old Covenant, is nearest to Christ and thus the most important of all, he takes a lower place than even the most insignificant member of the New Covenant. He belonged to the period of preparation and had not yet learned to know Jesus as the Crucified One, as the Risen Redeemer, and as the One who through His Spirit makes His habitation in the believer's heart and life." (Norval Geldenhuys, *Commentary on the Gospel of Luke*, [Grand Rapids: Eerdmans, 1979], 227.) Also Alfred Plummer, "By his office John belonged to the old dispensation; he was its last and highest product...but he belonged to the era of preparation. In spiritual privileges, in grace, and in knowledge any even of the humbler members of the Kingdom are superior to him. He is a servant, they are sons; he is the friend of the Bridegroom, they are his spouse." (Alfred Plummer, *A Critical and Exegetical Commentary on the Gospel According to Luke* [Edinburgh: T. & T. Clark, 1981], 205.)

11. Seeds from certain types of plants do not necessarily produce a tree true to the mother tree. That is why grafting is necessary. Also, many fruit trees are grafted because the root stock has some particular qualities—cold or disease resistance, rapid growth—that have value. Yet apart from being grafted, they would produce inferior fruit, or perhaps none at all.

12. I first came across this grafting picture as analogous with the miracle of regeneration in Abraham Kuyper, *The Work of the Holy Spirit* (Grand Rapids: Eerdmans, 1946), 311.

13. Though translations as a rule say "that the body of sin might *be destroyed*," scholars generally agree that the Greek word more pointedly underlines powerlessness or inactivity than actual destruction. See Leon Morris, *The Epistle to the Romans* (Grand Rapids: Wm. B. Eerdmans Pub. Co., 1988), 252. Though this was the divine purpose, Rom. 6:12 ("do not let sin exercise dominion in your mortal bodies") warns us against any simplistic assumption that sin is no longer a powerful foe.

For a clear refutation of a figurative rather than a physical interpretation of "body of sin," see John Murray, *The Epistle to the Romans*, vol. 1 (Grand Rapids: Wm. B. Eerdmans Pub. Co., 1968), 220–21.

14. The following is an example of an "as though" approach to Rom. 6: "The Bible says that in the present Christian life we are in practice to live by faith *as though we are dead* now. 'For in that he died, he died unto sin once for

all: but in that he liveth he liveth unto God. Likewise reckon (this is an act of faith) ye also yourselves to be dead indeed unto sin' (Romans 6:10, 11a)." (Francis Schaeffer, *True Spirituality* [Wheaton: Tyndale House, 1971], 40.) This statement is followed by ten "as thoughs" on the next three pages. The significance of this terminology is to be understood in light of his later statement: "judicially we are already dead and raised.... Judicially this is a reality" (p. 56). In other words, he understood Rom. 6 as still centering on justification rather than the actual infusing of resurrection life—regeneration.

15. See chapter 3, note 26.

16. A brief presentation of this point of view is found in Craig Massey, *Adjust or Self-Destruct, A Study of the Believer's Two Natures* (Chicago: Moody Press, 1977). For a more extensive study, see Renald Showers, *The New Nature,* (Neptune, New Jersey: Loizeaux Brothers, 1986). Showers prefers the term *disposition* rather than *nature*. At least he views the miracle of regeneration as being significant enough to say, "The sinful disposition wages war against that which would control the believer to go contrary to *what his inner self wills in accord with the holy nature and will of God*" (italics mine, p. 102). He also quotes with approval John Murray's statement, "this delight is not peripheral but belongs to that which is deepest and inmost in his moral and spiritual being" (p. 98). If Showers would have gone far enough to agree that since the "new disposition" characterizes the believer's inner self, it is therefore the expression of a believer's essential being, I would agree with much he has stated. In many ways, his book is excellent. Nevertheless, as long as the "two disposition" idea is seen as a parallel relationship, such a view is flawed.

17. See J. Dwight Pentecost, *Pattern For Maturity* (Chicago: Moody Press, 1966), 92–93.

18. Many attempt to avoid the radical nature of John's statement by pointing out that John uses the present tense, which conveys the idea of a continuous action. Hence "no one who is born of God *practices* sin." Regarding the inadequacy of this interpretation, see chapter 6.

19. Any nonprejudiced reading of Rom. 7:17, 20–22 also points away from any *parallel* "two dispositions" model of a saved individual. Though Paul acknowledged personal responsibility, he recognized that he most deeply delighted in the law of God; whereas the "law of sin" operated in his members.

20. At this point someone is bound to say, "That sounds like the false doctrine of sinless perfection!" In no way am I suggesting that after regeneration a second crisis moment must take place—"entire sanctification"—when one's bent toward sinning is completely removed. Nevertheless, with the continuing enablement of the Holy Spirit, our bodies can become "slaves of righteousness." This is John's expectation and the basis for my statement regarding our fully pleasing God.

But this does not change the natural bent of our flesh toward sin, "the law of sin that dwells in my members" (Rom. 7:23). The various demanding, sinful thought patterns programmed in our brains are still there—ready for instant retrieval. As long as this circumstance remains, we cannot claim total perfection, even though our behavior may be consistently righteous. Happily, when "the redemption of our bodies" at last takes place, we will experience that complete perfection.

21. Here (Gal. 5:16, NASB) Paul uses a double negative in order to underline the emphatic certainty of his statement.

22. See chapter 6.

23. The following may serve to illustrate the difficulties involved in making this adjustment. Imagine with me a great profit-making company whose essential purpose is to manufacture poisonous gas for the army. Department by department the company busies itself daily with this goal. In the chemistry lab they are absorbed in the search for newer, deadlier, more destructive gases. The bookkeepers bend over the records in pursuit of profit/loss comparisons. Salesmen thumb through well-worn synonym-finders in search of positive adjectives. Quality control inspectors rush about with clipboards and sharpened number three pencils. All busy. All geared toward that one consuming goal: producing poisonous gas for profit.

And then a remarkable thing happens to the poisonous gas company. The entire board of directors of the company changes hands. It is actually a brand new company, not only because of a change in leadership and name, but also because of a change in its essential purpose. The new company rejects the profit-making motive. It is now committed by its very nature to be a nonprofit company. Its new product? Making life-saving oxygen for hospitals. It is more than a corporate name change. More than a simple paper shuffle. It is an actual change of identity. Well, that solves everything! Everyone appreciates oxygen. This new company should work out just fine.

But it isn't quite that simple. All of the company's machinery and all of those varied departments are still geared-up for the same old poisonous purpose. If left to themselves, each of those departments would still measure their success as they always measured success—producing poison for profit. That's what life was all about for many of those old career poison producers. Just because the company changes doesn't mean all the departments automatically snap to attention. It's tough to teach the old hands new tasks. So management has a clear-cut job to do. An intense indoctrination program has to take place, filtering from the top right on down.

"Listen chemists, you must change your concept of success in this department. Junk your poison formulas. Success is now to be measured by the quality of lifesaving oxygen you produce. Bookkeepers, from now on you will have to forego the pleasure you used to derive from being the first to know the size of the company's profit. Forget profit. Management expects you to simply keep the books and keep them well. Understood?"

Understood perhaps, but not appreciated. "Why do we have to be so different? Every other company judges its success just like we used to!" "We've always measured ourselves against the competition. That added some spice to life!" "You're asking us to reject most of what we've learned. It may sound easy for you up there on the top floor, but not down here!"

CHAPTER 5

1.   Though I believe the following may be an overstatement, it underlines the difficulties involved in formulating definitions. "The New Testament neither implicitly contains nor explicitly teaches a philosophical anthropology as such or any theoretically precise or systematically consistent definitions of body, mind, soul, or spirit. Its use of anthropological terminology is extremely complex and diverse. Particular words such as *sarx, soma, psyche, pneuma,* and *kardia* have a variety of meanings that can vary from one New Testament book to another. Scholars cannot even achieve consensus in mapping the diversity of nuances and connotations." (John W. Cooper, *Body, Soul, and Life Everlasting*

[Grand Rapids: Wm. B. Eerdmans Pub. Co., 1989], 106.)

From a somewhat different perspective, regarding the occurrence of "spirit" in Rom. 8:16, Fee states, "By the very way Paul speaks of God's Spirit bearing witness with ours, he is saying something about his anthropological perspective—that we have 'a spirit' (are a 'spirit'?), which is distinguishable from the body. This is probably equal to 'the inner person' to whom Paul refers in 2 Cor. 4:16. This seems so clear, and so matter of fact, that all other *pneuma* texts in Paul that refer to the human spirit need to be heard in light of this one." (Gordon D. Fee, *God's Empowering Presence, The Holy Spirit in the Letters of Paul* [Peabody, Mass: Hendrickson Pub. Inc., 1994], 568.) Fee's uncertainty regarding our "being" a "spirit" is unnecessary. As synonymous with "inner person," at least some of Paul's references to the human spirit equate it with that level of selfhood we most deeply *are* rather than something we *have*.

2.   As an example, disembodied saints in heaven waiting the resurrection are described either as "souls" (Rev. 6:9) or "spirits" (Heb. 12:23). Also Mary's use of "soul" and "spirit" (Luke 1:46, 47) is better understood as an example of Hebrew poetry expressing synonymous parallelism. Guthrie may have some justification in assuming that 1 Thess. 5:23 ("body, soul and spirit") is an example of "piling up of terms…for emphasis rather than for definition." (Donald Guthrie, *New Testament Theology* [Downers Grove, Ill.: InterVarsity Press, 1981], 165.) This may also be the idea conveyed in Mark 12:30. See also George Eldon Ladd, *A Theology of the New Testament,* (Grand Rapids: Wm. B. Eerdmans, 1974), 457. Nevertheless there are exceptions to this synonymous idea. For example, Rom. 7:22-26 describes one's "inmost being" at odds with one's "flesh."

3.   Though we may be sure that the "material" aspects of the new heavens and earth will be quite different from anything we now know, we know we will have real bodies. Paul considered this as a matter of importance. See 2 Cor. 5:1–5 and 1 Cor. 15:35–54. In the latter passage, the NRSV contrasts "physical bodies" with "spiritual bodies," leading us to assume future bodies will not be physical. This is quite misleading since their word *physical* is actually the word *soulish*.

4.   Such an idea appears disturbing to some Christians because they needlessly fear that such a belief automatically paves the way to naturalistic evolution.

If one acknowledges that what exists is the product of direct, divine, personal, creative acts, all naturalistic explanations are automatically eliminated.

5. Among modern English versions, the NRSV (the major version used in this book), the NASB, and the NKJV are the most consistent in rendering the Hebrew *basar* and the Greek *sarx* as "flesh." Variations from this (as seen especially in the NIV), with few exceptions are not only unnecessary but often misleading.

6. "The Hebrew word for body occurs only fourteen times in the Old Testament and never stands in contrast to the soul (*nephesh*). More often the word flesh (*basar*) is used to designate the body (23 times). This word carries primarily a physical meaning. One significant usage is 'flesh' as a symbol of human frailty in relation to God. *Basar* appears as something that men and animals possess in their weakness, which God does not possess." (Ladd, *A Theology of the New Testament*, 458.) Also Robinson, "*Basar* stands for the whole life-substance of men or beasts as organized in corporeal form." (John A. T. Robinson, *The Body, A Study in Pauline Theology* [Philadelphia: Westminster Press, 1952], 13.)

7. Boivin states, "A Hebraic model [of personhood], though, tends not to distinguish between the physical and the metaphysical. It distinguishes between the physical in its fallen or maladaptive state and the physical in its completed or redeemed state (man and world in God's kingdom here on earth) Isa. 11:1–9, NIV.... A Hebraic model, therefore, conceptualizes the person within a physical and natural realm, without equating individuals with animals or eliminating those divinely inspired aspects of humanity." (Michael J. Boivin, "The Hebraic Model of the Person: Toward a Unified Psychological Science," *Journal of Psychology and Theology* 19:163, 164.)

8. Commenting on the distinction between the words *flesh* (*sarx*) and *body* (*soma*), Kreitzer states, "It is sometimes difficult to make sharp distinctions between *soma* and *sarx* ('flesh') as terms of human mortality, although the latter is almost always used negatively by Paul to describe the physical side of human beings as they are driven by purely human concerns and interests." (Larry J. Kreitzer, "The Body," *Dictionary of Paul and His Epistles*, ed. Gerald F. Hawthorne, Ralph Martin, Daniel G. Reid [Downers Grove, Ill.: InterVarsity Press, 1993], 72.)

Jesus' use of *sarx* in John 6:51–56 is unique. In speaking of his giving of his life "for the world" (6:51), Jesus pointed to the literal pouring out of his life at the cross involving his flesh and his blood. Nevertheless his reference to "eating" his flesh and "drinking" his blood is equated with "whoever eats me" (6:57). This carries us above a purely physical sense to a reference to ingesting *his life as our life*. The parallel he drew between himself as having life "because of the Father," is therefore identical for us. We live "because of" him. This unique nonphysical use of "flesh" is also supported by the fact he described himself as "living bread" prior to his incarnation.

9. Though in many nontheologically sensitive passages the NIV has kept the word *flesh* (*sarx*) as "flesh" (some 33 times), 23 times in crucial theological passages, the translators chose the term *sinful nature*, with an additional eight renderings expressing the same concept. Examples of this prejudiced and misleading rendering of "flesh" in crucial theological passages are Rom. 7:5, 18, 25; 8:3 ("sinful man"), 4, 5, 8, 9, 12, 13; Gal. 5:13, 16, 17, 19, 24; 6:8. By contrast, the NIV never renders the parallel OT Hebrew word for flesh (*basar*) as "sin nature."

A classic example of the NIV's (and several commentaries') aversion to equating *flesh* with the body and their resulting bent toward rendering *flesh* as "sin nature" is seen in 1 Cor. 5:5. There (according to the NIV), Paul commanded the church in Corinth, in confronting an individual who was involved in gross sin, to "hand this man over to Satan, so that the sinful nature [flesh] may be destroyed and his spirit saved on the day of the Lord." This issue is worth our careful consideration, not only because it confronts head-on the meaning of the word *flesh*, but also because it pointedly distinguishes the word *flesh* from the human spirit.

Fee accepts the NIV rendering, favoring some sort of metaphorical "destruction" of this individual's sin nature. By analyzing Fee's reasoning, I trust it will be clear this passage instead parallels 1 Cor. 11:27–32, and as such, corresponds to the normal physical sense of the word *flesh*. We have, therefore, a clear example of *flesh* used as distinct from the human spirit. Fee's arguments for the "sin nature" meaning of *flesh* in this passage (and my response) are as follows:

(1) *The context emphasizes the remedial nature of judgment.* Indeed it does,

"so that his spirit might be saved in the day of the Lord." So also is the goal of 1 Cor. 11:27–32. There Paul stated the purpose for God's harsh disciplines—including physical death—was "so that we may not be condemned along with the world." The great biblical moment for the world's condemnation is the day of the Lord. (The "spirit being saved" and to "not be condemned with the world" are clearly getting at the same idea.)

(2) *To assume Paul had in mind the actual destruction of the body is inconsistent with Paul's strong emphasis on the resurrection of the body, as though he viewed the believer's hope was in the salvation of one's spirit.* In response to this I suggest first, though Paul indeed emphasized bodily resurrection, it was due to his obvious belief that one's "soulish" body (1 Cor. 15:44–46) would need resurrection because of its prior destruction in death. Also, viewing "spirit" as referring to the deepest level of one's selfhood is compatible both with Paul and other NT writers. (Rom. 8:16; 1 Cor. 2:11; Heb. 12:23; cf. Rom. 7:22–25. See also my later comments in this chapter regarding the word "spirit.")

(3) *Because the 1 Cor. 11 passage is made "after the fact," it differs from 1 Cor. 5 which is "before the fact."* I see this as irrelevant. Peter's declaration regarding Sapphira was also *before* the fact (Acts 5:7–10). In other words, 1 Cor. 5 looks at the process while 1 Cor. 11 looks only at the result.

(4) *Since 1 Cor. 5:11 commands the church not to have any contact with this sinning individual, it "implies that no immediate death is in purview."* But what is there in the passage that requires "immediate death"? Perhaps Paul's hope was that as the individual became progressively "more weak and ill" (to use 1 Cor. 11 terminology), repentance might take place and avert the otherwise certain death.

(5) *It is not in keeping with the times of Paul's writing that an individual would lie outside of the prospect of restoration.* Both Acts 5 and 1 Cor. 11 are answer enough for this idea.

(6) *It would be against Satan's own interests to assist God in this manner.* In response, Satan *already knows* all of his efforts will be thwarted. He knows God will accomplish his purposes (the demons do). Nevertheless he does not know in advance how any particular individual will respond to his evil acts (cf. Job 1:9–11; 2:4–5). Perhaps Satan imagined his opportunity to kill this Christian might cause the church to become disillusioned, or to become so in dread of

God they would doubt his love. Regardless, we have a similar example in 1 Tim. 1:20. (Gordon D. Fee, *The First Epistle to the Corinthians* [Grand Rapids: Wm. B. Eerdmans Pub. Co., 1987], 208–14.) See also Manfred T. Brauch, *Hard Sayings of Paul* (Downers Grove, Ill.: InterVarsity Press, 1989), 96–102.

10. Walt Russell, "The Apostle Paul's View of the 'Sin Nature'/'New Nature' Struggle," *Christian Perspectives on Being Human, A Multidisciplinary Approach to Integration,* ed. J. P. Moreland and David M. Ciocchi (Grand Rapids: Baker Book House, 1993), p. 212. In his well-argued work, his reference to "redemptive-historical reasoning" has to do with his understanding that in several crucial theological passages, especially Gal. 5–6 and Rom. 7–8, the word *flesh* conveys not only that which is merely human in a bodily sense, but that which was "distinctly Jewish" with reference to the era under the Old Covenant when the Jews attempted to live under the Mosaic Law, in contrast with the New Covenant age of life "in the Spirit." Living "in the flesh," or "according to the flesh" would describe that prior condition.

11. "Man is an animated body rather than an incarnate soul.... Thus man does not *have* a body, he is a body—a psychophysical unity." (Robert H. Gundry, *Soma in Biblical Theology: With Emphasis on Pauline Anthropology* [Grand Rapids: Zondervan Pub. Co., 1987], 50. See also Bernard Ramm, *Them He Glorified* [Grand Rapids: Eerdmans Pub. Co., 1963], 93, and Clifford Williams, "The Irrelevance of Nonmaterial Minds," *Christian Scholars Review* 12 [1993]:310–23.) In supporting this point of view, Williams, an evangelical, argues well against accusations of atheistic materialism and determinism. Regarding the issue of existence after death, he suggests that "we cannot infer that people now possess nonmaterial minds simply because they must possess nonmaterial minds after they die" (p. 318). As to our knowledge of nonmaterial information, he argues that "God can give the brain that ability" (p. 321). He adds "It is, of course, absolutely mysterious how matter can have knowledge of God, but if I am right about the concept of no materiality, it is just as mysterious how something nonmaterial can have such knowledge. So I ask, 'What is the point of postulating nonmaterial minds?'" (p. 322) Though one may question some of Williams's conclusions, I believe he (along with others mentioned in chapter 1, note 13) provides an adequate basis for rejecting the belief that ethical references to flesh (*sarx*) "have no physical connotations."

(Cf. Ladd, *A Theology of the New Testament*, 474.) Note: My inclusion of Gundry and Ramm along with Williams is not to suggest that either of them would agree with all Williams presents.

12. Anthony A. Hoekema, "The Reformed Perspective," *Five Views on Sanctification* (Grand Rapids: Zondervan Pub. Co., 1987), 84. For a similar reference to "sins of the spirit," see John Murray, *The Epistle to the Romans*, vol. 1 (Grand Rapids: Wm. B. Eerdmans Pub. Co., 1968), 221, note.

It might be suggested that the Christian's sin not only arises from his flesh, but also from his spirit because of Paul's statement in 2 Cor. 7:1, "let us cleanse ourselves from all defilement of flesh and spirit, perfecting holiness in the fear of God." Out of a desire to keep Paul from identifying the source of sin as being the spirit, Nestle suggested that the grammar would allow for the following translation, "from all defilement of the flesh; in spirit perfecting holiness in the fear of God." Augustine considered this to be a possibility, although not acceptable to him. (See Alfred Plummer, *Second Epistle of St. Paul to the Corinthians*, The International Critical Commentary [Edinburgh: T & T Clark, 1956], p. 212.) Since such a translation would be abnormal, we should look for an explanation of the passage elsewhere. I believe the context provides an adequate explanation. The entire issue has to do with the *defilement* which may take place because of the association of something holy with something unholy. To say that one's spirit could possibly be defiled is to say something very different from one's spirit being the source of sin. It should also be noted that 1 Thess. 5:23 does not *require* the idea that one's spirit might possibly be "with blame" when Christ returns.

13. See Keith J. Edwards's brief response to J. P. Moreland's "A Defense of a Substance Dualist View of the Soul," *Christian Perspectives on Being Human: A Multidisciplinary Approach to Integration*, ed. J. P. Moreland and David M. Ciocchi (Grand Rapids: Baker Book House, 1993), 82–85. We rightly do not view animals as "sinning," because calling something "sin" involves a God-creature relational accountability the Bible does not ascribe to animals. It should be obvious that though Balaam's donkey had an encounter with a spirit being, this did not require its being "spiritual," nor would it be appropriate to say it had a "spiritual experience."

14. The following statement by Brauch is an example of "what we have

been told the Bible teaches." "When Paul speaks about 'being in the flesh' throughout his writings, he is not talking about our physical natures as such, about physical passions and desires, but about a way of life, an orientation of life, a life lived apart from God's purpose for us." Later, regarding Rom. 8:5–8 ("you are not in the flesh") Brauch adds, "Obviously *flesh* is used here not with any physical, biological connotations" (Manfred T. Brauch, *Hard Sayings of Paul* [Downers Grove, Ill.: InterVarsity Press, 1989], 44–45). Yet in light of the most obvious meaning of "flesh," in its overall biblical usage, what biblical grounds are there for rejecting this meaning? Certainly there are occasions when the Bible uses "in the flesh" as descriptive of a "way of life" as Brauch says, but it is a "way" that revolves around one's physical, mortal mind and body apart from the transforming miracle of New Covenant life. Clearly in Phil. 1:22–24; 1 Tim. 3:16 this expression is also used *not* as "a way of life" but as synonymous with "in the body."

15. Howard states both that "Man *is* flesh—that is his *basis of existence*," but also that flesh is something he has as "the sphere in which man lives out his earthly life." "To live *kata sarka* [according to the flesh] results in the improper satisfaction of the demands of the fleshly (human) body—its desires, propensities and wishes." (Richard E. Howard, *Newness of Life* [Grand Rapids: Baker Book House, 1975], 30, 33.) Though I agree with Showers in his definition of "flesh" as "all that man is by human birth" and "man in his weakness and mortality," I believe he unnecessarily complicates the issue by adding "sinful disposition" or "sin nature" as being distinct from flesh. Howard's comment above corrects this weakness. (Renald Showers, *The New Nature*, [Neptune N.J.: Loizeaux Bros., 1986], 95–96.)

16. Though the word *flesh* (sarx) occurs in Col. 2:5, translators have chosen to render it as "body." See Cooper, *Body, Soul, and Life Everlasting*, 42. (For another example of interchangeable uses of "flesh" and "body" see 1 Cor. 15:37–50.) Regarding this issue, Kreitzer comments, "Just to demonstrate how fluid the use of terms *sarx* and *soma* can be at times, it is worth noting that in 2 Corinthians 4:11 Paul describes the faithful as manifesting the life of Jesus in 'our mortal flesh' (*en te thnete sarki hemon*) and in Colossians 1:22 Christ's act of redemption is described as the reconciliation...brought about in 'his body of flesh'.... Most notable of all is the ease with which the apostle moves from

his discussion of *soma* in 1 Corinthians 15:35–38 to insert a (somewhat distracting) reference to *sarx* in 1 Corinthians 15:39, and then goes back to the use of *soma* in 1 Corinthians 15:42–44. In the main, however, the *sarx* acts independently of God and his Spirit, motivated by a spirit of independence and rebellion, captivated by sin and ultimately under eschatological judgment." (Kreitzer, 72.)

17. Murray rejected any nonphysical meaning of the word *body* in this passage. He also provides an extended list of other Scripture references. (Murray, *The Epistle to the Romans,* 1:220.) See also Showers, *The New Nature,* 71–72; Leon Morris, *The Epistle to the Romans* (Grand Rapids: Wm. B. Eerdmans Pub. Co., 1988), 252. Though Murray rejected any assumption that the body was the "source or seat of sinfulness," he also stated "there is an honest assessment of the sinfulness that characterizes the body and of the sins particularly associated with the body" (loc. cit, note, p. 221). In the same footnote he refers to "the sins of the human spirit," I assume in the same sense as Hoekema (see note 12).

18. At first, the fact that Paul described serving the law of God *with his mind,* but serving sin with his flesh, we might assume one's mental processes are not included in the word *flesh.* Yet obviously, all the "works of the flesh" begin in the mind. Literally Rom. 8:6–7 refers to "the mind of the flesh." In light of Paul's distinction between his inmost self (which he appears to equate with his mind) and his flesh, I believe it is reasonable to conclude that there are levels of the mind, the deepest level being a product of God's inner transforming work of both reconciliation and regeneration. (See Rom. 7:22–25, also my comments later in this chapter.) As we noted, it requires mental effort to covet, yet Paul recognized that this sin was not a product of his mind as his inmost self. See Murray, *Epistle to the Romans,* 265–66 for his somewhat inconclusive comments regarding this.

Countering the possibility that Eph. 2:3, "indulging in the desires of the flesh and of the mind" (NASB, NKJV), excludes the non-Christian's mind from being a part of his flesh, Wood states, " 'Thoughts' [Gr. *dianoia*] refers not to the mind itself, but to the projects it entertains with uncontrolled abandon." (A. Skevington Wood, "Ephesians," *Expositor's Bible Commentary,* vol. 11 [Grand Rapids: Zondervan Publishing House, 1978], 34.) Bruce comments that Paul "adds 'of our minds' probably in order to emphasize that the dictates of the flesh are not merely physical urges but include such qualities as pride and self-seeking." (F. F. Bruce, *The Epistles to the Colossians, to Philemon and to the Ephesians* [Grand Rapids: Wm. B. Eerdmans Pub. Co., 1984], 284.) Regardless, the expression "desires of the flesh and of the mind" is immediately preceded by the general statement, "all of us once lived among them in the passions of our flesh." Apparently Paul added the subsequent phrase to clarify the meaning of "the passions of our flesh" as to include one's thoughts or imaginations.

19. Russell, *Christian Perspectives on Being Human*, 222–23.

20. The word *crucified* is used in a similar way in Gal. 6:14, "the world has been crucified to me, and I to the world." In both cases, both the "world" and "I" are *dead to the other* as being in any sense where authentic life is to be found. Perhaps Paul's reference to "putting off the body of flesh" (Col. 2:11) as an accomplished event is getting at the same truth. See Appendix.

21. Among the most debated passages regarding a distinction between soul and spirit is Heb. 4:12. Some believe the passage allows for no distinction. (See F. F. Bruce, *The Epistle to the Hebrews* [Grand Rapids: Wm. B. Eerdmans Pub. Co., 1964], 96; Leon Morris, "Hebrews," *The Expositor's Bible Commentary*, vol. 12 [Grand Rapids: Zondervan Publishing House, 1981], 44; W. E. Vine, *The Epistle to the Hebrews* [Grand Rapids: Zondervan Publishing House, 1965], 44.) Others recognize a distinction (Donald Guthrie, *The Letter to the Hebrews, An Introduction And Commentary* [Grand Rapids: Wm. B. Eerdmans Pub. Co., 1983], 118–19; Paul Ellingworth and Eugene Nida, *A Translator's Handbook on the Letter to the Hebrews* [New York: United Bible Societies, 1985], 84). Though I doubt one's belief in a distinction should rest primarily upon this verse, the fact that even as "marrow" is a deeper entity than "joint," as unseen within the joint, so "spirit" may in this passage also refer to that deeper, unseen level of personhood. I believe the NRSV provides a justifiable rendering, "piercing until it divides soul from spirit, joints from marrow."

In his comments regarding 1 Thess. 5:23–24, Fee, who assumes some type of three-part distinction is involved, states, "Those who see this usage [of "spirit"] as denoting that part of human existence that serves as the place of intersection between the human and the divine by means of the Holy Spirit are most likely moving in the right direction." (Fee, *God's Empowering Presence, The Holy Spirit in the Letters of Paul,* 66.)

22. Since the word *spiritual* is commonly used as closely related to esthetics or to emotions or to anything religious (all of which may be nothing more than expressions of one's flesh), it is important to understand that as a biblical term it is expressive of anything directly related to God, most often, the Holy Spirit, and his involvement with human beings, especially those who are alive on the level of spirit. The products of that involvement would also be described as "spiritual." As an exception to this, evil angelic beings are described as "spiritual" (Eph. 6:12).

23. W. Harold Mare, "1 Corinthians," *The Expositor's Bible Commentary,* vol. 10 (Grand Rapids: Zondervan Publishing House, 1976), 202.

24. Fee, *First Epistle to the Corinthians,* 116.

25. Leon Morris, *The First Epistle of Paul to the Corinthians, An Introduction and Commentary* (Grand Rapids: Wm. B. Eerdmans Pub. Co., 1980), 60. Godet enlarges this idea as follows: "This word denotes a being animated with that breath of natural of earthly life (*psuche*) [Heb] which man possesses in common with all the living beings of creation." Frederic Louis Godet, *Commentary on First Corinthians* (Grand Rapids: Kregel Publications, 1977), 157.

It is in this sense that Paul uses the word *soulish* in 1 Cor. 15:44–49, "It is sown a *soulish* body ['physical,' NRSV; 'natural,' NIV], it is raised a spiritual body. If there is a *soulish* body ['physical', NRSV; 'natural,' NIV], there is also a spiritual body. Thus it is written, 'The first man, Adam, became a living soul ["being," NRSV, NIV]; the last Adam became a life-giving spirit.' But it is not the spiritual that is first, but the *soulish* [see above], and then the spiritual. The first man was from the earth, a man of dust ["earthy"]; the second man is from heaven.... Just as we have borne the image of the man of dust ["earthy"], we will also bear the image of the man of heaven." In making the decision to render *soulish* as they did, the translators believed that Paul had the same thing in mind as when he described people as "of dust" or "earthy." (See note 2, chapter 1.)

Usually throughout Scripture the word *soul* simply means "one's life." Harris comments, "The Hebrews counted 'souls' as we count noses." R. Laird Harris, *God's Eternal Creation, Old Testament Teaching on Man and His Culture,*

(Chicago: Moody Press, 1971), 10. He adds, "A few times the word *nephesh* [soul] even refers to a corpse, that is viewed as an individual." On rare occasions it refers to an individual after death. For example, Matt. 10:28, "Do not fear those who kill the body but cannot kill the soul; rather fear him who can destroy both body and soul in hell"; Rev. 6:9, "I saw under the altar the souls of those who had been slaughtered for the word of God…they cried out with a loud voice." Cf. Rev. 20:4.

26. This unwillingness to use the word *soulish* hinders the reader from appreciating the truth that there is, at least in some passages, a clear distinction between soul and spirit. See also James 3:15 where *soulish* is rendered "unspiritual" (NIV, NRSV), "natural" (NASB), "sensual" (NKJV, NEB). Jude also refers to non-Christians as "soulish" (Jude 19, "mere natural instincts," NIV; "worldly minded," NASB, cf. NRSV; "sensual," NKJV; "unspiritual," NEB). See also note 28. By contrast, translators have been fairly consistent in using the word *spiritual* as referring to that which directly involves either the Holy Spirit, the human spirit, or both.

27. Some argue that Paul describes three kinds of people, the third being the "carnal" Christian. The context requires that Paul perceived such an individual as a tragic, unnecessary aberration that God never intended.

28. See Acts 2:38; 10:47; 11:17; 15:8.

29. Peter H. Davids, *More Hard Sayings of the New Testament* (Downers Grove, Ill.: InterVarsity Press, 1991), 182, cf. p. 209. (It should be added that "the nature of the Father" is indeed also the nature of the Son. Cf. John 6:57; 17:23.) John's statements regarding the Christian and sin will be the emphasis of chapter 6.

30. Since it is occasionally presented erroneously that in the new birth *we don't change,* but rather, the Holy Spirit works in us (in spite of us!) to change our behavior, it is important to observe John's explanation of a believer's righteous behavior.

31. Though the OT normally describes persons as being homogeneous selves, the NT in various ways allows for some kind of "layered self" perspective. After reading a recent article in which the author attempted to remove some measure of confusion regarding humanness, I concluded that my "two level" terminology is most conservative. Within a few paragraphs, Roberts uses

the following terminology in referring to selfhood: First, there is one's "essential" or "truest" self, which apparently he also describes as one's "kingdom self." Next there is one's "actual self," which, he says, in itself is not bad. Apparently he also calls this "self" one's "inadequate" or "lesser" or "lower" self. But he also refers to another self—one's "false, pseudo" self which he seems to equate with one's "selfish" self, since this kind of self would be bad. The "lower self" he then equates with "lower nature, which needs taming and subordinating." On top of these, he says "we also have a sinful nature that needs to die." In his next paragraph he refers to one's "invidious self" which we must not simply subordinate to our "kingdom self," but we must "get rid of it altogether." This "invidious self" must be a different self than one's "lower self" which he has already described as simply needing "taming." Perhaps he uses it to refer to one's "sin nature" which "needs to die." Robert C. Roberts, "Psychobabble," *Christianity Today,* 16 May 1994, 24.

32. G. Appleton, *John's Witness to Jesus* (London, 1955), 29, quoted by Leon Morris, *The Gospel According to John* (Grand Rapids: Wm. B. Eerdmans, 1971) 219. Morris himself states, "[flesh] cannot give rise to anything other than what is earthly. But Jesus had been speaking of a spiritual kingdom, the kingdom of God. For entrance into that kingdom a spiritual birth is required." p. 219.

33. Regarding 1 Cor. 15:44–49, Guthrie comments, "Does this support the view that Adam had no natural *pneuma* [spirit]? Such a view would read too much into the context. What is important is whether, when he operates in man, the Holy Spirit transforms man's natural *pneuma* and then makes him a new creature; or whether the Spirit gives to man a *pneuma* at conversion which he did not previously possess. It is difficult to conceive of *pneuma* as something added to man's existing state. It is more reasonable to consider that man's natural spirit, which in his unregenerate state is inactive, is revived at conversion by the Spirit of God." (Guthrie, *New Testament Theology,* 166.) This appears to be wise advice as we grapple with this mystery. Wright states, "Meanwhile there still remains the original central control-house in man, namely the human spirit, which is of little use until it has been born again...until a man has been born again by the Spirit of God, he is 'natural' (*psychikos*), and only becomes 'spiritual' (*pneumatikos*) at the new birth (1 Cor. 2:14–15) even

though it has some awareness in light of 1 Cor. 2:11." (J. Stafford Wright, *Mind, Man and the Spirits* [Grand Rapids: Zondervan Pub. Co., 1971], 149.) Ladd comments, "the reception of the divine *pneuma* means the renewal of the human *pneuma* so that it acquires a new dimension." (Ladd, *A Theology of the New Testament*, 463.)

In light of Jesus' words "you are from your father the devil" (John 8:44), some believe that prior to regeneration, people are "Satan's spirit-offspring" or his "spirit children." (See also 1 John 3:8, 10.) This would suggest that in the Fall, Satan performed a regenerating miracle of his own, imparting his life to Adam and Eve. In light of the fact that the distinction in John 3:6 is between flesh and spirit, rather than from one type of spirit to another, it is more reasonable to conclude the expression "children of the devil," should be understood as a figure of speech referring to the truth that the unsaved are in the same state of rebellion as Satan, rather than their being a product of a supernatural birthing act of Satan. Closely related to this, some may argue that since unsaved individuals can be possessed by spirit demons, they must be functioning as spiritual beings. We need only to remember the demon-possessed pigs to dispel this idea (Matt. 8:31–32). This fact in no way minimizes Satan's obsessive activity "in the sons of disobedience" (Eph. 2:2; 5:6, NASB).

34. "'The inward man' is the true self, which answers to the Divine pattern; which is contrasted with the 'outer man' (2 Corinthians 4:16), the material frame, through which for a time the 'self' finds expression in terms of earth." See B. F. Westcott, *St. Paul's Epistle to the Ephesians* (New York: Macmillan, 1952), 51. It should also be noted concerning the present dualism in a believer's life, that it would be misleading to say that dualism is the necessary corollary to humanness. God's original *and* ultimate intention in people is that there be no dualism whatsoever. A believer's present state results from the fact that he/she temporarily exists as a redeemed spiritual being joined with an unredeemed mortality.

35. "Man's existential identity can no more be conceptualized than the being of God. God is divine spirit, a reality which evades capture by human thoughts and ideas. Man is made in God's spiritual image and is fully nondefinable as God. Ideas about feelings of spirits can be conceptualized but not man's identity as a human spirit." (Earl Jabay, *Search for Identity* [Grand Rapids:

Zondervan Publishing House, 1967], 56.) Though I question the biblical support of the original image of God in man as being a "spiritual image," his statement is relevant to those who, by the new birth, have the image of Christ progressively imparted to them.

36. The scriptural norm for believers is that their inmost self would be so strengthened by the Spirit that their bodies would indeed be "slaves to righteousness," manifesting in word, expression, and action, the attractiveness of Jesus Christ. But the fact is that there may be times when the travailings of our bodies will be so intense, that this norm is virtually impossible.

The Bible also assumes the reader is capable of logical thinking, adequate enough to handle, for example, the careful progression of the Book of Romans. Yet there may be extended periods when, for example, a person is so plagued with migraine headaches that he despairs of such a prospect.

We must therefore conclude that God knows and delights in the *true nature* of every child of his, whether he is an aged saint with Alzheimer's disease who pinches cute nurses and delights in children's cartoons or an emotionally distraught mother with an endocrine gland malfunction who through her tears cries out, "I don't know what's wrong with me. I don't want to be irritable, I don't want to be depressed. God knows I want to please him!"

By all means the world desperately needs to see Jesus Christ in our flesh. But it would be a most serious error for us to conclude that one of God's children is of less worth when an affliction would limit or even appear to oppose that purpose, as though that were the only reason for which God made him part of his family. Just try for a moment to visualize the thousands of horribly treated human beings (some of them Christians) who down through the centuries have been locked and chained and mocked and tortured and killed because they were spastic or epileptic or abnormally intelligent or autistic. The same would be true for those whose lifelong circumstances produce behavior that may appear to be far removed from the fruit of the Spirit. The speechless spastic, the eccentric, even the offensive person who unknown to everyone carries with him a slow-growing brain tumor; the once cheerful little lady now wasting away with Parkinson's disease who can only read Galatians 5 and weep. May God protect us from the horrid cruelty of judging men according to the flesh!

Awareness of spiritual identity is fundamental to any comprehensive appreciation of the value of persons. The new birth *always* produces God's workmanship. Whatever is born of God "is spirit." Every child of God is after God's own nature whether outwardly seen or not. How carefully we must guard ourselves from misjudging God's precious creations! Perhaps if we only knew the intensity of the pressures some have known, we would have to admit that we would have been crushed by them long ago. Could it be that unknown and unseen to us and to them, God is faceting their deep, inner selves with the most marvelous reflective surfaces, which will shine throughout eternity with a brilliance beyond all others? Who knows? Perhaps too, though their witness to people in the world may be tragically limited, their inner witness to principalities and powers in the spirit may be bringing glory to God in dimensions we cannot comprehend.

CHAPTER 6

1. Though God commanded holiness under the Old Covenant (Lev. 19:2), it is clear he expected them to fail miserably. One of the clearest examples of God's Old Covenant expectations is found in Deut. 31:19–21, 27–29. So also was the expectation of his covenant people as seen in Solomon's intercessory prayer, 2 Chron. 6:21–30, 36–39. By sharp contrast Christ's New Covenant intercessory prayer (John 17) was full of positive expectations, as were the expectations of the apostles (Rom. 6:1–2; Heb. 13:20–21, etc.).

2. I would not be surprised someday to hear church members defend their pastor's immorality by saying , "If King David had his Bathsheba, confessed and remained as Israel's ruler, why shouldn't we let our pastor keep his pulpit as long as he confesses?" Such a question might be reasonable if we were still living in Old Covenant times. Categorically God's New Covenant instructions regarding church leadership are the opposite of this type of thinking. Until the church adjusts to the radicalism of God's New Covenant expectations, any hope of revival based primarily on repentance and rededication will produce results parallel with Old Covenant revivals—short-lived and largely skin deep.

3. In view of John's use of the singular "sin" in his gospel (e.g., John 9:41; 15:22), Kubo argues that 1 John 1:8 has reference to the denial of guilt, rather

than the denial of a sinful disposition. He also concludes that the distinction between verse 8 and verse 10 is to be found in the severity of the consequences rather than in emphasizing a significant distinction between "have not sinned" and "have no sin." In verse 8, "we deceive ourselves," in verse 10, "we make him a liar." (Sakae Kubo, "1 John 3:9: Absolute or Habitual?" *Andrews University Seminary Studies* 7 [1, 1969], 51–52.) Also see Law: "The phrase 'to have sin' *(echein hamartian) is* peculiar to St. John, and has quite a definite sense. Thus in John 15:22 our Lord says, 'If I had not come and spoken to them, they had not had sin; but now they have no excuse for their sin.' Here, beyond question, 'to have sin' specifically denotes the guiltiness of the agent. In John 9:41, 15:24, 19:11 the sense is equally clear; and those parallels must be held as decisive for the meaning here." (Robert Law, *The Tests of Life, A Study in the First Epistle of St. John* [Grand Rapids: Baker Book House, 1968], 130.) Reference to this interpretation is also made in a footnote in John Stott, *The Epistles of John, An Introduction and Commentary* (Grand Rapids: Eerdmans, 1964), 77.

On the other hand, even if the singular "sin" is assumed to refer to a disposition toward sin (cf. Rom. 7:23), rather than guilt, such a view does not require one to believe a Christian always has sin in his/her life in terms of attitudes and/or actions. Clearly a Christian's flesh *has such a disposition*, which may be overridden by "the law of the Spirit of life in Christ Jesus" (Rom. 8:2). If indeed this is the meaning of the singular "sin," no Christian should make such a denial. (Cf. Stephen S. Smalley, *1, 2, 3 John*, vol. 51, *Word Biblical Commentary* [Waco: Word Books, 1984], 29.) Nevertheless it is crucial to understand there is a huge difference between possessing a propensity to sin and succumbing to that propensity.

4. There is no hint of the "when" idea in the grammatical structure of 1 John 2:1.

5. Referring to Christians, Berkhof states, "Confession of sin and prayer for forgiveness are continually required." (L. Berkhof, *Systematic Theology*, [Grand Rapids: Wm. B. Eerdmans Pub. Co., 1953], 540.) Also Packer, "the Christian finds that his heart is never absolutely pure, nor does he ever do anything that is absolutely right." J. I. Packer, *Keep In Step with the Spirit*, (Old Tappan, N. J.: Fleming H. Revell Co., 1984), 36. (See also p. 154.) 1 John 1:7 would also be used to support this view. Some argue that since the word *cleanses* is in the present tense,

this means that Christ's blood is constantly cleansing us, because, of course, we are constantly sinning. Such a conclusion is grammatically unwarranted. One would also use the Greek present tense to say "Our washing machine washes our clothes." Does that require the machine to always be running? Regardless, such a view fails to take at face value both 1 John 2:1 and 3:7–9.

Nevertheless John should not be understood as teaching that a believer in this life can come to a point in time when sin is no longer a powerful threat—some supposed state of sinless perfection. A believer's flesh by itself will always have a propensity toward sin. Happily, God's evaluation of his children as to personal holiness is not determined by the existence of that propensity, but by the degree to which that propensity is entertained. This most important distinction is often ignored, especially in explaining 1 John 1:8.

It is also important that we distinguish between progress in maturity and amounts of sin. Maturity includes growth in knowledge and wisdom. A young believer, with much growth yet remaining, may still experience times of genuine practical righteousness—times when there is nothing that needs to be confessed. It is unnecessary to assume that Paul's recognition that he had not yet "arrived" was also an expression of a belief that there was always some measure of sinning occurring in his life. The fact that Jesus "learned obedience through what he suffered; and having been made perfect, he became the source of eternal salvation for all who obey him," does not imply a measure of sin in his life either. Cf. Phil. 3:12–16; Heb. 5:8–9. The word *perfection* (*teleios*) more often expresses the idea of maturity or completion. It should be added that neither the Lord's Prayer nor James 5:16 require the belief that a Christian is always sinning.

6. This fact is acknowledged by most authors of commentaries on 1 John. In light of 1 John 2:19, perhaps none of these apostate teachers remained in the Christian fellowship to whom John is writing. Nevertheless John felt it necessary to alert those in the fellowship to the "antichrist" nature of their heretical teachings. This warning was especially important in view of John's later statements expressing the truth that sin is both abnormal and irreconcilable with authentic Christianity. To affirm this required that John first expose the "sinlessness" heresy of those who were also denying Jesus (2:22) and therefore were not Christians.

7. I. Howard Marshall, *The Epistles of John* (Grand Rapids: Wm. B. Eerdmans Pub. Co., 1978), 15.

Referring especially to 1 John 1:10, Barker states, "It makes a mockery of the gospel. It states that the reason God acted in grace and mercy toward us for the sake of our sins is false, that God first deceived us about ourselves and then himself becomes the Deceiver. The author's statement 'his word has no place in our lives' means that the Word proclaimed, the tradition received, or the witness from the OT Scriptures has no place in those who deny their sin. The most elemental presence of the Word of God in the heart and conscience has been denied. Consequently the possibility of hearing a redemptive Word is denied. The ability to live by the Word is removed.… The possibility of receiving the forgiveness offered by God is lost." (Glen W. Barker, "1 John," *The Expositor's Bible Commentary,* vol. 12 [Grand Rapids: Zondervan Publishing House, 1981], 313.)

The existence of incipient Gnosticism as a factor in John's audience is acknowledged in most commentaries on 1 John. These would be the same individuals who John later described as being identified with antichrist by denying Jesus was the Christ (the Messiah) who came in the flesh (1 John 2:22; 4:1–3; 2 John 7). It should be noted that later Marshall allows for the possibility that the statements of 1:8, 10, though originated by John's non-Christian opponents, may also be said by Christians who had been misled by these opponents. (Marshall, 112–14.) See also Stephen S. Smalley, *1, 2, 3 John,* Vol. 51 *Word Biblical Commentary* (Waco: Word Books, 1984), 21. I believe this is an unnecessary assumption, and to some degree appears inconsistent with Marshall's earlier quoted statement. If indeed this were so, it would have involved extreme confusion as to the nature of the gospel.

Though Brown may be accurate in his statement, "Most scholars take for granted that the adversaries were believing Christians whose faith was different from that professed by the author," it suggests an exceptionally broad definition of "believing Christian," far broader than I (or Marshall, for that matter) would be willing to accept. (Raymond E. Brown, *The Epistles of John* [Garden City, N.Y.: Doubleday & Co., 1982], 520.)

8. *New Testament Abstracts,* 14; vol. 1, 1969 (Cambridge, Mass.: Weston College School of Theology), 80.

9. In its first occurrence in verse 6, the "we" involved people who claimed fellowship with God yet who were walking in darkness. They would be the same individuals described in 2:4 who claimed to know God though they did not know him at all. (The "we" in this passage would be the equivalent of "anyone." A similar use is illustrated in Heb. 2:1–3 and 3:14.)

By contrast, in 2:1 John identifies his audience as "my little children" which identifies the "we" throughout the remainder of the book as representing genuine Christians.

10. So states Smalley, *1, 2, 3 John,* 51:30.

11. This is the most common view among standard commentaries.

12. Klyne Snodgrass, *Between Two Truths* (Grand Rapids: Zondervan Publishing House, 1990), 50. See Also Robert H. Stein, *Difficult Passages in the Epistles* (Grand Rapids: Baker Book House, 1988), 56, 57.

13. Though this approach is used by individuals such as Berkhof and Packer, it contradicts their belief that there is always some measure of sinning taking place in a Christian's life. See note 5.

14. Marshall, *The Epistles of John,* 180; S. Kubo, *1 John 3:9, Absolute or Habitual,* 47–56; Peter H. Davids, *More Hard Sayings of the New Testament,* (Downers Grove, Ill.: InterVarsity Press, 1991), 208. Though Fanning recognizes that the present tense may be used to express habitual action, he concludes that such does not appear to be the case in 1 John 3:4–10. Buist M. Fanning, *Verbal Aspect in the New Testament Greek* (Oxford: Clarendon Press, 1990), 214–17. Such is also the case with Dodd who states, "Yet it is legitimate to doubt whether the reader could be expected to grasp so subtle a doctrine simply on the basis of a precise distinction of tenses without further guidance. Moreover, it is not clear that this distinction of tenses is carried right through with the precision which would be necessary if the whole weight of the argument rested upon it." C. H. Dodd, *The Johannine Epistles* (London: Hodder and Stoughton, 1946), 79.

15. Marshall, *The Epistles of John,* 178–81. Cf. Stott, *The Epistles of John, An Introduction and Commentary,* 130–35, for a description of seven views.

16. Marshall, *The Epistles of John,* 182, 183. The following comments by Barker (referring to 1 John 2:1) appear to express the same perspective: "Lest any conclude from his previous statements [1:8–10] that sin must be consid-

ered inevitable in the life of the believer and not a matter of urgent concern since forgiveness is present by confession and the blood of Christ, John hastens to add, 'I write this to you so that you will not sin.' There is no question at all in his mind that sin and obedience to God are irreconcilable. Sin is the enemy…. And always the intent of the believer remains the same—not to commit sin!" (Barker, "1 John," 313).

17. Dodd, *The Johannine Epistles,* 81.

18. The irrationality of sin is also evident in 1 Peter 2:11. "Abstain from the desires of the flesh that wage war against the soul." Why would anyone in their right mind entertain such an evil enemy? Certainly Peter understood this as the logical result of having *already* "escaped the corruption that is in the world by lust" (2 Pet. 1:4, NASB.) See Blum's correction of the NIV's rendering of this verse. (Edwin A. Blum, "2 Peter," *Expositor's Bible Commentary,* vol. 12 [Grand Rapids: Zondervan Publishing House, 1981], 268.) Chamblin writes, "It is illogical and senseless for Christians to live according to the flesh, for they are not 'in the flesh' but 'in the Spirit'; yet they may choose to live illogically and irrationally (8:5–9, 12–13 [Rom.])." J. Knox Chamblin, *Paul and the Self, Apostolic Teaching for Personal Wholeness* (Grand Rapids: Baker Book House, 1993), 176.

19. Berkhof states, "Sins committed on purpose, with full consciousness of the evil involved and with deliberation, are greater and more culpable than sins resulting from ignorance, from erroneous conception of things, or from weakness of character. Nevertheless the latter are real sins and make one guilty in the sight of God." (Berkhof, *Systematic Theology,* 252.) It is noteworthy that under the Old Covenant, there was no sacrifice or forgiveness available for acts of open defiance against God. See Lev. 4:22–5:19; Num. 15:27–29. Though sin is often defined as rebellion, not all sin is an expression of rebellion. See Anthony A. Hoekema, *Created in God's Image* (Grand Rapids: Wm. B. Eerdmans Pub. Co., 1986), 181–82.

20. Dodd, *The Johannine Epistles,* 79.

21. Paul's use of the present tense, "I am the foremost [sinner]," and "I the very least [saint]" (1 Tim. 1:15; 1 Cor. 15:9; Eph. 3:8), points not to the present sinfulness of his life, but to the fact he still deserved these claims in light of sinful acts committed thirty years before. If by using the present tense he

had wished to expose his present wickedness, one would expect he would have chosen more recent examples.

Another passage erroneously used to support the essential sinfulness of Christians is James 4:8, "Cleanse your hands, you sinners, and purify your hearts, you double-minded," as though this were an appropriate description of believers—including James himself. His earlier reference to double-minded individuals (James 1:8) demonstrates that James assumed the bulk of his readers were *not double-minded* (cf. 1:1–7; 5:7–12), any more than the bulk of his readers were the wicked rich described in 5:1–4 or the "adulterers" of 4:4. Nevertheless in light of the danger of falling into sin, James concludes his book by making reference to the importance of rescuing the believer who "wanders from the truth" (5:19–20).

It is commonly taught that the beatitude, "Blessed are the poor in spirit," refers to believers who are aware of their spiritual bankruptcy (Matt. 5:3). Would it not be more reasonable to assume Jesus was expressing that which was also true of himself when he said, "I am gentle and humble in heart" (Matt. 11:29)? The next beatitude, "Blessed are those who mourn," is assumed to refer to mourning over one's sins (Matt. 5:4). Not only is there nothing in the context to support this idea, but five verses later we find Jesus' words, "Blessed are the pure in heart." Jesus was "a man of sorrows" (Isa. 53:3, NIV). He both grieved and wept. If God intended us to assume automatically that "mourning" referred to sorrow due to sin, it is surprising that none of Paul's references to his sorrows were due to continuing sin in his own life. (See comments later in this chapter regarding Rom. 7:24.)

Some argue that since in the Lord's Prayer, "forgive us our debts" is preceded by "give us this day our daily bread," we must assume Jesus expected sinning in the Christian life to be as continual as our need of daily bread (Luke 11:3–4; cf. Matt. 6:11–12). Rather, the parallel Jesus made was between God forgiving us and our forgiving our debtors. In both cases, forgiveness happens whenever it is needed.

22. The Greek word *huperechontas* was more commonly used to express the idea of prominence, importance, rather than relative moral goodness (cf. Phil. 3:8; 1 Peter 2:13).

23. Though it is not his own view, Barclay M. Newman does an excellent

job of summarizing this view in his article, "Once Again—The Question of the 'I' in Romans 7:7–25," *The Bible Translator* 34 (Jan. 1983):126–27.

24. Translating the Greek word *katargeo* as "rendered inactive," is in agreement with most scholars, even though many English versions use the word *destroy*. See F. F. Bruce, *The Epistle of Paul to the Romans* (Grand Rapids: Wm. B. Eerdmans Pub. Co., 1963), 138; *The New International Dictionary of N. T. Theology*, vol. 1, ed. Colin Brown (Grand Rapids: Zondervan Publishing House, 1975), 73; John R. H. Stott, *Men Made New, An Exposition of Romans 5–8* (Downers Grove, Ill.: InterVarsity Press, 1966), 44. Stott comments, "It means rather to 'make ineffective or inactive', and is used of unproductive land and unfruitful trees. They are still there. They have not been destroyed. But they are barren." John R. H. Stott, *The Cross of Christ* (Downers Grove, Ill.: InterVarsity Press, 1986), 240.

25. Regarding Rom. 6, John Stott writes, "if we have died with Christ and risen with Christ, it is inconceivable that we should go on living in sin." He then comments that "Each [of the two parallel sections of Rom. 6] elaborates the same general theme, that sin is inadmissible in the Christian." (Stott, *Men Made New, An Exposition of Romans 5–8*, 30.)

26. Because Paul's concept of himself as expressed in Rom. 7:14, "but I am of flesh, sold in bondage to sin," is in direct contradiction with Rom. 8:5–13, it certainly was not a description of Paul's present state as he was writing, but rather he was standing in the shoes of a pious Old Covenant believer who was struggling with the demands of God's moral law without a personal awareness of Rom. 6 or 8. See D. Martin Lloyd-Jones, *Romans, the Law: Its Functions and Limits, Exposition of Chapters 7:1–8:4* (Grand Rapids: Zondervan Publishing House, 1974). Harrison assumes that Paul was describing a hypothetical situation reflecting the despair of a Christian who still lives as though he were under the law. Everett F. Harrison, "Romans," *Expositor's Bible Commentary*, vol. 10 (Grand Rapids: Zondervan Publishing House, 1976), 84–85. (See Appendix.)

27. Seifrid, representative of this view, states, "The salvation which Paul describes in Rom. 8 is extrinsic, building on the earlier argument. Deliverance from 'the law of sin and death' is an act of God external to the believer (8:2). 'The law of the Spirit of life' which frees the believer is based on the

resurrection of the incarnate Son whom God sent to overcome sin (8:3). God will raise to life those who belong to Christ, just as he raised Christ from the dead (8:11)." I assume that by this Seifrid meant that the despair expressed in Rom. 7:14–25 has *no answer* outside of the eventual redemption of the believer's body.

Seifrid notes that the word *fulfilled* in 8:4 is a passive form of the verb pointing to the truth that since "believers will continue to sin as long as they remain in this life," that the fulfilling is "realized by an external act by God in 8:2, 3, 11." Later he states, "The juxtaposition of a description of extrinsically accomplished salvation in Rom. 8:1–4 with the intrinsic plight of the *ego* described in 7:14–25 makes it clear that the argument of Rom. 7, and of 7:14–25 in particular, is related to Paul's earlier explication of 'justification by faith alone'" (Rom. 1:16–5:21). Mark A. Seifrid, "The Subject of Rom. 7:14–25, *Novum Testamentum XXXIV* 4 (1992):331–32. See also Francis Schaeffer, *True Spirituality* (Wheaton: Tyndale House, 1971), 56. Though Packer would appear to hold the same perspective by stating "the holiest saint is never more than a justified sinner and never sees himself any other way," (p. 105) he also states, regarding Rom. 6–7, "they have been raised with him to walk in newness of life; this means that the power that wrought Jesus' resurrection is now at work in them, causing them to live differently *because in truth they are different at the center of their being* in what Paul in Rom. 7:22 calls 'my inmost self' and Peter in 1 Pet. 3:4 calls 'the hidden person of the heart.'… This change wrought by what John Wesley and his apostolic namesake, following Jesus himself, called the 'new birth'." (Packer, *Keep in Step with the Spirit*, 107, italics mine.)

28. For the sake of simplicity I will occasionally refer to regeneration as inclusive of reconciliation in the sense that both involve God's interior change in believers. A similar combination appears in Toon's question regarding whether Old Testament believers were regenerate. "If by 'regenerate' is meant that they had a right relationship with God and enjoyed communion with him, then certainly they were regenerate." Peter Toon, *Born Again: A Biblical and Theological Study of Regeneration* (Grand Rapids: Baker Book House, 1987), 61. I believe it would be more accurate to connect "right relationship" and "communion" with God to the truth of reconciliation, yet because it involved an

interior work of God as does regeneration, his approach is understandable.

29. Though happening simultaneously, justification and regeneration are in some sense sequential. For example, in Rom. 5:9–10, the "much more" of being saved from God's wrath because of justification and reconciliation, is followed by the "much more" of being "saved by his life." In 7:21, justification *leads to* eternal life. In Titus 3:5–7 the "rebirth and renewal by the Holy Spirit" is based upon one's already "having been justified by his grace." Justification saves us from God's wrath, but it does not qualify us for a holy heaven. This requires a new quality of life, the impartation of life from God—his own divine nature. Jesus' answer to Nicodemus was not "You need to be justified," but "You need to be born again."

30. This fact is often missed due to the standard outline for the book of Romans—"Sin," chapters 1–2; "Justification," chapters 3–5; "Sanctification," chapters 6–8. Actually, Rom. 6–8 is loaded with "regeneration" truth. Toon states, "what God declares believers to be as he views them in Christ is also what he intends they shall truly be: thus justification leads to their actually being made righteous through the inner renewal of the Spirit (Rom. 6)." In the same paragraph, Toon equates the renewal of the Spirit with the new birth. (Toon, *Born Again,* 64. See also F. F. Bruce, *Paul, the Apostle of the Heart Set Free* [Grand Rapids: Wm. B. Eerdmans Pub. Co., 1977], 205, 206; Millard, J. Erickson, *Christian Theology,* vol. 3 [Grand Rapids: Baker Book House, 1985], 944; Ronald Mayers, *Evangelical Perspectives* [University Press of America, 1987], 139–42; Renald Showers, *The New Nature* [Loizeaux Brothers, 1986], 11, and throughout his comments regarding Rom. 6–8.)

Regeneration has been understood by many as the initial miracle in God's overall work of sanctification. See Toon, *Born Again,* 67.

31. The distinctly Jewish context surrounding Rom. 6 requires us to recognize that the "old self [man]" terminology pointed to Israel under the Law in contrast with the "new self [man]" pointing to the New Covenant people who now possess Christ's risen life (cf. Eph. 4:15, "one new humanity [man]"). This by no means eliminates the personal impact of the passage, as is clear in light of the intensely individualistic focus of Rom. 6:11ff. (The same may be said of the portions of Rom. 7 in which the "I" may be understood as both representative and personal.) A more corporate view is represented by Mark W.

Karlberg in his helpful article, "Israel's History Personified: Rom. 7:7–13 in Relation to Paul's Teaching on the 'Old Man'," *Trinity Journal NS,* (1986):64–75. A more personal view is represented by John Murray, *The Epistle to the Romans* (Grand Rapids: Wm. B. Eerdmans Pub. Co., 1968). See Appendix for extended comments regarding this.

32. The only passage using the terminology "old self" which might be seen as contradictory to the perspective of Rom. 6:6 is Eph. 4:22–24, in which the "putting off" of the old self is commonly translated as being a command. (See NASB, NIV, NRSV, KJV.) In contrast with the translators who give the infinitives, "to put off" and "to put on," an imperative force, John Murray believed that both the grammar allowed and the exegesis demanded that the infinitives were "infinitives of result." He translated v. 22 as follows: "so that ye have put off, according to the former manner of life, the old man." (See his extended argument in *Principles of Conduct,* 214–18. See also L. S. Chafer, *Systematic Theology,* vol. 6 [Dallas: Dallas Seminary Press, 1947–48], 270, and John Eadie, *A Commentary on the Greek Text of the Apostle Paul to the Ephesians* [London: William Mackenzie, 1854], 346.) Moule also expressed a past tense perspective in his paraphrase, "you were taught in Christ with regard to the fact that your old man was laid aside" (H. C. G. Moule, *Studies in Ephesians* [Grand Rapids: Kregel Publications, 1977], 118). Martyn Lloyd-Jones, while accepting the standard translation, believed that it in no way contradicted the past tense perspective of the "old self" of Rom. 6 and Col. 3. "What the Apostle is saying in effect is 'Do not go on living as if you still were that old man, because that old man has died; do not go on living as if he was still there; put that off.'" (*Romans, the New Man, An Exposition of Chapter 6* [Grand Rapids: Zondervan Publishing House, 1973], 64.) He felt Paul's terminology was comparable to someone today saying to a full grown man, "Don't be a baby because you are indeed a man." Though the Ephesians passage may be debated, there is no question as to the past tense perspective concerning the old self in Col. 3:9. In spite of this fact the NASB has used the imperative in the heading, "Put on the New Man" at the top of the page containing this verse.

33. John Murray writes in connection with Rom. 6, "The old man is the unregenerated man; the new man is the regenerate man created in Christ Jesus unto good works." John Murray, *Principles of Conduct; Aspects of Biblical Ethics*

(Grand Rapids: Wm. B. Eerdmans Pub. Co., 1957), 218.

34. David Wenham, "The Christian Life: A Life of Tension? A Consideration of the Nature of Christian Experience in Paul," *Pauline Studies,* ed. Donald A. Hagner and Murray J. Harris (Grand Rapids: Wm. B. Eerdmans Pub. Co., 1980), 81.

35. Ibid., 89.

36. See also 1 Cor. 4:11–16; 6:3–10; 1 Thess 1:5–6; 2 Thess. 3:7–9; 2 Tim. 3:10–12. Another "example" type of passage, Phil. 3:17, is preceded by Paul's reflections that he had not yet "arrived" (3:12). There was yet more for him to grasp (3:10). But one would be hard pressed to prove from Scripture that the three areas he longed to know more fully implied his present, lesser knowledge was the equivalent of greater sin any more than that was true of 1 Cor. 13:12.

37. Wenham, "Christian Life," 82.

38. *The Book of Common Prayer* (New York: James Pott and Co., 1892), 4.

39. See Rom. 6:1–2; Col. 3:1–17; 1 Cor. 15:34; Gal. 5:16; Heb. 13:20–21; 2 Pet. 1:3–4.

CHAPTER 7

1. Though the OT records many examples of individuals who approached God directly, nevertheless, the book of Hebrews makes this distinction.

2. A list of such individuals would also include some mentioned in the NT prior to the Day of Pentecost; individuals such as John the Baptist, his father, and Elizabeth, who also were filled with the Spirit (in light of their activity of prophesying). John was filled "from his mother's womb."

3. Job. 1:1; Ps. 1; cf. Jer. 11:20; 12:3; 21:12. See also David's personal testimony in Ps. 18:20–24.

4. "Life" in this context was understood as temporal rather than eternal life. It is a common but false assumption that Old Testament believers shared with the apostles the treasured hope that death ushered them into a "far better" state. Though OT believers did have hope in future bodily resurrection, this is rarely mentioned (e.g., Isa. 26:19; Dan. 12:2). Long earthly life, rather

than the immediate joy of immortality, was the normal evidence of divine blessing. An unusual exception to the "long life" expectation is described in Isa. 57:1–2. This is in a context of a society so evil that a premature death for a righteous man was to be understood as a divine kindness.

5. To render "righteousness under the law" as "legalistic righteousness," as does the NIV, is to force upon the text an interpretation that may not have been intended.

6. See chapter 6 for a clarification of 1 Tim. 1:13–15.

7. The OT repeatedly anticipated the radical, inward change that some-day would come. Not only is this expressed in the actual statements of the New Covenant (Jer. 31:31–34; Isa. 59:21; Ezek. 36:26–27; cf. Isa. 60:21; 62:12, especially those passages anticipating the coming of the Holy Spirit), but also in the deep-felt agony of the prophet who realized that the day of that New Covenant had not yet arrived (Isa. 59:9–15; 64:5–7). Ladd underlines that "the idea of newness is distinctly eschatological," and then goes on to say, "The Pauline statement that in Christ the old passed away and the new has come is an eschatological statement." George Eldon Ladd, *A Theology of the New Testament* (Grand Rapids: Wm. B. Eerdmans Pub. Co., 1974), 479.

Were Old Covenant believers regenerated? Peter Toon responds as follows:

> The answer to our question as to whether the faithful believers of the old Israel were regenerate is, then, both yes and no. If by "regenerate" is meant that they had a right relationship with God and enjoyed communion with him, then certainly they were regenerate. They were assisted by the Holy Spirit in their relation-ship with the covenant God. However, if by "regenerate" is meant that the Holy Spirit was permanently present in their souls, then the answer is that they were not regenerate, for they could not have enjoyed the benefits of the New Covenant before it had been inau-gurated.

Toon, *Born Again: A Biblical and Theological Study of Regeneration* (Grand Rapids: Baker Book House, 1987), 61. More precisely, the relational work of God in an individual's life, as we have noted, involved the interior miracle of *reconciliation*.

Toon's distinction is of greater significance than is often perceived. Are not the benefits of the New Covenant central to the significance of regeneration? Ladd states, "The ascended Christ has not only entered the realm of spirit; he has become a living-giving spirit, able because of his new mode of existence to impart life to men as he could not do in the days of his flesh." Ladd, *A Theology of the New Testament*, 490. Bruce writes, "the prime function of the indwelling Spirit in the believing community, as in the individual believer, is for Paul the reproduction of the Christ-likeness in his people, until the whole body corporate attains 'the measure of the stature of the fullness of Christ' (Eph. 4:13)." F. F. Bruce, *Apostle of the Heart Set Free* (Grand Rapids: Wm. B. Eerdmans Pub. Co., 1977), 210. In its article "New Creation, New Creature," the *Baker Encyclopedia of the Bible* states: "According to the NT, the new creation is a present reality dating from the resurrection of Christ…. The Holy Spirit is the power of the new creation (cf. Heb. 6:5). Where the Spirit is at work as the gift of the glorified Christ, the new creation is present." Vol. 2, ed. Walter A. Elwell (Grand Rapids: Baker Book House, 1988), 1545.

By contrast, Lewis in arguing for regeneration under the Old Covenant refers to the time when the Spirit came upon Saul and he not only was changed "into a different person," but "God gave him another heart" (1 Sam. 10:6, 9). Are we to assume this was the point of Saul's "regeneration"? Hardly. Rather it describes a brief period when Saul functioned as a prophet. He also refers to David's prayer, "create in me a clean heart" (as though that was when David was born again [Ps. 51:10]). As noted above, an inner attitudinal change toward God relates to God's reconciliating, rather than his regenerating work. (Arthur H. Lewis, "The New Birth Under the Old Covenant," *The Evangelical Quarterly* 56 [Jan. 1984]:35–44; cf. Millard J. Erickson, *Christian Theology,* vol. 3 [Grand Rapids: Baker Book House, 1985], 981.)

Though earlier in this note I quoted Ladd, Murray, and Bruce as expressing the uniqueness of New Covenant regeneration, all of them believed regeneration also took place under the Old Covenant. Admittedly, it is difficult to draw a fine line between reconciliation and regeneration, both resulting in inward change.

8. This statement finds a direct parallel in Gal. 6:3, "For if those who are nothing think they are something, they deceive themselves." Apart from the

operation of Jesus' risen life within, we are nothing on any divine scale of worth. "The Spirit gives life; the flesh counts for nothing" (John 6:63, NIV).

9. Jesus' deity is declared emphatically in John 1:1, 14, 18; 8:58; Titus 2:13; Rev. 22:13–16; cf. Rev. 1:8.

10. Note in the following passages the way in which people related the miraculous events Jesus performed to the presence, not of God, but of a prophet in their midst: Luke 7:16 (raising the dead); 7:39 (supernatural knowledge; cf. John 4:19; also Mark 2:8; John 1:48; 2:24–25); John 6:14 (feeding the multitude); Luke 24:19 (two of Jesus' disciples described him as "a prophet mighty in deed and word"—spoken after they had been told of his resurrection).

11. Why have we been taught that his miracles proved his deity? I believe there are two reasons. One relates to the necessary evangelical response to those who have denied Christ's deity. In declaring his deity, using clear scriptural resources, some have succumbed to the temptation to load on whatever else they might think of in order to overwhelm the opposition. His miracles have been the "whatever else." (Sadly, strong arguments are always weakened by adding weak or incorrect arguments.) In their zeal, they may well have cast an unintentional shadow upon the sacred truth that Jesus in every sense was a real man.

Another inadequate argument used to show that Jesus' miracles proved his deity is John's stated purpose for his Gospel (20:30–31). On the surface this is a reasonable argument. But if John intended to say that it was the signs in themselves, apart from the discourses, that proved Jesus' deity, then we are confronted with at least two problems: (1) It was pointedly *not* Jesus' miracles that disturbed the unbelieving Pharisees, but his words, "I and the Father are one" (10:32–33). (2) Jesus twice declared that the works were from his Father (10:32, 37). Also it is significant that Peter, in using a similar sign attestation argument in Acts 2:22, not only does not use miracles as proofs of Jesus' deity, but declares they were accomplished by the Father ("God") through the man, Jesus. We find a similar sign attestation argument used in Hebrews 2:3–4 for the exclusive purpose of verifying the truthfulness of the words spoken. It is therefore reasonable to conclude that the proof of Jesus' deity was accomplished not by the signs in themselves but by the discourse context related to several of his miracles and most especially by the final sign of his resurrection from the dead. The miracles, then, were the Father's means of verifying his Son's integrity. (See D. A. Carson, *The Gospel According to John* [Grand Rapids: Wm. B. Eerdmans Pub. Co., 1991], 395–400, esp. 399–400).

12. John 14:12. Helpful explanatory comments are found in Leon Morris, *The Gospel According to John* (Grand Rapids: Wm. B. Eerdmans Pub. Co., 1971), 645–46.

13. Some have suggested that when Jesus declared that his words and miracles (his "works") were not from himself (John 5:30; 8:28; 12:49; 14:10), he simply was affirming that he, as a part of the Trinity, functioned "as a team" in union with the other members of the Trinity—never independently. The NIV rendering of John 14:10, "The words that I say are not just on my own," would suggest that idea. But the Greek text neither says "just on my own" or even "on my own" (suggesting cooperative action), but rather "not from myself." Consistently Jesus affirmed what he said and did were the Father's actions *in contrast with* their being his actions. Even when he stated "My Father is still working, and I am also working" (John 5:17), by his comments in 5:19–21 he made it clear he was not suggesting an equal "team" imagery. A parallel to this is found in Paul's comments, "for this I toil and struggle with all the energy that he powerfully inspires within me" (Col. 1:29). By contrast, when it comes to the ultimate judgment day, it will be the Son, not the Father, who delivers the verdicts (John 5:22; 2 Cor. 5:10; Matt. 23:31–46).

14. This fact was first expressed seven hundred years before in Isaiah's prophesy regarding the Messiah's dependence upon and obedience to his Father. See Is. 50:4–7; cf. 49:1–7.

15. Cf. Morris, *Gospel According to John*, 689–90.

16. During the earthly stay of the Son of God until his resurrection, we may assume his deity never interfered with his experiencing humanness, including all of its limitations. Now, in his post-resurrection glory, his humanity never interferes with the expression of the glory of his deity.

17. This statement finds a direct parallel in Gal. 6:3, "For if those who are nothing think they are something, they deceive themselves." Apart from the "umbilical cord" idea, we are nothing on any divine scale of worth. As Jesus said, "apart from me you can do nothing" (John 15:5). Remember too that

during his self-emptying on earth, Jesus said much the same thing of himself! "I can do nothing [from myself]" and "I live because of the Father, so whoever eats me will live because of me" (John 5:30, 6:57). "It is the spirit [or Spirit] that gives life; the flesh is useless" (John 6:63).

18. Ephesians 1:20; 2:6.

19. Not only does Luke describe Jesus as one who was "full of the Spirit," but also that he entered his ministry "filled with the power of the Holy Spirit" (Luke 4:1, 14). Though the descent of the Spirit upon Jesus at his baptism has special significance, we would be in error to assume that Jesus was not filled prior to that event. If John the Baptist was described as one who was filled with the Spirit "even before his birth" (Luke 1:15), it is impossible to imagine anything less with Jesus who was given the Spirit "without measure."

20. John 1:14. Scripture is quite clear in declaring that Jesus was fully a human being. Jesus called himself a man (John 8:40; cf. 1 Tim. 1:5; 3:16, "He was revealed in the flesh"). Heb. 2:17 states that "he had to become like his brothers and sisters in every respect." See also Erickson, *Christian Theology*, vol. 2, 711–12. Cullmann's discussion of Jesus' humanness is also most helpful. (Oscar Cullmann, *The Christology of the New Testament* [Philadelphia: Westminster Press, 1963], 93–96.)

21. See *The New International Dictionary of Theology*, vol. 2 (Grand Rapids: Zondervan Publishing House, 1976), 503–4.

22. For constructive evaluation of the genuineness of Jesus' temptations, see David H. Peters, *More Hard Sayings of the New Testament* (Downers Grove, Ill.: InterVarsity Press, 1991), 93.

23. See Isa. 53:5–12; Mark 10:45; John 1:29, 36; 1 Cor. 15:3; 2 Cor. 5:21; Heb. 9:26, 28; 1 Pet. 1:18–19; Rev. 1:5.

24. Since the original Greek text was written entirely with capital letters, it is the task of a translator to determine, for example, whether the "s" of the word "spirit" should be capitalized. When did the writer intend to refer to the human spirit and when to the Holy Spirit? In a few contexts it is difficult, if not impossible, to be sure. Gordon Fee suggests that due to the intimate participation of the Holy Spirit within the human spirit, some references may be best translated as "S/spirit" in order to convey the truth that the human spirit finds expression only by the presence of the Holy Spirit within. Though his

comments are made with reference to 1 Cor. 5:4 and 14:15, I suggest the same thought may have been in Paul's mind in such passages as Rom. 8:9–10, "you are not in the flesh, but in the S/spirit...the S/spirit is life;" and also Gal. 5:17, "for what the flesh desires is opposed to the S/spirit, and what the S/spirit desires is opposed to the flesh." See Gordon D. Fee, *The First Epistle to the Corinthians* (Grand Rapids: Wm. B. Eerdmans Pub. Co., 1987), 205, 670, 671. Fee nevertheless assumes that Paul "would undoubtedly understand the human 'spirit' as a distinguishable constituent of the human personality" (p. 112).

25. This statement should in no way cast a shadow on the future, actual realization of the New Covenant by God's unique covenant people, the nation Israel. See Rom. 11:24–27.

CHAPTER 8

1. A. W. Tozer, *Knowledge of the Holy* (New York: Harper and Bros., 1961), 9–10.

2. Among the many fine books available for increasing your confidence in the authority of the Bible, two of the more popular ones are Paul E. Little, *Know Why You Believe* (Downers Grove, Ill.: InterVarsity Press, 1967) and Josh McDowell, *Evidence That Demands A Verdict* (San Bernardino, Calif.: Here's Life Pub., 1979).

3. David C. Needham, *Close To His Majesty* (Portland, Ore.: Multnomah Press, 1987). Earlier I quoted from A. W. Tozer's book *Knowledge of the Holy*. It is excellent. Another classic is J. I. Packer, *Knowing God* (Downers Grove, Ill.: InterVarsity Press, 1973).

4. See John 3:3–8; Eph. 2:8–9.

5. One may assume that since Paul said "I have learned," he was describing an extended process. Indeed, he learned through each experience over the years. Yet we dare not deny the radical transformation following Pentecost in which contentment in suffering came so quickly to so many.

6. See Rom. 7:9–11. It is in light of this realization he then cries out, "Wretched man that I am! Who will rescue me from the body of this death?" (7:24) This sense of hopelessness as to finding life (a sense of personal worth,

significance and love) is what Paul meant by the word "death" in Rom. 8:2, 6, 10, 13a. This unique use of "death" should be seen in sharp contrast with his references to life in the same verses.

7. "Lecherous flesh" is the same flesh (functioning independently) which must be made a slave to righteousness. When this is taking place, a believer's flesh takes on a beautiful significance as being the means by which the life of Jesus is expressed, physically, emotionally, and verbally by the enabling of the Holy Spirit.

8. I believe Ray Stedman has done an excellent job of exposing the inadequacy of viewing a Christian as having either ego (self) on the throne or Christ on the throne. (Ray C. Stedman, *Authentic Christianity* [Portland, Ore.: Multnomah Press, 1984], 90–91.)

9. The one Scripture section around which there is a special mystery is the record of Christ's struggle in Gethsemane. There it would appear that he expressed a wish contrary to the will of his Father. "My Father, if it is possible, let this cup pass from me. Yet not what I want, but what you want" (Matt. 26:39; cf. Mark 14:36, Luke 22:42). Some have suggested this was simply an expression of his human will that naturally would draw back from the cross. I suggest an alternate view. Could the repulsion he felt rather be the expression of his essential will as a person of absolute righteousness and spotless purity who most properly would react not so much against the impending suffering as against the impending reality of being "made sin" (2 Cor. 5:21)? The "will" of holiness would rightly stand against personal contamination. How could it ever properly be the will of a holy person to become unholy? Only the overriding purpose of his Father—which encompassed not only holiness but love, grace, and the necessary satisfaction of his own righteousness—would be adequate for the Savior to say, "Your will be done."

10. Concerning self-denial, 2 Cor. 5:15 needs to be evaluated. It is important to see that the statement "those who live might live no longer for themselves," comes right in the middle of an important progression of thought. Paul begins the chapter by making a clear distinction between one's deepest self and his mortal house. This follows with a contrast between those who take pride in appearance, who recognize people according to the flesh, over against the fundamental fact that a Christian is God's new creation, God's

ambassador. To make the "oneself" concept of 5:15 a reference to one's deepest self would be to go against the entire flow of thought. Paul would say "sad are the Christians who live as though they were still out to fulfill life as if they had not died with Christ, as if they were not 'a new creation'." Paul is saying essentially the same thing as Gal. 2:20. This distinction is most important. The Bible repeatedly asserts as sinful anything that is selfish, anything that manifests one's concern or interest in oneself without regard for others. Thus Paul stated, "for Christ's love urges us on" so that "those who live might live no longer for themselves, but for him who died and was raised for them." Jesus expressed words quite similar when He spoke not only of the proper self-denial of his followers, but also of his own self-denial (see Mark 8:34; Mark 10:45; John 8:28).

11. In Gal. 2:20 Paul was not declaring that he had lost his own distinct selfhood; he pointedly stated, "I live." But the "self" he was now was alive because it was inseparably linked to the will and life of Christ. The "self" that he once was—the "old self" of Rom. 6—that "self" had been "crucified with Christ." Nevertheless for very practical reasons, this risen, New Covenant life which now was his, was being lived "in the flesh."

12. See Matt. 23:15 for Jesus' criticism of the Pharisees' evangelistic zeal.

13. Though the product and the purpose are completely different, it is possible for the Bible teacher, pastor, missionary, or evangelist to discover their identity precisely the same way as any hard-driving insurance salesperson whose goals may be measured in terms of monthly quotas, earning gold keys, or having one's name mentioned for special commendation at the next conference. Biblical scholars may find fulfillment in their word studies on the same mind-flesh level as the scientist who analyzes the vocabulary of a chimpanzee. Similarly, a Christian teacher may go over her books, sharpen her notes, develop stunning illustrations, utilize modern audio-visuals, and assume that if she does these things she is fulfilling life. Truthfully, she may be scarcely touching life at all—authentic life, resurrection life. To compound the loss, many Christians will put such individuals on spiritual pedestals.

14. Standing in our theological orthodoxy, we as evangelicals may pride ourselves that we have not forsaken the fountain of living water as Judah did so long ago (Jer. 2:13). Instead, we may well be missing the fundamental

purpose of the fountain. Somehow that seems even more tragic.

15. Shame is the expression of that agonizing assumption that I in myself should have been able to behave properly, that I should not have messed up, that I have lost the respect and honor I could have had if only I had done better. Shame is a direct product of a denial that "in my flesh dwelleth no good thing." It is in that sense that shame is a counterpart to pride.

16. Annie Johnson Flint, "He Giveth More Grace" (Kansas City, Mo.: Lillenas Publishing Company, 1941).

17. The fact the epistles repeatedly urged the early churches to stop whatever sin was occurring argues strongly for the apostles rejecting any thought that sinning was normal behavior. Though under the Old Covenant, God's people were also challenged to holy living, a major emphasis was placed on *the expectation of their failure.* A classic example of this is found in Solomon's failure-obsessed intercessory prayer. (1 Kings 8:30, 33–36, 46–50. For another example, see Deut. 31:16–29.) This radical contrast between the Old Covenant expectation of defeat in sin and the New Covenant expectation of victory in holiness was central in Paul's mind as he wrote the book of Galatians. See also Jesus' intercessory prayer in John 17 (not even a hint of any expectation of failure). Since justification by faith and reconciliation were realities under both covenants, the difference lies in the distinctives of the New Covenant miracle of resurrection life—regeneration—wrought by the "Spirit of life."

18. Observe Paul's repeated question, "Do you not know?" 1 Cor. 6:2, 3, 9, 15, 16, 19; cf. 3:16 in light of 3:3. Clearly, Paul was shocked as to their ignorance regarding the radical miracle that took place when they were saved. Their values were wrong because their concept of themselves was wrong.

19. Tremper Longman III, *How to Read the Psalms* (Downers Grove, Ill.: InterVarsity Press, 1988), 28. As we have noted, such an obsession with confession is far removed from the perspective of 1 John.

20. "James clearly distinguishes sin from evil desire and temptation. Evil desire 'gives birth to sin,' but it is not sin. Temptation may lead to sin, but it is not sin. We must not get down on ourselves because we are tempted to sin, nor because we hear the voice of evil in our thoughts. These occur because of our human condition. We cannot help that. Sin occurs when we heed that evil

voice and yield to that temptation. To overcome these and listen rather to the voice of God is the perseverance of faith." (William R. Baker and Paul K. Carrier, *James and Jude* [Cincinnati: Standard Publishing Co., 1990], 26.)

21. See Millard J. Erickson, *Christian Theology*, vol. 2 (Grand Rapids: Baker Book House, 1984), 596–98.

22. See chapter 7 regarding this concept and the temptations of Christ.

23. It might be argued this disagrees with Jesus' words "it is from within, from the human heart, that evil intentions come" (Mark 7:21). In response, it first should be noted that Jesus said this in order to underline the simple truth that defilement does not come from the outside in, but from the inside out. As with so many words, *heart* is used in a variety of ways in the Bible. Here, it is more probably a synonym for the mind (see Col. 2:18). It is unnecessary contextually to require the word to take on the deeper spiritual sense of one's inmost self as used in Rom. 7:22, which Paul equates with his mind (7:23, 25). Since animals produce many of the sinful expressions listed in Mark 7:21–22, yet are nothing more than flesh, one needs to look no deeper than the fleshy mind in human beings to explain the same attitudes. True, for the unregenerate individual, there is no life deeper than flesh. Therefore their "heart" or "mind" is indeed what they most deeply are. What a beautiful contrast we find in "the pure in heart" who will see God! (See Matt. 5:8; cf. Titus 1:15; also those who possess a "sincere [pure] mind," 2 Pet. 3:1, Gr. *dianoia.*)

24. Though we may be encouraged that God evaluates motives, we should be sobered by the fact that when the Scripture draws clear lines regarding moral issues, our disobedience is sin no matter how good our motives may appear to us. For example, it is always a sin to break up an unhappy marriage no matter how much you may think another prospect is in need of your intimate devotion. It is always a sin to fudge on our income tax even though the money we save goes to missions. Pure motives will always be rooted in our joyful acceptance both of *who we now are and the resulting spheres in which life will be found.*

CHAPTER 9

1. See Appendix 2.

2. See John 17:13; Neh. 8:10; Prov. 8:27–31; Phil. 2:13; Eph. 1:5, 9; Heb. 2:12.

3. See David C. Needham, *Close to His Majesty*, chapter 4, "Happiness Is Holiness" (Portland, Ore.: Multnomah Press, 1987), 70–79.

4. Taking the time to reflect over the sequence of events that led up to any particular sin is crucial. As we follow the sequence, we must not be satisfied until we have identified the real *why?* for each wrong step we took. In searching for the answers, we must avoid the cop-out of the simplistic answer, "It was just my sin nature acting up." By understanding the true whys of any sin, we have some reason to hope we might avoid the sequence the next time—now that we understand where and why we went wrong. Sin is *not* avoidable if we continue to remain ignorant regarding this. (See Action step 2 in this chapter.)

5. In the past I have found this kind of response difficult to do. The reason I found it so hard to imagine that God was smiling at me was because this is not the way it is in most human relationships. If I have offended or hurt someone, it seems to take time for that hurt to heal; time for the one I grieved to be convinced of my sincerity; time to restore their trust in my love for them. Happily God is not bound by these *time* necessities. His grief changes to joy in an instant because he knows automatically the sincerity of my heart. How quickly we need to enter into the awareness of God's joy! (See Zeph. 3:17; Hebrews 9:14; 10:19–22.)

6. "Most defense mechanisms, adjustment-to-need conflicts, are attempts to maintain self-equilibrium. This urge for balance expresses itself most fundamentally in the universal human need for meaning in life, without which some measure of the person will cease to exist. The organization of personality around some focal center designates the locus of meaning—reason for being." (C. Carl Leninger, "Man's Basic Need for Meaning," *Church Administration,* January 1972, 12–13.)

7. The Greek word, *alazonia,* "describes a pretentious hypocrite who glories in himself or in his possessions…. 'Pride of life' will be reflected in whatever status symbol is important to me or seems to define my identity." Glen W. Barker, "1 John," *Expositor's Bible Commentary,* vol. 12 (Grand Rapids: Zondervan Publishing House, 1981), 322.

8. Cheryl Forbes has done a beautiful job of presenting the positive aspects of the gift of imagination in her book, *Imagination: Embracing a Theology of Wonder* (Multnomah Press: Portland, Ore., 1986). Though I suggest she went beyond Scripture when she stated that imagination is the image of God in us (pp. 19, 39, 185), she nevertheless rightly emphasizes its importance.

9. As a general rule, Christians have appeared to be more righteous if the culture in which they lived maintained more rigid moral boundaries. In our times, as culture collapses morally, Christians tend to collapse in tandem. Clearly, culturally conditioned righteousness is neither the product of the Holy Spirit nor evidence of the power of resurrection life, but rather a product of conformity.

10. For a comprehensive description of this present tragedy, see David F. Wells, *No Place for Truth: Whatever Happened to Evangelical Theology?* (Grand Rapids: Wm. B. Eerdmans Pub. Co., 1993).

11. "The New Testament calls upon us to take action; it does not tell us that the work of sanctification is going to be done for us. That is why it does not put us into a clinic or hospital where the patient is told 'It will be done for you,' and 'Allow the Lord Jesus to do it for you.' It calls upon us to take action, and exhorts us to do so. And it tells us and commands us to do so for this reason, that we have been given the ability to do it. If we had not been given the ability, if we had not received the new nature as the result of the new birth, if we had not been given the new life, if the Spirit was not in us, then, of course, we should need someone to do it for us. But as we have been given the power and the ability and the capacity, the New Testament quite logically, and in perfect consistency with itself, calls upon us to do it. 'Do not let sin reign in your mortal body' it says. 'Do not present your members as instruments unto sin or unrighteousness.' Do not do it! This is something that you and I have to do; it is not going to be done for us." (D. Martyn Lloyd-Jones, *Romans, The New Man* [Grand Rapids: Zondervan Publishing House, 1972], 179.)

12. Sometimes individuals discover they are a terribly weak-willed people. They feel helpless even to begin the process. What do they need? Using my earlier illustration in which a person's will is their car battery, what they need is a "jumper cable" linked to some strong-willed person to temporarily support

their weak will until their own "spiritual engine" is able to carry on its generating task. One-on-one supportive relationships and "caring groups" are invaluable. If your own church is not actively participating in such a program, perhaps God will use you to awaken in that local body a fresh commitment to fulfill Scripture's commands. "Bear one another's burdens, and in this way you will fulfill the law of Christ." "And we urge you, beloved, to admonish the idlers, encourage the faint hearted, help the weak, be patient with all of them" (Gal. 6:2; 1 Thess. 5:14).

13. Forbes, *Imagination*, 29–30.

14. This explanation is in sharp contrast with the common nonbiblical answer which says Christians find it easier to sin than to produce holiness because their essential natures are sinful.

15. Paul recognized that no matter how successfully he exercised his spiritual gifts, God still might have judged him as "disqualified" (1 Cor. 9:27). The primary spiritual gifts in this case may have included the gifts of apostleship, teaching, and evangelism.

16. The emphatic verb form used could be rendered as "be at home." Clearly Christ is *in* every true believer (2 Cor. 13:5). Paul's prayer moves beyond this fact.

17. It is tragic when Christians are misled into thinking that the truly great demonstrations of God's power are seen in miracles of healing rather than in believers who spread the fragrance of the love of Christ, the fruit of the Spirit, wherever they are.

18. I believe it is no coincidence that immediately following "Pray without ceasing," are the words "In everything give thanks" (1 Thess. 5:17–18). Each of us will have to discover the most effective ways of developing this important habit. I discovered years ago that my best prayer times were when I prayed audibly with my eyes open as I took long night walks with God. This has made it easier to nurture the practice of this ongoing, often interrupted, conversation during the day.

19. I have purposely omitted a variety of "Disciplines of Abstinence" as listed by Dallas Willard (*The Spirit of the Disciplines* [San Francisco: Harper & Row, 1988], 158), including solitude, silence, fasting, frugality, and sacrifice, because I understand these activities to be appropriate by-products of one's

ongoing response to both the heart and will of God and one's resulting love for people rather than their being disciplines which one sets about to practice in order to promote spiritual maturity. Instead of their being tools God uses to change our lives, they are among the evidences (if rightly understood) that life has been changed. It is noteworthy that Jesus was led by the Spirit into the wilderness rather than that he planned to perform a particular discipline. I would imagine it would have taken a tough act of discipline *not to go*. On the other hand, those "things I must believe" along with "things I must do" as described in this and the preceding chapter are indeed tough disciplines out of which fullness of life flows. For example, I am convinced when Paul described his own harsh discipline of buffeting his body, the toughest buffeting involved his thought life rather than some form of physical deprivation. Always preceding physical acts are mental decisions (see 1 Cor. 9:27).

20. To see this more clearly, let's take a very graphic illustration. I have a nose that prefers good smells over bad ones. Let's assume God places me in some filthy aboriginal village where the stench is so intense I can scarcely breathe—even through my mouth. In this state I will find it most difficult to be content. And to be discontented with the will of God is sin. Obviously the mechanics of my problem are quite simple even though the resulting sin is among the most pervasive of all sins. My nose simply sends a message to its control center in my brain. Because of its urgency, it interrupts all other communications with one loud "I can't take this any longer! I deserve some fulfillment. I demand something pleasant to smell." Before long the console of the conscious department of my brain flashes in bright red, "Coveting."

Unless my true personhood comes across with overriding decisiveness, I will be in real trouble. Either I will struggle on, bombarded with guilt and repeated confessions, or I may simply pack up and leave. But wait a minute. Life for me is *not* what I smell. "Sorry nose, you simply are going to have to suffer. Life for me is in displaying Jesus, and believe me, this place needs Him—'a fragrance of life unto life!'" In dealing so harshly with the desires of the flesh, I am really only agreeing with the ground on which I stand.

21. Can you imagine standing before God's judgment seat some day and hearing him say to you, "Well done, my child, you discovered a cure for cancer—you won an Olympic medal—you made it to the top of your chosen

field—you fulfilled the American character." Or even "Well done, my child, you didn't let your birth defect, your blindness, your miserable childhood break you. No, instead you proved to the world that you could still earn that college degree, support your family. Congratulations!" What will God say? How will he measure the quality of the lives we have lived? Certainly he will evaluate our stewardship of every aspect of life. But the fundamental, overriding issue is Christ. The sphere of expression may be the Olympics or a medical lab, health or sickness, abundance or poverty. But the sphere will always be secondary to the essence—dependent resurrection life. This is the great leveler, the great equalizer of the relative significance of each believer's life.

22. It is for this reason that the expression "the Spirit-controlled life," is not only inadequate but contrary to Scripture. The ministry of the Spirit is to energize, to enable, to lead. "Control" suggests that I must be "restrained," as though the direction I desire to move is opposed to God's direction—as though God and I were at odds. We aren't, regardless of what our flesh may signal. Righteousness is our deepest desire. We are to "walk" or "live" by the Spirit. He is the enabler. It is by the Spirit. Happily, in keeping with this truth, at least some scholars agree that the phrase "so that you do not do what you want" (Gal. 5:17, NIV, as parallel with Rom. 7:14–23) expresses the wish to do righteousness, which is possible through living by the Spirit (Gal. 5:16, 18). See James Montgomery Boice, "Galatians," *Expositor's Bible Commentary,* vol. 10 (Grand Rapids: Zondervan Publishing House, 1976); Walt Russell, "The Apostle Paul's View of the 'Sin Nature'/'New Nature' Struggle," *Christian Perspectives on Being Human: A Multidisciplinary Approach to Integration,* ed. J. P. Mooreland and David M. Ciocchi (Grand Rapids: Baker Book House, 1993), 217. Regarding this passage J. P. Packer writes, "Any idea of holiness as a manful refusal to do all that one most wants to do must be dismissed as the unregenerate mind's misunderstanding. True holiness…is the doing of that which, deep down, he now most wants to do, according to the urgings of his new, dominant instincts in Christ." (J. I. Packer, *Keep in Step with the Spirit* [Old Tappan, N.J.: Fleming H. Revell Pub. Co., 1984], 108.)

23. Though many are familiar with 1 Cor. 10:13, there is a remarkable message hidden away in Isa. 28:23–29. God describes the wisdom he gives to

farmers as they carefully plant different kinds of seeds, and with equal care, thresh the seeds at harvest time. Dill and cumin are soft seeds with thin hulls. They need only the careful tapping of a rod to release the seed. Barley has a tough hull which requires the heavy turning of the cartwheel. As the farmer, so also with our God. He knows the kind of seed you are. Perhaps you are a "barley" kind of personality, needing the cartwheel—what to the dill seed would appear terribly harsh treatment. But to release you—to free you to experience life in its fullness—it is perfect, because our wise "farmer" God will never allow the cartwheel to turn one too many times. It is also good to remember that to the "dill," the tap of the rod would seem as harsh as the cartwheel to the barley. How sensitive we need to be in accepting the varied "faceting" methods God chooses to use in the lives of his distinctively different children! "This also comes from the LORD of hosts; he is wonderful in counsel, and excellent in wisdom."

CHAPTER 10

1. Westminster Shorter Catechism. Cf. Is. 46:9–11; Eph. 1:4–12; Rom. 11:33–36; 2 Tim. 1:9; Rev. 4:11.

APPENDIX 2

1. Though the NT affirms that the OT made direct references to the deity of the Messiah (Acts 13:33; Heb. 1:5; 5:5 [referring to Ps. 2]; Matt. 22:42–46; Mark 12:35–37; Luke 20:41–44; Acts 2:30–36 [referring to Ps. 110]), nevertheless there is no biblical reason to assume even the most devout Old Covenant Jewish believers *understood* the Messiah would also be God. Rather he would be a most special human descendant of David.

2. We may assume this was part of Jesus' instruction to them as "he interpreted to them the things about himself in all the scriptures." Soon after, he shared the same with all the disciples (Luke 23:27, 44–47). We may be sure that Thomas was not alone in his response to Jesus—"my Lord and my God!" (John 20:28). As we see later in Acts 9:30–35, there was no confusion in Philip's mind as to the relation between Jesus and Isa. 53. The substitutionary atonement was by that time truly appreciated.

3.   By the time of his writing of Romans (25+ years after the resurrection), Paul considered the individuals of Rom. 10:2 as needing to be saved. Had the New Covenant age not yet arrived, perhaps God would have accepted many of them as "saved" as any other zealous believer within the Old Covenant. It is impossible for us to know with certainty the limits of God's grace during this transitional Old Covenant/New Covenant period. ("Saved" certainly has a relative use in Acts 11:14.)

4.   This parallels the adjustment level of at least some of the original readers of the Book of Hebrews.

5.   Though Peter may have expounded on the substitutionary nature of Jesus' death during those early days, what is recorded gives us no hint that repentance and the promise of forgiveness of sins were viewed as different from the Old Covenant pattern of the call to repentance under John the Baptist, except that it involved acknowledging Jesus as Lord. See also notes 1 and 2.

6.   Though "the Lamb of God who takes away the sin of the world" identity of Jesus had been introduced by John the Baptist (John 1:29, 36), there is no reason to assume that either he or Jesus' disciples grasped the implications of this prophetic utterance until after the resurrection. John's later question reveals his lack of comprehension (cf. Matt. 11:2–6). Note also the disciples' repulsion regarding Jesus' announcement to them of his impending death. Cf. Matt. 16:21, etc. According to 1 Pet. 1:10–12, prophets did not necessarily comprehend the messages they delivered.

7.   It appears, then, the effect of Christ's resurrection relates more to the truth of regeneration (newness of life) than to justification, although the fact he rose affirmed divine acceptance of Christ's substitutionary death, enabling God to justify sinners. This issue indirectly relates to Rom. 4:24 as to whether Christ was "raised for our justification" (NIV, NRSV), or "because of our justification" (NASB). Harrison provides a careful analysis of both the grammatical and theological issues involved, concluding with a belief that "because of" is the more probable rendering. "Justification, considered objectively and from the standpoint of God's provision, was indeed accomplished in the death of Christ (5:9) and therefore did not require the resurrection to complete it. Paul does not mention the resurrection in his definitive statement on justification in 3:21–26." (Everett F. Harrison, "Romans," *The Expositor's Bible Commentary,*

vol. 10 [Grand Rapids: Zondervan Publishing House, 1976], 53–54.)

8.   Though on one hand, Paul emphasized the degree to which his message was a product of divine revelation, passages such as 1 Cor. 7:10–12 demonstrate how fully he was aware of the specific truth Jesus had taught his disciples. During his several visits to Jerusalem, we can only imagine the eagerness with which Paul must have consumed every bit of information regarding the words and actions of his Lord. In Gal. 1:18; 2:9 he mentioned time spent with Peter, James, and John. Along with so much else, this undoubtedly would have included the crucial "you in me and I in you" truth of John 14–17. We may also surmise he had a good visit with his fellow Pharisee, Nicodemus (certainly among the true believers, cf. John 19:39).

9.   In his comments on Rom. 6, I agree with Showers's repeated emphasis that the doctrine of regeneration underlies this text. (Renald Showers, *The New Nature* [Neptune, N.J.: Loizeaux Brothers, 1986], 65–67, cf. p. 11.)

10.   I believe it is more reasonable to understand Rom. 7:1–6 as a clarification of the freedom spoken of in 6:18 and 22 in terms of the Old Covenant bondage to the law rather than as the beginning of a new section which includes the remainder of Rom. 7. Another clue that 7:7 begins a new section is found in the expression "What shall we say then?" (NASB), which is identical with the beginning of chapter 6. Packer also appears to see 6:1–7:6 as a unit. (J. I Packer, *Keep in Step with the Spirit* [Old Tappan, N. J.: Fleming H. Revell, 1984], 128.)

11.   Examples are as follows: "In baptism we affirm that the life of the one who is baptized is henceforth to be determined by the fact that Christ died and was raised, that *in relationship with him* as justified persons, we are delivered from the dominion of sin and freed for life." (Manfred T. Brauch, *Hard Sayings of Paul* [Downers Grove, Ill.: InterVarsity Press, 1989], 40.) "This death and resurrection is not a mystical experience that *ipso facto* changes one's inner nature when he believes, nor is it a transformation accomplished by the sacrament of baptism. It is rather an eschatological fact that has happened in the mission of Jesus Christ but which can only be perceived by faith.... Believers are to recognize this change of dominion, and *for this reason* they are to change their alliance from sin to God (vv. 17, 18, 22 [Rom. 6]). It is because this change has occurred in Christ that believers are exhorted to yield themselves to righteousness (v. 19)." (George Eldon Ladd, *A Theology of the New Testament*

[Wm. B. Eerdmans Pub. Co., 1974], 485–86.) To support this view, some have used Paul's expression "For whoever has died is freed [lit. 'justified'] from sin" (6:7). To the contrary, I believe the translators were correct in concluding in this context that Paul's intent was to declare (in agreement with rabbinical usage) that "death cancels all obligations."

12. See John R. W. Stott, *The Cross of Christ* (Downers Grove, Ill.: Inter-Varsity Press, 1986), 240; F. F. Bruce, *The Epistle of Paul to the Romans* (Grand Rapids: Wm. B. Eerdmans Pub. Co., 1963), 138; John R. W. Stott, *Men Made New, An Exposition of Romans 5–8* (Downers Grove, Ill.: InterVarsity Press, 1966), 44; W. E. Vine, *An Expository Dictionary of New Testament Words* (Old Tappan, N. J.: Fleming Revell Co., 1940), 13; Larry J. Kreitzer, "Body," *Dictionary of Paul and His Epistles,* ed. Gerald F. Hawthorne, Ralph Martin, Daniel G. Reid (Downers Grove, Ill.: InterVarsity Press, 1993), 73.

13. See John Murray, *The Epistle to the Romans,* vol. 1 (Grand Rapids: Wm. B. Eerdmans Pub. Co., 1968), 220–21. Such an understanding of "body of sin" fits well with Paul's later expressions, "do not let sin have dominion in your mortal bodies, to make you obey their passions;" and "For just as you once presented your members as slaves to impurity and to greater and greater iniquity, so now present your members as slaves to righteousness for sanctification" (Rom. 6:12, 19). In light of these passages, it would be inconsistent to render "body of sin" as a metaphorical expression.

14. The determination of several scholars to remove any physical connotation from both the expression "body of sin" and "the body of this death," is wholly without justification and does nothing but hinder understanding the text. (E.g., Barclay M. Newman, "Once Again—The Question of 'I' in Romans 7:7–27," *The Bible Translator* [Jan. 1983]:131. See also Showers, *The New Nature,* 71–72, for both his reference to others who hold this view and his own reasons for rejecting it.) Nevertheless, by no means do these expressions point to some wish of Paul for a bodiless state. See Rom. 8:23; 2 Cor. 5:1–4; 1 Cor. 15:35–54.

15. If we remember the Jewish context in which Paul wrote, plus the fact that Paul concluded this section with Rom. 7:1–6 and its reference to being dead to the Mosaic law, the crucifixion of the "old man" may indeed refer to the Old Covenant law "way of life." This would have included even devout Jews and proselytes who, because they had not yet received New Covenant life

by the Spirit, were still "in the flesh," struggling to please God by their own earnest efforts. In receiving Jesus as both their Messiah and their once-for-all Sacrifice, they also received the "Spirit of life." In that moment the "old man" died. Attaching this perspective to the expression "old man," is also in harmony with the strong Jewish contexts of both Gal. 2:20 containing the parallel words "crucified with Christ" and Col. 2:11–14. Karlberg defines "old man" "as Israel as a corporate body under the covenantal administration of death and condemnation" and also as "fallen humanity represented by Israel under law." (Mark W. Karlberg, "Israel's History Personified: Romans 7:7–13 In Relation to Paul's Teaching on the 'Old Man,'" *Trinity Journal* [1986]:68, 70.) From a different perspective, Murray defines the "old man" as "the unregenerate man in his entirety in contrast with the 'new man' as the regenerate man in his entirety." *Epistle to the Romans*, 219. See also Showers, *New Nature*, 65–67.

16. "Old man/new man" terminology is also used in Col. 3:9–10 and its parallel, Eph. 4:22–24, in a "putting off/putting on" imagery rather than the crucifixion context of Rom. 6. Using this analogy, it is clear Paul's emphasis was on the believer's behavior. It was as though Paul saw a believer standing before two wardrobes; one contained the clothing (lifestyle) of an unregenerate person. "Take them off," Paul urged. "They don't fit, they're out of style, totally unbecoming of who you are, and, if that were not enough, they don't belong to you." The other contained the clothing (lifestyle) of a regenerate person. "They're yours!" Paul exclaimed. "Wear them. Don't worry, they'll fit!"

17. Regarding the new birth, Toon states, "The divine begetting causes new life. What happens to the believer is an inner resurrection in anticipation of the bodily resurrection that will occur at the parousia. It is a passing from death to life." (Peter Toon, *Born Again, A Biblical and Theological Study of Regeneration* [Grand Rapids: Baker Book House, 1987], 32.)

The following statements by Murray underline the centrality of regeneration in Rom. 6. "It is a mistake to think of the believer as both an old man and a new man or as having in him both the old man and the new man, the latter in view of regeneration and the former because of remaining corruption. That this is not Paul's concept is made apparent here by the fact that the 'old man' is represented as having been crucified with Christ and the tense indicates a once-for-all definitive act after the pattern of Christ's crucifixion. The 'old man' can no more be regarded as in the process of being crucified than Christ in his sphere could thus be regarded." (Murray, *Epistle to the Romans*, 219–20.)

"Paul announces the definitive cleavage with the world of sin, which union with Christ insures. The old man is the unregenerate man; the new man is the regenerate man created in Christ Jesus unto good works. It is no more feasible to call a believer a new man and an old man, than it is to call him a regenerate man and an unregenerate. And neither is it warranted to speak of the believer as having in him the old man and the new man. This kind of terminology is without warrant and is but another method of doing prejudice to the doctrine which Paul was so jealous to establish when he said, 'our *old man has been crucified*.'" (John Murray, *Principles of Conduct; Aspects of Biblical Ethics* [Grand Rapids: Eerdmans, 1957], 218.)

18. See my earlier comments regarding this passage in chapter 6.

19. Walt Russell, "The Apostle Paul's View of the 'Sin Nature'/'New Nature' Struggle," *Christian Perspectives on Being Human: A Multidisciplinary Approach to Integration,* ed. J. P. Moreland and David M. Ciocchi (Grand Rapids: Baker Book House, 1993), 221. See also Douglas J. Moo, *The Epistle to the Romans* (Grand Rapids: Wm. B. Eerdmans Publishing Company, 1996), 461. Though Moo uses the "pious Jew" terminology, and describes such an attitude as genuine delight of "one who took his religion [O. T. Jewish faith] seriously and sought to do what was required of him" (p. 461), he nevertheless also depicts such individuals as "condemned, bound for hell" (p. 466). Much to be preferred is to assume that such "genuine delight" reflects the true piety of saved individuals under the Old Covenant (cf. Psalm 119:97). Indeed they were pre-Christian, but not unsaved; they had been reconciled (profoundly changed in their attitude toward God), but not yet regenerated (possessing resurrection life and power).

20. In agreement with Russell, I believe any effort to distinguish "in the flesh" from "of flesh" to support a major break between Rom. 7:7–13 and 7:14–25 (the former referring to the unsaved, the latter to the saved), is an unnecessary splitting of a hair.

21. Paul's later statement, "Anyone who does not have the Spirit of Christ does not belong to him" (Rom. 8:9), must be understood as being true in the New Covenant age. Because resurrection life and having the Spirit of Christ are

so closely related, it must be questioned if such was available to Old Covenant believers. Ladd states: "The ascended Christ has not only entered the realm of spirit; he has become a life-giving spirit, able because of his new mode of existence to impart life to men as he could not do in the days of his flesh." (Ladd, *Theology of the New Testament*, 490.) Toon states, "The Jews had to allow God to transfer them from the Old Covenant into the New Covenant; and for him to effect this transfer, they had to receive the Messiah and believe in his name. In doing so, they would receive the permanent gift of the Holy Spirit to enable them to truly know, worship, love and serve the Lord" (Toon, *Born Again*, 61). Tenney went so far as to write, "Nicodemus knew nothing of the Holy Spirit experimentally. In the Old Testament teaching, the Spirit came upon prophets and other specially chosen men for unusual reasons, but nowhere in Judaism was taught the coming of the Spirit upon all men for their personal regeneration." (Merrill C. Tenney, *John, The Gospel of Belief* [Grand Rapids: Wm. B. Eerdmans Pub. Co., 1953], 87.) I assume Tenney might have added "except as a yet future event." An example of this "special" work of the Spirit is illustrated by Peter's reference to "the Spirit of Christ" within the prophets (1 Pet. 1:11).

Some twenty-five years after the beginning of the New Covenant age, Paul encountered disciples of John the Baptist (certainly "believers" in an Old Covenant sense) who, when asked if they had received the Spirit, replied, "No, we have not even heard that there was a Holy Spirit" (Acts 19:2).

22. More recently, several scholars have rejected any autobiographical approach to Rom. 7:7–25 in place of the "I" being metaphorical (as representing corporate Israel). Regardless, what was true corporately was also true individually. The crucial issue, then, is the historical perspective from which this section is written. See Karlberg, "Israel's History Personified," 70–74.

23. Moo, *Romans 1–8*, 468.

24. It is important that we understand this conflict as involving two levels of mind. Coveting, the sin which brought Paul such despair, is a "thinking" type of sin, yet he identifies its source ("my flesh") as distinct from his mind, which is a "slave to the law of God" (Rom. 7:25; cf. 7:23). One level represents the independent operation of an individual's brain/mind—a central aspect of one's flesh. The second, deeper level represents the divinely initiated "God dependent" operation of an individual's brain/mind as a result

of God's interior changes in a person. It is on this level that we have the mind of Christ (1 Cor. 2:16). That deeper level alone represents one's authentic selfhood, hence it is only that level which receives the full force of "I." Yet both levels possess attributes of personhood—thought, emotion, and will.

From a somewhat different perspective, in light of 1 Cor. 14:2, 14–17, we may assume it is appropriate to identify this deep level as being one's spirit. Though controversial, most scholars agree this passage describes one's spirit praying, expressing thanksgiving to God, apart from one's choosing the words to be expressed and also without one's understanding of the communication (apart from the gift of interpretation); it is in a language foreign to one's flesh-mental programming. Passages such as Rom. 1:9; 8:16 may also support this deeper level of mind as being one's spirit, although the understood "witness" of one's spirit involves no special spiritual gift.

25. See chapter 3, note 26.

26. Representative of this view, the McGraths write, "Sin and righteousness thus coexist; we remain sinners inwardly, but we are righteous extrinsically in the sight of God.... From our own perspective we are sinners; but in the perspective of God, we are righteous." This is followed by quoting Martin Luther, "Now the saints are always aware of their sin and seek righteousness from God in accordance with his mercy. And for this reason, they are regarded as righteous by God. Thus in their own eyes (and in reality!) they are sinners—but in the eyes of God they are righteous, because he reckons them as such on account of their confession of their sin. In reality they are sinners; but they are righteous by the imputation of a merciful God. They are unknowingly righteous, and knowingly sinners. They are sinners in fact, but righteous in hope." (Joanna McGrath and Alister McGrath, *The Dilemma of Self-Esteem* [Wheaton: Good News Pub., 1992], 98–99.)

27. Though this "death" may include ultimate "eternal separation from God," (cf. Murray, *Epistle to the Romans,* vol. 1:293–94), I believe it is possible to limit its meaning to "death" as understood in Rom. 7:9–11, 13, 24. See also chapter 8, note 6.

28. Ibid., 289.

29. I believe it misses the point to press the thought that since according to Paul *we* have crucified the flesh, rather than God doing it, we have appar-

ently done such a poor job of it we must continue to do it, therefore making this passage parallel with Rom. 8:13. (See Stott, *The Cross of Christ*, 279.) Later, in contrast to the text, he states, "According to verse 24 [Gal. 5] we are to 'crucify' the flesh, with its evil passions and desires" (p. 348). (This one negative comment in no way suggests my lack of appreciation of this book as among the best ever written on the cross of Christ.)

Another inadequate approach conveys the thought that "the believer in Christ has already repented of his former way of life to the degree of actually having executed the old nature," yet "as in actual crucifixion, life lingers even though the criminal has been nailed to the cross." (James Montgomery Boice, "Galatians," *Expositor's Bible Commentary*, vol. 10 [Grand Rapids: Zondervan Publishing House, 1976], 500.)

30. The NRSV renders "spirit" as "Spirit." For supporting arguments for "Spirit," see Murray, *Epistle to the Romans*, 289–90, including his footnote referring to Sanday and Hedlam who argued for "spirit." Fee assumes the possibility in some passages of a dual meaning, hence "S/spirit." (Gordon D. Fee, *The First Epistle to the Corinthians* [Grand Rapids: Wm. B. Eerdmans Pub. Co., 1987], 204–5.) Vine finds several references to the human spirit in Rom. 8. (W. E. Vine, *The Epistle to the Romans* [Grand Rapids: Zondervan Publishing House, 1965], 114–16.) See endnote 24, p. 284.

31. Norman F. Douty, *Union With Christ* (Swengel, Penn.: Reiner Publications, 1973), 183. Regarding Col. 1:17, "Christ in you, the hope of glory," Bruce states, "The fact that here and now, as members of his body, they have his risen life within them, offers them a stable basis for confidence that they will share in the fullness of glory yet to be displayed, on the day of 'the revealing of the sons of God' (Rom. 8:19)." (F. F. Bruce, *The Epistles to the Colossians, to Philemon and to the Ephesians* [Grand Rapids: Wm. B. Eerdmans Pub. Co., 1984], 86.)

Note: Leader's study guide materials, discussion suggestions, and a set of colored overhead transparencies are available from the author.

For more information write to:
David C. Needham
9501 N.E. Sacramento Street
Portland, Oregon 97220
(503) 255-9853

Please leave your name and address on the answering machine. (We are sorry but we will not be able to return phone calls.)